*A Million Miles*

The Defiance House Man colophon is a registered trademark of the University of Utah Press. It is based on a four-foot-tall Ancient Puebloan pictograph (late PIII) near Glen Canyon, Utah.

LIBRARY OF CONGRESS CATALOGING-IN-PUBLICATION DATA

Names: Olsen, Jody K., author.

Title: A million miles : my Peace Corps journey / Jody Olsen.

Description: Salt Lake City : The University of Utah Press, [2024] | Includes index. |

Identifiers: LCCN 2024016339 | ISBN 9781647691851 (hardcover) | ISBN 9781647691974 (paperback) | ISBN 9781647691981 (ebook)

Subjects: LCSH: Olsen, Jody K. | Peace Corps (U.S.)--Officials and employees--Biography. | Women volunteers in social service--United States--Biography. | Volunteer workers in social service--United States--Biography.

Classification: LCC HC60.5 .O53 2024 | DDC 361.6 [B]--dc23/eng/20240612

LC record available at https://lccn.loc.gov/2024016339

# A MILLION MILES

*My Peace
Corps Journey*

JODY OLSEN

THE UNIVERSITY OF UTAH PRESS
*Salt Lake City*

*For my family*
*and everyone who has been touched*
*by the Peace Corps*

I repeat for the last time: to understand me, you'll have to swallow a world.

   —Salman Rushdie, *Midnight's Children*, 1981

# Contents

# Acknowledgments

My ever-broadening circle of Peace Corps colleagues and friends has made my story possible. I thank my former husband, Bob Olsen, and my two children, David Olsen and Kirsten Andersen, for helping create the loving and sharing family that gave me support for writing this memoir in both joyous and painful detail. Letters, notes, and an autobiography left behind by my parents, David King and Francine Timothy, rekindled memories of pleasure and pain. I am grateful to them for their honesty in describing the heartaches each experienced.

Numerous Peace Corps colleagues encouraged me to write my Peace Corps story, helping me clarify details of events in DC and abroad and refining memories nearly lost. Special thanks to my then-husband, Bob Olsen, who lived each day's two-year Tunisian experiences with me. As a Peace Corps Volunteer at age twenty-three, I traveled the country with him, exploring Roman ruins, mosques, and the vast north Sahara Desert. A newly minted architect, he taught me how to observe both people and places and catalog my memories.

His early optimism about becoming a Volunteer gave me the adventures that have made possible my professional life recounted in this memoir. Fellow Volunteers Karen Primm Hurst and Diane Wilson and sister Cindy Mahak reviewed the section on our calamitous trip in the Tunisia desert from which we weren't sure we would return. Over fifty years later, we still marvel at its happy ending.

Two dozen friends and colleagues reviewed all or sections of the book as I wrote, taking valuable hours and even days to nudge me toward describing inner feelings about painful situations I had kept private. They added facts and suggested changes to many Peace Corps scenes throughout.

Isabel Swift's early mentoring helped organize the book's sequence. A former publishing house vice president, she knew what writers need to create a consistent story arc. I owe my creating an Excel spreadsheet of my life's events to her gentle questions of "Why?" "How?" "So what?" This gave coherence to the book and to what, reluctantly, ended up in my electronic "outtakes" file.

Jon Keeton shared his journals and trip notes about central and eastern European countries critical to descriptions in chapter 11. Peace Corps colleagues Claudia Kuric, Maryann Minutillo, Meghan Donahue, and Earl McClure helped me strengthen descriptions of my Peace Corps staff positions. Each had worked with me and knew my quirks and foibles as well as my strengths. I am grateful for their ongoing friendships built through Peace Corps time together.

Dick and Karen Cook, Volunteers in Venezuela the same years as my time in Tunisia and subsequent social work colleagues, give reality checks on my perceptions of the Volunteer experience and how it shaped our lives. Dick is honest and direct, thank goodness. My Peace Corps mentee and fellow University of Utah graduate, Deanna Blackwell, offered further perspectives on Salt Lake university life and its connection to subsequent Peace Corps service.

Close friends have seen me as a mother, grandmother, wife, colleague, and neighbor. They added detail to many of my life's Baltimore and Washington stories. Judith Bird, a close friend for five decades, added more depth to my accounts of being a mother, juggling a career, and my divorce. Barry Fulton, a friend, Foreign Service colleague, and writer, gave invaluable structural edits as well as nudging me to write in my authentic voice. "This work is not an academic paper," he often commented.

Anne Callier and Jean Sullivan-Finn were longtime friends of my mother, Francine. They filled in spaces of her life less known to me as they talked of her humanity and generosity. Susan Leviton reviewed scenes of my years in Baltimore, as my former husband, Bob, designed her and her husband's house, which began a long friendship. Jane Lipscomb added editing perspectives from our years together at the University of Maryland. Deborah Gordis, a former editor and now social worker, challenged me to dig deep about my feelings after Francine's leaving and my complex relationship with the Mormon Church. Her directness led me to write about my pain and subsequent recovery. Connie Freeman, Jennifer Presley, and Margo Stern all know me well from years in Washington, DC, and helped me frame the larger political and social fabric during my Peace Corps leadership roles.

My cousin Susie Scherr, whose mother was Francine's sister, added insights to the early years in Ogden with my grandparents. Liz Fannin, a former editor whom I met at a conference, offered to review the manuscript for clarity as a reader who did not know me or the Peace Corps. Her suggested changes have made the memoir more accessible to readers.

My daughter, Kirsten, gave me courage throughout my three years as Peace Corps director, particularly during my last two difficult months in that position. During those two months, she created a daily countdown to January 20, 2021, hidden on note cards for me to find each morning. This routine gave us smiles against the January 6 political upheaval as I closed out my long professional career.

Jedidiah Rogers at the University of Utah Press held my hand through the publication preparation process. His patient understanding helped guide me through the realities of publication mixed with conversations about the science behind the failing Great Salt Lake. The two University of Utah Press peer reviewers, Claudia Kuric and Jana Riess, devoted weeks to detailed reading, offering numerous additional suggestions for tightening the text and noting any inconsistencies as well as giving overall positive reviews.

I am also lucky to have so many general supporters—Peace Corps colleagues, students, young women I have mentored over the years—who have encouraged me to write this book.

I thank all who have given me the enriched life I share in this memoir.

# *Preface*

Why a memoir? For my daughter and son. For my grandchildren. And generations beyond. For everyone who has ever served in the Peace Corps—and for their parents who saw them off and welcomed them home. For the thousands of families abroad who invited Volunteers into their homes. For the hundreds of thousands in scores of countries whose lives were touched by an American Volunteer. For generations of administrators and legislators who supported the Peace Corps. For the tens of thousands of returned Volunteers who have enriched our country.

And for you. For opening this book to share my adventure from a child in Utah abandoned by her mother to a Peace Corps director. After serving in Tunisia, Togo, and Kazakhstan and visiting another 115 countries, I have stories.

Who am I? Shy, frightened, quiet. True as a young girl. But also curious, earnest, and impatient. And now, decades later, this memoir recounts a journey that has led to renewal, compassion, and strength. For that, I thank my family, my friends, and the men and women of Africa, Asia, Inter-America, and Europe who have given back as much as or more than they received.

Some suggested two volumes: one to chronicle my personal growth and the other to describe my twenty-two-year association with the Peace Corps. Impossible, as my professional and personal lives are so intertwined that a separation would be artificial.

I invite you to join me on this many-decade journey, to weep with me when disaster strikes and celebrate with me at moments of joy. Stand by my side at my marriage, the birth of my children, my experience as a Peace Corps Volunteer in Tunisia, my reconnection with my birth mother, and numerous other life-changing events culminating in my appointment as Peace Corps director. You will also feel my grief over deaths, stumbles, and setbacks. And I trust you will share with me the pride of growing stronger, learning compassion, and embracing renewal.

# PART ONE
## *Growing Up*

# 1

# The White-Gloved Wave
## 1945–48

The plane filled with passengers, doors closed, silent, as if waiting for one more goodbye. A hand, one white-gloved hand, waved weakly from a tiny round window midway along the sleek frame. I raised my right arm to respond, to acknowledge the wave, just as Daddy took my left hand and turned his back on the plane, the window, and the last moment to see my mother. Daddy said nothing. Nana and Grandpa stood beside him. They said nothing. The outside air felt heavy, as if expecting rain. My father looked down at me, resignation in his eyes. That moment is all my three-year-old brain remembers of my mother, Francine, leaving.

The plane, the limp wave, the silence of unhappiness, all bound up in that moment, created the acute memory of my loss. The image of the fragile gloved hand in the window lived in my dreams, my thoughts, and when asking "Where's Mommy?" to faces that turned away without words. I asked, "Did I make her go away?"

"You did nothing," the adults responded.

"Why can't you tell me something?" I learned to remain silent, still, alone. I stopped saying her name when talking, but the wave stuck in my mind. The memory of that shadowed face seemed sadder each year.

*

David Jr., my one-year-old brother, and I moved from the family redbrick duplex on Ninth Avenue, Salt Lake City, to my mother's parents' house in Ogden, forty miles north. They baked me a chocolate cake with sprinkles for my fourth birthday.

I wandered around their house quietly, came to dinner when called, watched Nana vacuum while whistling off-key to outdo its noise, room by room, determined to achieve visual perfection. Grandpa, when home, sat in an overstuffed chair with enormous arms and stacked papers for reading. The curtains stayed closed, the room dark except for the lamp over his shoulder. I sat on the stool by his feet, looking up to get his attention. Sometimes he picked up a picture book and read aloud. His gentle, firm voice pronounced each word.

Nana said to me, "When someone dies, their soul flies to heaven." I stood at the open kitchen door one sunny afternoon, looking into the blue sky to see our neighbor's soul fly. He had just died. Is that what happened to my mom? No, her soul stayed on earth. But to me, it flew into that blue sky.

The pictures of Francine in Nana and Grandpa's house disappeared. Gone. David Jr. slept in her childhood bed in the room where she learned to dress and begin school. Yes, she also left David Jr., only a year old. Why did she leave him? Still a baby. We played, slept, and kept silent in the same house where Nana and Grandpa had raised my mother and her three sisters and two brothers. One of her brothers, Hugh, died at two when tangled in his crib. His soul went to heaven.

Daddy drove the forty miles from Salt Lake to Ogden to visit for a few hours most weekends. If on a Sunday, we attended church together. He looked pale and skinny.

"I have to work," he said. "My job is in Salt Lake. You have a loving family here." He took me across the street to play at Ogden High School. The tall school building had the same gold rust bricks as my grandparents' house. The matching bricks made our house as important as the school.

Twice during my year with Nana and Grandpa, Daddy drove me to his apartment. "Where do you live?" I had asked. Salt Lake seemed far away.

"I'm nearby," he said as he opened the apartment door.

"No, you're not," I said. The drive had taken a long time, way past lunch. "Can I stay?" I asked, not wanting to go back to Nana's house. He hesitantly walked across the room to the sofa.

"Come here," he said. "Sit on my lap." I climbed over his legs as they extended, long and thin, and tucked my body into his arms. They seemed heavy, slow. "I have to work. I earn money to take care of you and David Jr."

"But I can be here," I said. He had a tired smile, and I wanted to take care of him.

"Nana and Grandpa are taking good care of you and David Jr.," he added. I asked no more questions, wanting to be good, to please Daddy.

I sat on the sofa, quiet, looking at stacks of papers. They looked just like Grandpa's papers. Daddy must read a lot. I wanted to learn to read a lot. I wanted Daddy to love me.

*

During this year with Francine's parents, Daddy drove me to the This Is the Place Monument at the mouth of Emigration Canyon on the Wasatch Range edge of Salt Lake. The tall white tribute to Mormon pioneers towered over the valley below, the Great Salt Lake shimmering in the distance. The city's downtown buildings huddled in the north corner of the county. Mountains circled the valley, making it seem protected, safe.

"The monument is where Brigham Young and the first pioneers came through that canyon," Daddy said as he pointed to the mountain and the canyon behind us, "and saw this valley for the first time." I imagined the oxen, wagons, ladies in bonnets and long billowy dresses, and men wearing suspenders that crossed in the back, pictures I studied in Sunday school.

"Brigham Young was ill," Daddy continued, "and lay in the back of the wagon." I pictured an old, sick man with a long beard and a shirt with large sleeves. "When told he could see the long-sought valley, he sat up, looked out across a flat desert valley to the lake on the other side." Daddy became animated as he told the story, his voice determined. "Brigham Young's body hurt from all those rocks on the trail. He had been in this wagon for months, trekking across plains and mountains, leading hundreds of people.

"Brigham Young put his arm out just like this," Daddy said, thrusting his arm forward, "and said, 'This is the place… drive on.' Brigham Young knew the Mormons would be safe here."

Daddy continued, "Trappers and explorers told Brigham the valley existed, but nothing would grow. However, this leader believed with God's help, it would blossom as a rose." That phrase came from church. But standing on the edge of the valley, I saw no roses.

"Your great-great-grandparents were among those first pioneers to see this valley in 1847. They had been kicked out of Illinois for being Mormons. They had the strength to walk and ride west in wagons with all their belongings. They believed." I liked standing on the very spot where pioneers stopped traveling and found a home.

Daddy looked proud as he said, "You belong to this city, this state, and this church, the true church." He wanted me to appreciate this story, our family story. I stared into the valley, to houses with smoke from chimneys. I heard car engines.

Did my relatives build log houses when they arrived? Did they cook over fires? How did they grow food? In Sunday school classes, I found myself in pictures of children walking aside oxen. One of those ladies had been my great-great-grandmother, Matilda Robison, an immigrant from England who walked across the plains. Her granddaughter, Eliza Lythgoe, had written about the death of Matilda's daughter, Emily: "They traveled so terribly slow, ten miles often a day. Grandfather took boards out of the end of both wagons for the coffin to bury her in. They laid her by the road. Made brush fire on the grave so the coyotes could not tell it was a body underneath. How Matilda could look back the next night and tell right where it was. She could hardly keep from running back."

My place was here in Salt Lake. Ancestors sacrificed for me. Because of them, I stood proudly looking over the city. I wanted to honor their sacrifices.

\*

A few months later, Daddy said Nana and Grandpa needed a rest away from David Jr. and me.

"Did I do something wrong?" I asked. "Was I not good?" Sent away? Maybe I'm not quiet enough. Daddy dropped David Jr. and me at the door of a long white house with many children. What is this place? Is this where bad children go? We all slept in a room with white walls and ceilings, beds and cribs crowded close. The children made noises in the dark. Each morning, I looked at David Jr. in his crib. He sometimes cried. The ladies in white uniforms sent us outside to play. Sun glared against the white walls and cement. I didn't want to play on the cement, so I hid under the bed.

Daddy came back the next weekend. He hugged me so tight, I couldn't breathe. I didn't want him to let go. "We can go back to Nana's now," he whispered.

"I will be good," I said. That house remained a mystery and still haunts me today.

*

I was certain this had happened. The image of the white-gloved wave from the airplane window stayed with me. Mother left. I didn't know why. Adults kept silent. Where did my mother's shadowed face go after the plane landed? Did she think of me? Did I matter? I occasionally overheard whispers about her from my grandparents, followed by "Oh, Jody, I didn't see you here," and then no more words. She remained a secret. She only had a waving hand and a shadowed face. That moment became my reality, my story.

Why she left two young children behind tore at me throughout my life. Growing up, I feared doing something similar, even leaving my own child someday. This anxiety lingered in the background, the thoughts hidden.

It is now seven decades after she disappeared. As an adult, I reconnected with her, called her Francine, but never asked about that day she left. She never said why. After she died, I discovered typewritten papers. They appeared to be personal notes from years earlier. In those papers was her answer:

> I don't know how accurately I remember my escape (desertion in the divorce), since I know that I had "lost it," stopped "tracking," or "slipped a cog," depending on who was describing me. Later, a psychiatrist told my mother-in-law that staying would have ended in a mental institution, but, sadly, no one told me then that he said that. It would have lightened my dead weight of guilt and diluted other words used about me, such as "wicked" and "coward."
>
> Five years into this disastrous marriage, someone inside me walked me to a train and away from every familiar thing I had known, even my two small children....
>
> The only thing I remember clearly about that day was my taking my two children to a babysitter I hadn't met before and leaving them there at her house. Jody, my five-year-old, ever-trusting daughter, seemed calm about me leaving her, but she had always been an accepting child who rationalized bad things away. Two-year-old David Jr., however, wouldn't let go of my hand until I released it one clinging finger at a time, and then he held onto my leg, his arms so tight, his trembling body became part of mine. How did he sense,

when I didn't, that I wouldn't see either of them again for a very, very long time?

Now it was a hot day, and the three of us were bedraggled and untidy in the way I had let us become, since any effort on my part often seemed more than I could handle. The babysitter wore a limp cotton housedress and would have been described by Mother as "stringy," no fat on her bones. She greeted the children in a casual manner, bordering on disinterest, and assured me they would be fine with her.

Where was my mind? Where was my heart that strange day about which no amount of trying to remember can retrieve anything except the vivid scene of leaving my children? The mechanics of what I did after are still, all these years later, erased. I can truly vouch for the fact that temporary insanity does exist.

I didn't even take that one last look at my children, since I certainly didn't imagine it would be a last look. I was a loving mother, a very loving mother, and I did my inadequate best to show them my love, not deliberately, but because I felt it every minute I was ever with them.

Francine's writing continued in this painful follow-up:

I fled across the country to my mother-in-law [Vera King, Senator King's wife], the kindest person I knew. She put me to bed, took an appointment with a psychiatrist, and informed my family I was safe, though ill.

Days of sleeping and convalescence went by before I received a letter from my parents [Grandpa Evans and Nana]. They told me they were legally disowning me, that I was no longer a child of theirs, and that they knew they would not be with me in heaven because I had disqualified myself. My emotionally astringent husband wrote that he was divorcing on his terms and taking the children. The church then "cast me out" (the expression actually used). My heart was broken.

Loss, unthinkable loss, possessed my memory and changed my life forever, as it did Francine's. But memories are fickle. We creatively construct our own realities and live within these constructs. The inner and outside worlds get muddy, but does anyone know what is true? Was my three-year-old memory accurate? Were passenger planes flying out of Salt Lake City in 1946? Did my mother wear gloves? How much did I invent? Is it important to know what really happened? It doesn't matter. I remember being three years old, a plane, and white gloves. Francine remembers me being five, a babysitter, and a train. My memory haunted me growing up, the truth of this memory driving my need to be good, to be accepted. These moments, true or not, remain clear to me.

*

Daddy also had his memory of this time, his truth, and it drove his future. He wrote his memories after he retired:

> Then came the catastrophe. It must have been in May 1946. Francine, without my knowledge or consent, went back to Washington to spend some time with my mother, as my dad was a U.S. senator from Utah. One day my mother called me from Washington, DC, and with great emotion and grief dripping from her voice, said that Francine was in no condition to return home ... maybe never. ... I couldn't have received news of the start of the apocalyptic battle of Armageddon with greater shock. There had been absolutely no warning. It was like a clap of thunder coming out of a clear-blue sky. ... I had the devastating feeling of having been rejected and forever abandoned by one's beloved.
>
> For the next few months, I did everything I could think of to get Francine back. I wrote her incessantly—I drew pictures and cartoons—I sent her funny records and serious records on the theme: "I can't live without you," etc. I sent her everything my imagination could suggest but to no avail. I wanted Francine back as I wanted nothing else in all the universe.
>
> For me, there was also the pain of humiliation, which is punishing to a proud individual when circumstances make him look ridiculous. The rack was given an extra twist, as I had a leadership position in the Salt Lake region of the church. I preached about the sanctity of eternal marriage. Divorces? No one could have despised them more than I. They were the scourge of the human race.

During my childhood, Daddy never spoke about Francine's departure. He said almost nothing about her, except to comment on her beauty. He never let go of his first image of her:

[Paris, September 2, 1939] As soon as the church meeting started, I saw a young lady, sixteen, at the piano accompanying the singing. That moment marked the awakening of a profound feeling of love for her, which soon consumed me entirely. To me, she seemed so pure, so chaste, so like an angel, and exactly what I, at twenty-two, was yearning for. Had God spoken? I had never seen a girl who so fascinated me. What drew me to her was her abundant repertoire of artistic talents, her beauty and femininity, and an exquisite capacity to make herself charming in the eyes of her beholders. She was the quintessential princess, and I was absolutely enthralled by her dazzling array of captivating graces.

Daddy recorded these words fifty-five years after he first saw her, after a political career, a second wife, and a large family. His writings confirmed what I felt but did not say—that he never lost his love and passion for Francine. He kept it hidden, deep, unspoken. He knew I knew, but silence prevailed. That known love kept me attached to both parents, even with their complete estrangement. They never saw each other again.

Francine's writings said something quite different about the five-year marriage from that of my father's:

I married at seventeen [actually eighteen], since my parents were delighted that a serious, thirty-year-old [actually twenty-four-year-old] lawyer chose me. This humorless suitor probably wouldn't have proposed if he had suspected how pleased and astonished I often was at the ridiculous side of life. I had to be colorless before marriage but became even more so in my new life in a rigid church under the domination of a fanatically religious man. Just at the age when I should have flourished, all my latent effervescence was flattened with the metaphorical rolling pin of his personality.

Marriage was oppressive despite my pride in my intellectual and handsome but emotionally deficient husband. I had been an obedient child, but not as obedient as I became to this man and his church.

I was slender but then became gaunt; I was mere but then became invisible. My self no longer counted.

Finding these writings later in life, I see myself in each parent, opposite as they appeared to be. I inherited my father's ambition, serious study, fear of humiliation, and need to prove he was not a failure. He fought back and achieved much in his ninety-one years. He was my father, my guide to understanding my instinct to achieve. Words he wrote in his autobiography might have described my own instinctive push to prove personal success for my family and my heritage:

> The impact of my divorce on my life's objectives was a reaction to the feelings of inferiority, which the divorce left me with. I would spend the rest of my life "proving" that I was not a failure. My life was to "fight back." As a result, I probably rose higher than my natural abilities would otherwise have carried me.... I had been intensely ambitious.... I was ready to surmount everything that stood in the way of success. I was playing the game exactly the way I had been led to believe it was supposed to be played.

I also understood Francine's words: "I was a loving mother, and I did my inadequate best to show them my love, not deliberately, but because I felt it every minute I was ever with them."

I feel love for others, assume love of others, and share this love. As with Francine, my love is not frequently expressed because it is always there. I hope my actions have shown this feeling for others.

Much later in her life, Francine showed me her love was "simply always there." I knew it growing up, even during her twenty years of disappearance and the silence of others. I know because I am like her.

# 2

# No Glass Slipper
## 1948–53

David Jr. and I moved in with the Hansen family, one of my father's Salt Lake clients. He described in his autobiography my grandparents' decision to move us out: "The Evanses gave me a friendly ultimatum—'Take your children. I can't involve myself any further. Whatever you have to do, do it quickly. I can't stand this any longer.' They were right. I took the children and placed them with the Hansens."

Another rejection.

The three Hansen kids made the house noisy. Mr. Hansen sometimes drove David Jr. and me to the Union Pacific train station where he worked. I enjoyed playing in the passenger cars and smelling the leather seats as I sat, pretending to be traveling. Passengers ate at tables with silver salt-and-pepper shakers and candle-shaped electric lights. I wanted to live on a train, to go away.

One afternoon in early January, as heavy snow fell outside, Mrs. Hansen yelled upstairs from the basement, "Get down here now! Everyone." Her voice filled the house, her substantial frame adding volume to her command. The wooden stairs shook while we clamored down, trying not to trip over each other. The sawdust smell from Mr. Hansen's carpentry project permeated the grim space as we gathered and looked into Mrs. Hansen's glazed eyes. I stood in front of David Jr. to protect him, just in case. She seemed unfocused as she moved to the wooden workbench, her face blank. She waved an enormous hammer, one used for smashing rocks, in circles around her head. Mrs. Hansen had powerful arms.

She came closer, now eyeing each of us. "If you don't stop your noise, your screaming, your disobeying, I will kill myself with this hammer," she yelled. With force, she continued to wave it, shouting again, "I can't stand you, any of you, anymore!" She caught her breath. "I really will kill myself!" We stood still, without words. As she stared, she put the hammer down slowly, looking tired, used, defeated. She turned her back to us, crying. I pushed David Jr. ahead of me as we slunk upstairs, shaking.

"I'm scared," he said, tears forming. "Can't we go away?"

"I don't like it here either," I whispered. "But we have no place else to be." I climbed into bed to hide and pulled up the covers, keeping David Jr. close. I said nothing to Daddy when he visited. That memory amplified my fear of what people can do. I became even more quiet, invisible, fearful of doing wrong.

*

Daddy heard my thoughts. When the doorbell rang a few weeks later, it had to be him. Same time every week. He smiled at Mr. Hansen as he entered. A woman, a foot shorter, with curly blond hair, accompanied him. She beamed. "Bring the family together, everyone," Daddy asked of Mr. Hansen. His voice commanded attention, even in someone else's house. He had trained that voice for giving speeches.

We gathered, sat crowded on two sofas, waiting, watching. I nervously picked up a crocheted doily that had fallen from the armrest onto the floor. Once he had silence, Daddy turned to the woman at his side, smiling. He put his arm around her waist, lowered his head, and radiated as he looked into her eyes. The ticking clock overtook the moment. No one moved or talked. Daddy stayed silent as he stepped toward us. He lifted his hands, cleared his throat, lowered his voice. He spoke as if giving a practiced speech.

"This is Rosalie Lehner. She just agreed to be my wife."

More silence. Then "Congratulations," Mr. Hansen shouted. The Hansens jumped up and hugged my father and Rosalie. I remained numb, silent. David Jr. looked confused at what had happened.

"Wow, a new mother," someone yelled to me. I looked toward the window. Tears. Daddy hadn't told me. A new mother? I wanted the real one, wherever she might be.

*

Before the marriage, Rosalie and I opened a new coloring book together filled with outlines of little girls in frilly clothes. We sat on the floor in Daddy's apartment.

"Don't color outside the lines," she said.

"I won't," I replied. I learned early not to go outside the lines, ever.

The morning of their wedding, she helped me put on a long white dress, white bows on the sleeves, buttons in front, and white shoes. My blond ringlets reached to my waist.

"You are elegant," Rosalie said as she arranged the last ringlet. "And call me Mother."

I liked the appearance of my five-year-old self in the floor-length, gold-gilded mirror of the Hotel Utah banquet room. People's faces towered over me. I saw creased dark pants, long flowery skirts, and bows worn by people who seemed important. My grandfather had been a senator in Washington. In a photo Daddy showed me, Senator King stood tall behind President Roosevelt as he signed the first Social Security legislation. At the wedding, guests gathered around the senator. When Daddy and my new mother cut the three-tiered white flowered cake, I stared at the tiny bride and groom dolls on top under a ring of flowers. Daddy and my new mother seemed happier than the dolls' faces.

*

Our new family settled into a modest, redbrick house near a ravine at the mouth of Parley's Canyon on Salt Lake's East Bench. David Jr. and I chased grasshoppers, climbed rocks, gathered wildflowers, and ran with friends on the sides of the hills above the creek. Adults didn't come into the ravine. We owned the hiding places, tumbleweed forts, and make-believe battles. It was our own world.

At home each morning, my new mother vacuumed the rugs and dusted. She put pots on the stove in the afternoon. I stirred soups and gravies. We sat at the dinner table at 5:00 p.m.

Every Sunday after church, Daddy read me the *Prince Valiant* comics in the newspaper while listening to Beethoven symphonies and smelling the aroma of roast and potatoes. When we ate, I made holes in the mashed potatoes on my plate to hold the gravy. Red Jell-O salad melted into the white potatoes, turning them red. "Eat the salad first, before it melts," Mother said.

We held to the family routine for over a year.

Daddy, as a proud father, wrote of David Jr. and me during this first year of marriage: "Jody and David Jr. seemed to adapt very well to their new life. Both of them were remarkable children, exhibiting great seriousness of purpose and great sensitivity."

I'll take his word for it, as my memories are limited. Nothing was said about my birth mother, Francine.

*

I walked home from kindergarten the summer I was six, about a mile, at noon. Hot, all blue sky, neat redbrick houses—with sheets and towels drying in the backyards. I didn't enjoy hanging wet clothes. Mothers came onto porches, one by one, down several blocks:

"Timmy, come in for lunch."

"Jennifer and Sarah, lunchtime. Sandwiches are ready." Kids ran toward them on the front lawn. The clothes kept drying in the back. I don't want to be like the mothers. I don't want to live in a hot little house, fixing sandwiches every noon, bringing in sheets and towels from the line every afternoon, putting water on the stove to begin dinner every night. These thoughts screamed inside me. I don't want that daily routine. Were these tiny houses like my house when I had a real mother? Did she have a daily routine? Did she do laundry? Did Mommy tire of that routine and leave?

*

A few months after my sixth birthday, Mother gave birth to a baby boy, Elliott. They brought him home, but no one smiled. *His head's too big for his body.* He had an operation the following week. Afterward, Mother said, "He'll be normal in a couple of years. We are praying for him." I overheard Daddy and Mother talking at night about Elliott. They cried to each other.

"He'll never be normal," Daddy said to me months later. "Elliott has hydrocephalus." I practiced the new word. "He was born without proper drainage from his brain," Daddy continued. I told my friends at school about Elliott and used this medical term but didn't understand what this meant for Elliott and our family. My personal time with my new mother ended the day Elliott arrived.

Elliott defined our daily routine for eight years. We cared for him, a forty-pound baby with no more understanding than that of a six-month-old. He learned to sit up, but then his development stopped. He never stood. His body stayed little, his head big. We cut slits in his shirts to get them over his head. My job was to wash, dry, and fold the diapers to have them ready on the bassinet. The song from the dryer at the end of each cycle, "The Near Future" (with the lyrics "How dry I am, how dry I am, nobody knows, how dry I am"), was my signal to run to the basement and fold. I resented the song and the diapers.

"Please put Elliott to bed," Mother sometimes called out. I sang to him at night, holding his warm bottle of milk as he sucked. He held onto my little finger. I made up songs and stories sitting in the dark with him. Elliott didn't understand, and no one else listened to my invented stories.

My grade school years included folding diapers, fixing bottles, and singing to Elliott. I grew, I changed; he did not. With his baby face in his oversized head, I could do nothing except love and cradle him.

Mother returned to her earlier work as a nurse, night shift at the hospital, two days a week to help with medical bills. "I need some time away from Elliott," she said. During Mother's evenings at the hospital, Daddy and I cared for Elliott. We understood the sadness underneath our love for him and acknowledged helplessness to make him better, our unconditional love.

"I don't want to bring friends home anymore," I announced to Mother when in the fifth grade, as I sat on the kitchen chair watching her cut up carrots. "Last week, when I brought them here, they noticed Elliott sitting on the living room floor tearing up newspaper strips. They laughed at him."

Mother stopped cutting, put the knife away, and looked at the floor, saying nothing.

"I don't want anyone to see him. They don't understand why he is this way." I cried. Mother came over, put her hand on my head, and sat next to me. Her tears matched mine.

I grew up fast during grade school, no longer a little girl. We felt stuck in a present that wouldn't change.

*

Elliott's convulsions began at age seven, another disability to manage. Mother watched me withdraw further from friends.

One day, looking at me, she said, "Let's talk for a minute." I put my books on the dining room table. "Neither you nor David Jr. are bringing friends over."

"I know," then blurted out, "we can't do anything about it. Nothing can happen." She sighed, her face buried in her hands. She just looked at me, not knowing what to do next.

Mother paused and then asked, "How bad is this hurting you?" Silence.

"A lot," I finally said. We, as a family, had ceded ourselves to his care for seven years. Daddy had minimized his political and religious ambitions to take his turn with Elliott.

"I want to study and be with friends, but I can't. It's just Elliott, Elliott, Elliott all the time."

Mom continued, her voice sad, "Daddy and I are looking for a new home for Elliott. He needs total care we can no longer give. We're tired." She slumped lower, exhausted.

"I'm sorry." I leaned over, hugged her, and walked away. She didn't move.

*

"We found a temporary home for Elliott," Mother told me as I left for school a couple of months later. I skipped the entire route.

The next week, our family drove south one hour to Salem, Utah. Elliott had a new home with a caring family. Mrs. Theisen's effusive smile put me at ease. Elliott would be fine here. Mrs. Theisen had a large frame under her blue cotton flowered dress, which swung gently below her knees as she reached out to greet us. I rushed over and hugged her, shouting "Thank you" over and over. "I love Elliott, and you will love him even more."

We told Elliott goodbye and drove home, the four of us wordlessly staring at farms along the county road and at Mount Timpanogos—the "Sleeping Maiden"—rising nearly twelve thousand feet above the eastern slope of the Wasatch Mountains.

Daddy interrupted my drifting mind when he turned his head and proudly, yet humbly, explained, "Mormon senior officials asked me to be president of the youth program for the entire church. We have said goodbye to Elliott. I can say yes."

His face looked sad when he mentioned Elliott, and then he smiled as he continued to talk. He loved Elliott. We all loved Elliott, but I wouldn't miss him.

"We can now do new things," I blurted out. No one in the car disagreed.

Our home felt empty and silent when we returned. The center of our actions, thoughts, emotions for eight years, Elliott, now slept in a bed in Salem. The Theisens would sing songs to him and change his diapers.

We drove to the Theisens' house monthly until space opened at the American Fork Training Center, a state institution for those who could not live without self-care support. We visited Elliott every two months in his new home. As we walked through the front door into the waiting area for the first time, I gathered my courage and then said to Daddy, "I love Elliott but can't see him. I get sad looking at him. I can't help him."

Daddy gently responded, "None of us could do more. You appreciate that."

"Yes, but I keep asking myself why." Daddy understood me.

I went with our family on the regular visits but stayed in the waiting room and talked with caregivers. Daddy and Mother never asked me to see Elliott, only to come to American Fork with them.

From the staff I met, I observed the institution's rhythms in caring for the residents—schedules, times, food preparation, cleaning systems.

"Where are meals prepared? Who does the laundry? How do those who are more able help those less able?" This information fascinated me. Other visitors didn't ask these questions, and the staff greeted me warmly each time I came. I wanted to know how the institution worked, an interest that always stayed with me.

Daddy had mentioned another resident at American Fork, Joanne Evans, Francine's younger sister. He had met her when dating Francine, as Joanne still lived with her parents in Ogden. Daddy explained Joanne's condition. "She had a high fever as a young child, which affected her development. She matured only to the mental age of five. If you see her, be nice to her."

Nana and Grandpa lost a son at age two, and now Joanne. How had these losses affected my grandparents? Francine?

I occasionally sat with Joanne when my family visited Elliott. I wanted to be a niece talking to an aunt.

"What do you like to do here?" I asked Joanne as we sat side by side on metal chairs in the game room.

"I like to knit. Do you want to see my scarf?" Without waiting for an answer, she pulled out a long blue scarf from her cotton bag. She was clearly pleased with her work. "I have another one. Want to see it?"

Joanne lived in the present. No past, no memory of her sister, Francine, and little of her family. I could learn nothing from her but could share in the joy of being present.

*

The silence about Francine held when Daddy, David Jr., and I visited the Evanses. They had left that golden brick family home and moved near Ogden Canyon into a new slate house with wall-sized windows facing west, overlooking Ogden and the northern end of Great Salt Lake. A side stream flowing from the canyon nearby offered a chance for David Jr. and me, accompanied by Grandpa, to wade, skip rocks, and laugh at each other getting soaked. I had not seen this side of my grandfather before, not this free-spirited, joyful, and exuberant man. I wouldn't again. He died a year later.

"You are wet. You will catch a death of a cold," Nana remarked upon our return, not "Did you have fun?" In little time, Grandpa was back in the house, with his white hair, metal-rimmed glasses, and rigid body, settling comfortably into his wingback chair with the stacks of paper he studied.

I still saw no photos of Francine and heard no words. I felt, but could not name, what the Evanses had done to my mother—disownment. We didn't discuss Joanne either. She, too, had been banned.

We visited Elliott over four years before moving to Washington, DC, when I turned sixteen. He died at eighteen as I trained for Peace Corps service without my ever seeing him again. I held onto the memory of holding him, loving him, and telling him stories. Elliott taught me to love without expectations, without conditions, and to draw strength even from what could not change. This took years to understand.

# 3

# On the Campaign Trail
## 1953–58

Our return to a four-person family gave me freedom from the dryer, diapers, and seizures I didn't understand. Elliott's baby shirts with extra large necks remained folded neatly on the bassinet, silent. All seemed quiet after seven years of bedtime preparations, feedings, or stroller walks around the block. I still tiptoed to not wake him and worried about having friends over. Habits die slowly.

This calm ended abruptly one morning a year later. Mother walked into the kitchen and spoke excitedly to David Jr. and me as we finished breakfast.

"We're bringing home a new baby boy in two days."

I put my spoon down, stunned. "Oh no, not another baby," I whispered to myself. "What?" was the only word said. Our small family gave me the freedom to plan my own time, a luxury.

I sunk lower into the chair. Mother saw me, walked over toward me, pulled out a chair, and dropped down, elbows on the table, head in her hands. She sobbed, quietly at first, then uncontrollably. Tears, held back for seven years, ran down her face, her arms, and onto the placemat. Her body shook, shoulders hunched. She couldn't stop. In those moments that February morning, she let the years of pain and anguish over Elliott go and prepared to begin motherhood anew.

The depth of her sadness had not shown as she gave full love and care for over a half decade. My distress obscured my understanding of her grief, exhaustion, and sadness. Around the table that morning, we grieved for Elliott and ourselves. Then we let him go.

My parents both wanted more children, which church teachings encouraged. But pregnancies didn't happen. Francine had given birth to David Jr. and me. Mother ached for her own.

In fourth grade, one afternoon, I sat in the kitchen near the telephone, absently thumbing through a directory of Mother's college nursing classmates. Each classmate, most now married and mothers, had described a wish: a new home or car, not unusual for young women in Salt Lake. Rosalie King's name then appeared.

She had written, "I hope to have a daughter of my own." The words left me numb. Empty. Did I not belong, even while trying so hard?

Although David Jr., Daddy, and I said nothing about Francine, her ghost lived with us. Mother's own children could erase the haunting. Her occasional negative references reaffirmed her resentment of this unspoken presence.

"Were you aware," she began as I loaded the dishwasher one evening, "that Francine and your daddy got a full set of sterling silver cutlery at the wedding?"

"No."

"She took it all when she left." Her voice dripped with disapproval. "The cutlery should have stayed with your daddy. I deserve it."

I said nothing but grabbed the dishes and noisily stacked them, trying to drown out the words.

*

Baby Stephen arrived on February 23, 1956. My father's description of him at that moment reflects his own eagerness for new fatherhood after years of pain.

"He was a blond bundle of joy—well built, with an abundance of curly blond hair, a cherubic face, and all smiles. To us, he seemed to have come right out of heaven. We cherished him with all the love and devotion that could be given to any baby. Our arms were hungry for a little one, and we had waited a long time."

Daddy wrote a perfect description of Stephen. No one else had curly hair.

Six months later, in the heat of August, we packed the used green station wagon, made a baby bed for Stephen in the rear, and drove to the port of New York City to greet the ship, the SS *United States*. Down the plank with a caregiver came three-year-old Frank, our newly adopted brother from France. Daddy had negotiated the adoption, even flying to Paris in April to meet Frank in a hospital and sign the papers.

Frank had an Algerian father and French mother, lived in fifteen orphanages during his three years, and arrived with a contagious smile and a severe ear infection. He screamed as men approached him, even Daddy. Yet only Daddy could speak to him in his language, French. Driving back to Utah, Daddy tried to cuddle him while singing in French, but Frank screamed and struggled. Finally, he tired himself out and slept in Daddy's arms as Mother drove. Baby Stephen remained in my care.

Two weeks later, Frank's ear cleared up, English words appeared, and Daddy became his friend. With daily cuddling, they became buddies.

As Frank became part of the family, Mother announced she was pregnant. Matt arrived in April 1957. In fourteen months, I became the oldest of five, including two babies (Stephen and Matt) and a three-year-old (Frank) adjusting to America. Noise, toys, bottles, diapers, strollers reentered our daily patterns. My being a babysitter resumed and continued until college. Mother gave birth to Christine two years after Matt and then to Christopher two years after Christine, as I headed to the University of Utah. With Francine as the mother of David Jr. and me, Frank and Stephen adopted, and Rosalie as the mother of Matt, Christine, and Christopher, our brood claimed three fathers and four mothers, a case study of nature and nurture's bumpy ride together.

*

All families have tensions, as did ours. Frankie's disruptive adjustment posed difficulties. Neighbors and friends inadvertently added confusion to his integration. As family members went to the store, church, or park, others stopped us with "Is he yours?" pointing to Frank. "Where did he come from?" or "Why does he look different?" Frank, small for his age, had black hair, brown eyes, and olive skin. Other family members showed our Scandinavian and British roots—blond hair, blue eyes, and tall. Our neighborhood looked like us, our church congregation looked like us. No one looked like Frank.

These innocent, curious, and yet stinging comments about Frank were noticed. We, and Frank himself, internalized the comments. He knew he was different.

"Frank might not grow as fast," Mother commented. "Our Frank might have a harder time in school." Those words that emphasized differences impacted him—and us as we grew. They were innocently said but kept Frank apart, outside. Watching their impact stayed with me. I learned to not speak out about differences. Stay mum.

*

Daddy's church-wide responsibilities increased, including giving talks to church congregations throughout Salt Lake and Provo. Sunday became another day without Daddy.

"Do you want to come with me when I speak this afternoon, Jody?" Daddy asked one Sunday morning before our own church service. Mormon church services were both Sunday mornings and afternoons.

"Sure," understating my excitement. During the twenty-minute drive that afternoon in our green station wagon—which had taken us to New York City and back and sported a fresh nick from Daddy's misjudged parking effort—he lectured me on how to prepare speeches. Daddy didn't have small talk; he lectured while he drove, and they continued on our Sunday drives to and from churches where he frequently spoke for three years. His engaging words, distinguished vocabulary, crisp enunciation made listening easy.

"Think of a train," he began, looking over at me, hoping for an interest in the topic. "A train has boxcars, sometimes a hundred cars." He had my attention. "Each boxcar is chosen by the trainmaster for the day's journey. Some boxcars remain in parking lots, while others cross thousands of miles before resting." Daddy talked in metaphors, even to his family.

He continued, "Giving speeches is like being the trainmaster. I go through my boxcars, actually five-by-seven note cards, and choose those that suit my subject and audience. I think of a religious topic relevant to today here in Salt Lake. I look at news headlines. I imagine moral and spiritual issues the congregants face."

Daddy's cards about hope were more yellowed and frayed than those about raising money for new churches. Some cards remained in their appointed spaces. Others joined new topics each week as speeches changed. Those card images live with me today. They are the metaphor for my own speech preparation, filed by topic on the computer, waiting to entertain an audience.

These car rides with Daddy stirred my interest in speaking, taking new ideas or found quotes, adding them to cards, and holding them as I spoke, giving confidence to my voice.

But giving a speech is more complex than choosing cards from a box. It is a craft that requires practice, courage, and a voice that carries confidence and knowledge. A speaker's goal is to have listeners feel passionate, confident, or knowledgeable while listening. I learned from my father to offer listeners my passion and confidence. I have to care if I want my audience to care.

During car rides, Daddy recounted his own fears and later recorded them in his autobiography. His fear of not offending mirrored my own: "I was born timid. I never seemed able to please my father, who cut a very overpowering figure and was known as Utah's silver-tongued communicator.... Maybe I was just super sensitive and never wished to offend anybody. I conclude that during my early teens, I must have gotten awfully mad at myself and decided to fight back. The escape from my timidity torture lay in the success of my plan to develop such excellence that I could eventually show the world that I was worthy of its approval and admiration."

Daddy spoke each Sunday, me in the front row, alone, looking at his face, long and thin, with blue eyes that became larger as his voice gathered strength. He stood straight—tall at six feet, two inches—and spoke directly into the microphone, his eyes fixed on the audience, even as he held his cards. He had them memorized.

Occasionally, I turned around unobtrusively to look at the audience, about a hundred families, parents and children, from babies to teenagers. Church members dressed up for church, bows in girls' hair, clip-on ties for their brothers, suits and white shirts for fathers, and cotton dresses below the knee with jackets for mothers. Congregations looked similar, whether in Draper, Sandy, or American Fork. Families going to church together dressed their best, even while carrying babies, bottles, and cloth activity books for toddlers, a Mormon Church tradition.

The congregation looked straight at Daddy. Unlike with other speakers, congregants stayed still as he spoke. Babies stopped making noises. Daddy gave audiences confidence in what they could be and do.

After meetings, members hovered around my father as he stood in front of the pulpit. They introduced themselves, thanked him, and shared their own stories. I listened, interested in the banter of adult conversations.

When he introduced me to others, I gave a few practiced, gracious words, hoping Daddy would be proud.

"Yes, I am now in seventh grade, and I like school." "Yes, Daddy and Mother also say I am pretty. Thank you." "Does your son also like middle school?" My comments got easier, gave more information, but not too much.

I met city, state, and church leaders, all men, after these church meetings. Before each service, Daddy gave me a list of important people who might attend. He wanted to introduce me. His pride showed in his gleaming eyes and knowing grin as he brought me close. His words made me feel good.

"Jody is my oldest. I am so proud of her. Straight As in school, plays the piano, and loves books." Each sentence, each word, made me stand straight and tall like him.

*

I came home from church each Sunday full of excitement but expecting the inevitable as the door opened: "Jody, you need to fold the diapers," or "Stephen is crying. You need to pick him up. Help me, as I have church friends coming over tonight."

Mother used an angry voice, the tone resonated as shrill, loud. She sounded bigger than her five-foot, two-inch stature. She rushed from room to room, giving orders. Her jealousy was clear, home managing the kids while I spent time with Daddy. She wished to be with him and me at home, the oldest child babysitting the others. As always, my body tightened, my smile disappeared, my greeting to her remained unsaid as I began picking up toys in the living room.

During these early teenage years, my struggle with Mother defined our interaction. I liked to study, read, and play the piano. I didn't like picking up toys, putting kids to bed, cleaning three bathrooms, and folding clothes. Was I the maid?

My mother and I sparred over the use of my time. I tried to hide to read or do homework; she tried to find me to wash, clean, fold, or tend to the kids. These tasks never ended. We had to eat. We had to have clean clothes. We had to have scrubbed bathrooms. Kids shouldn't be alone. Mother wanted me in her sight, ready to do whatever and whenever. No discussing schedules.

Instructions flew at me in short, curt phrases and at random moments. "The bathrooms need an extra cleaning. Do it now and use the brush better next time." Or "Some of the dried dishes still had grease. You didn't wash them properly."

She didn't thank me, just told me how to improve. At school, math, English, and history came easily, with compliments from my teachers, gushes of joy from my father when looking at my grades, and praise from other students. Yet at home with Mother, I was never good enough at stacking the toy cardboard blocks, chopping the celery, or folding clothes.

Since then, nagging memories have stayed with me when doing chores in my own home. As a Peace Corps Volunteer, I asked Tata, a Tunisian neighbor, to help me clean. I paid her, hugged her, and thanked her each time. We became friends, laughing together and joining family holiday ceremonies. When I returned to the States, any help I asked for would come with praise and thank-yous. I always thank others. I know how it feels to not be thanked.

*

In June 1958, five months ahead of the congressional elections, the Utah Democratic Party asked my father to run for Congress, representing Utah's Second Congressional District.

Later, Daddy wrote in his notes, "Despite my nonconfrontational temperament, with its penchant for pleasing everybody, I also had some of the maverick in me. This captured the maverick."

I resonate with his words "pleasing everyone" and "maverick."

He spoke to the family about his decision that evening during dinner.

"This gets your daddy better known. Good for his law practice," Mother said.

"Will you win?" I asked, finishing my apple salad. I already visualized walking into the U.S. Capitol through the bronze front doors.

With my question, Daddy paused, thought, and then said, with unexpected honesty, "The Democratic leaders pointed out that Eisenhower is president for two more years and Utah is a Republican state. They said, 'We think we can win the seat in 1960, but not this year.' They told me I am a respectable candidate, which gets the Democratic Party ready for the big one in 1960. They said, 'If you run now, you might be the candidate who wins in two years.'" Faint praise.

A few minutes later, as Mother brought in bowls of bottled peaches for dessert, Daddy continued, voice raised over the kids squabbling, "With the state Democratic convention in a month and the election four months after that, we have to move quickly. I begin tomorrow." His tone silenced the kids. "Remember, I will use all my energy, but don't get your hopes up."

Daddy had only run for a state elective position once, a decade earlier, and lost. He had never held elective office, but the state party was asking him to go straight for the big prize—Washington. They knew the magic my grandfather had brought to Utah, a senator for twenty-four years. Our last name, King, still carried recognition. Daddy's reputation for his church speeches added glitter. But even with the family name reputation, the party thought this effort unwinnable.

My babysitting duties increased as both Mother and Daddy campaigned day and night. Newspapers wrote about his unusual campaign strategy: "King shakes eight hundred hands a day. He walks streets, neighborhoods, grocery stores shaking hands. When will he slow down?" That story grew during the fall.

"I have no money," Daddy said after the first article. "I only have my smile, my hands, and my long legs that can walk fast."

\*

That fall, as a sophomore in high school, I occasionally joined my father's campaign. As October began and the first snows covered the nearby Wasatch Mountains, we drove over the Point of the Mountain, the passageway that separates Salt Lake and Utah Counties. We continued to Vineyard, Utah County, and the Geneva Steel Mill, best known for heavy, sooty smoke from its four smokestacks and the pervasive smell of rotten eggs.

"We'll see workers pouring out red molten steel slag. You have curiosity. I bet you want to see the mill in operation," he said knowingly. He understood me. We had passed the mill many times driving to see Elliott and remembered tall, billowing smokestacks.

After our tour of the mill, keeping a respectful distance from danger, we walked to the small one-story brick house of Mr. Thurman, the union leader. It was located on mill property where the sound of slag pouring resonated as we approached the house. We sat on metal chairs in the tiny living room as Mrs. Thurman passed homemade oatmeal cookies. Their aroma made me hungry. A baby whimpered in the next room.

Mormon households did not offer alcohol, coffee, or tea—just water if asked for something to drink. Mrs. Thurman poured our glasses of water from a large plain glass pitcher. No ice. She smiled but said nothing. Mr. Thurman talked about his job, the union, and the need for higher wages and health coverage.

He turned to Daddy. "Can you promise to fight for unions if you go to Washington? We'll give you our vote if we get your support."

"Yes, you have that support," Daddy responded. "I am proud of my Democratic heritage and what I can do for unions." Mr. and Mrs. Thurman seemed satisfied.

As we returned to Salt Lake in our tired station wagon, Daddy lectured me quietly in his familiar baritone voice. "I learned much today about the steelworkers' union and the needs of its members. I support them."

He drove for a few minutes in silence. Then he continued, "As I think about our visit, I couldn't be a steelworker." This had been my thought. After more silence, he said, "Each day seems to be the same, all routine, safety risks, repetitive motions each worker makes to produce and cool the steel. He comes home to the same house, the same dinners, and the same factory sounds in the background." The scene he painted brought back the memory of my summer walk home from kindergarten ten years earlier, looking at mothers calling kids in for lunch while sheets dried in the backyard. My fear of routinized motherhood returned.

He continued, "I would get too bored." His honesty surprised me. "I need ideas, intellectual problems to solve, stimulating people to challenge me. I like to debate issues, grand problems." His voice grew even stronger as he burrowed further into his psyche.

At home, he often drove himself to study and seek answers as he hunched over books and papers on the dining room table. No one disturbed him. Details mattered less to him than the broad structure that held the details together. He continued talking, and as he did, I realized why he had to run for Congress. He couldn't *not* run.

I have since viewed that conversation as permission to be like him—to study, learn, be with people in offices solving problems. I pictured myself sitting at a desk, typewriter, phone, others asking questions. I didn't see myself staying home as the church suggested women do.

*

Election Day came. Friends at school knew about Daddy's campaign. One teacher asked me to explain the process. "We all should learn what a campaign is. You can be our student expert."

"Your father can't win," some at school said. "He's a Democrat."

These comments didn't surprise me. I was aware since the second grade of the paltry number of Democrats in Salt Lake. That year, just a week before the 1952 election, my teacher asked the class, "How many of your parents are voting for Eisenhower?" Most hands sprang up. Then "How many of your parents are voting for Stevenson?" Two hands, mine being one. I was different... and proud of it.

*

On election night, Daddy and Mother sent us to bed at 9:00 p.m. to avoid seeing him lose. Daddy had worked hard and then harder still. His loss would hurt him deeply. Then—the votes were tallied. From Daddy's autobiography: "The returns, up until midnight, showed the Democrats to be trailing by several thousand votes. Rosalie and I got out our sackcloth and ashes in preparation for our concession speech. But about midnight, my vote tally began inching up toward my opponent's. About two in the morning—the miracle happened. The sweet taste of victory. The ecstasy was worth the agony. I passed him up.... When it was all over, at about three in the morning, I had won by six hundred votes."

Mother shook me awake, screaming, "We won! We can go to Washington! We won!"

"What?" I cried. I hugged her, jumping out of bed. "We weren't supposed to win."

"But we did. We won." The news now sunk in.

"I'm beginning to believe it.... Yes, it's true, it's true!" my voice yelled out. Images of being at the Capitol flooded my mind.

"Congratulations" from my homeroom friends as I came into school, sat straight, all five feet, nine inches of me, and kept smiling.

"How much money will your father make?" asked someone in class.

"Forty-two thousand dollars!" I replied excitedly, a question already asked of Daddy.

"That's a lot. What will you do with it all?"

No answer. Most classmates asked about money. They didn't

understand what a congressman did, but they appreciated what they could do with money. I wasn't sure what a congressman did either.

"I am ready to move. Washington looks good," I said to Mother. Giving up the orchestra, straight As, the Salt Lake bus system, and my piano lessons seemed fine for something new, something bigger.

We packed our station wagon and began our family's second drive across the country on December 21, 1958. The crowded car included Matt, now one; Stephen, three; Frank, six; David Jr., thirteen; me, sixteen; Mother, seven months pregnant; and Daddy. I have blessedly forgotten the details of that difficult 2,100-mile trip.

Daddy promised me mountains on the East Coast and around Washington. "You love the Wasatch Mountains, our canyon picnic suppers, hikes, views of the city," he said as we left Ohio and entered Pennsylvania. "But we have mountains here too. Keep your eyes peeled for them."

As we left Hagerstown toward Frederick, Maryland, I asked, "When do we see the mountains? I didn't see any."

His reply: "Didn't you see the Appalachian Mountains?"

"Those hills? They're not mountains." We both laughed. I became an easterner, exchanging mountains for green trees, parks, forests, and rain—lots of it.

# 4

# Mr. Speaker, It's Me in the Gallery
## 1959–61

My new school, Walter Johnson High School in Bethesda, Maryland, carried the name of a famous Washington Senators pitcher, one of the greatest pitchers of all time. I loved baseball, knew how to keep score, knew players' names. Growing up in Salt Lake City, autumn meant canning cherries, peaches, apricots, and tomatoes, all to the sound of Major League Baseball. I looked forward to listening to the World Series while mashing apples for apple butter.

"WJ," as we called the school, became my academic home on January 3, 1959, where two thousand strangers would pass me in the hallways. Although shy, belonging became my goal. But how?

After pondering the question, I said to David Jr. as we loaded the dishwasher, "I want to say hi to at least one person I know between every class every day."

He laughed. "That's a stupid idea. I don't care how many kids I meet. Why does belonging matter?"

My project began. The number of students responding to my greeting was few the first month but then increased quickly. At dinner on March 5, I turned to David Jr.: "Success! I've said hi to at least one person between every class today."

"Silly. I'm working on good grades."

Like my father, my drive to belong, to succeed, even with small goals, pushed me past my cautiousness throughout my professional life.

\*

The school bus rides gave opportunities for gossip and new ideas for belonging. To Janet, my regular seatmate known for her bulky sweaters and a quick smile, I asked, "Am I dressing right? Should I roll my socks down? Wear Mary Jane shoes?"

She looked surprised by the question, but I continued: "I don't know what to wear. In Utah, we dressed like the cheerleaders who led the fashion fads. Belonging depended on looking like them."

Janet laughed. "I've never heard of something so stupid. Why do you think it matters?"

Was she serious? It didn't matter? Of course it mattered. In Salt Lake, friends thought wearing the right clothes beat studying. My secondhand clothes from cousins had kept me on the social outer edge in my high school. WJ was my chance for a fresh start.

Janet continued with emphasis, "Worry about grades. That's what counts."

"Are you joking?"

"I'm serious. I want to go to Cornell. Worrying about clothes doesn't get me there."

Good news. Fashion remained a mystery to me. But a decade later, Francine would show me I did need to think about clothes. Women are often judged by what they wear.

*

Surrounded by open fields with grazing cows keeping watch over the football field, WJ's reputation was that of the "cow school" but with an academic catch. It had the highest number of graduates going to Ivy League colleges in Montgomery County.

My rude academic awakening at WJ came at the end of my first month. Bad habits die hard, and mine was getting As with minimal studying. My father's hugs and praise with each report card encouraged my further achievement without effort.

My joy in academics moved east with me. On the first morning at WJ, Mr. Humphrey, my math teacher, said, "You already have first-semester As from Salt Lake, so we'll give you a practice mark at the end of January. It won't count."

"I'll do well," I said, head high.

"Good luck. We work hard here." Other teachers proposed similar plans, all As assured.

"I'm disappointed in you," Mr. Humphrey said as he gave me my practice D at the end of the month. Other teachers joined with Cs and Ds: a dullard from Utah who couldn't cut it in Washington.

My study habits immediately changed. "Could you review formulas with me so I will understand?" I asked Mr. Humphrey. To my English teacher: "Could you critique this paragraph I wrote for any errors?" Help came from all my teachers, even the gym instructor, who patiently encouraged my volleyball spike.

I pushed harder, spoke up more, studied longer, read with care. Achievement required work.

My competitiveness came from my father. In his autobiography, he said, "In my youth, I was very timid and easily frightened. But I became personally ambitious and competitive, a paradox in life I am at a loss to explain."

Two and a half years later, I graduated tenth in a class of 570 students. The fear of failing drove my academic competitiveness.

*

To make moving to Washington easier, my father bought the Kensington, Maryland, home owned by the person he defeated in the election, and it remained the family home for forty-five years. The split-level, two-story, redbrick house had four bedrooms and three baths, a tight fit for a family of seven. With Christine's birth two months later, we became eight. David Jr., Frank, Steve, Matt, and now Christine shared two bunk bed bedrooms upstairs. I, being a teenage girl, had my own bedroom with a desk downstairs, a generous gift from Mother given the growing family.

Mother and I renewed our housekeeping tug-of-war—her asking me to take care of the kids, tend to laundry, and clean bathrooms, and my retreating to my orderly desk with textbooks and three-ring binders.

Mother would call down to my bedroom, "Jody, fold the diapers now." She heard me carrying diapers upstairs on tiptoe. "Jody, now could you set the table for dinner?" That done: "And now cut the carrots." Tasks continued as afternoon turned to evening. Studying began again after 8:00 p.m. after stacking toys in the playroom and helping the kids to bed.

My careful nighttime study routine kept my grades up. Based on six hours of sleep, 11:30 p.m. to 5:30 a.m., it did not include TV, reading for pleasure, or parties. During this time, my father stayed aloof, sitting at the dining room table, typing notes on his old Royal typewriter, keystroke by keystroke, click by click, as if encased in a cocoon with the sign "Do not disturb." Mother ran the house.

*

At 5:45 every weekday morning, I called into David Jr.'s bedroom, "Ready?" We left for the daily 6:00 a.m. Mormon seminary class on Western Avenue near Chevy Chase Circle.

"Great to see you. I see Danny and Emma Jean didn't wake up in time today. Are they coming?" Brother Samulson, our instructor, asked as the twenty of us shuffled in, yawning, sinking into our desks, doing a quick catch-up with friends before class began.

All chatter then stopped as Brother Samulson said, "Open your Book of Mormon to Nephi, chapter 2, verse 1, our subject for today." Our daily religious education began.

Because of the early morning seminary, friendships grew among us, all Mormons, scattered thinly among three area high schools. We dated, partied, studied scriptures, and shared stories. Our group had common Mormon roots and Utah-Idaho heritages, and we knew church rules. We knew not to drink alcohol, coffee, tea, Coke; wear immodest clothes; or include petting on dates. These rules made our parties easy—punch, cookies, games, music, and talk. We stayed close, reducing the temptation to join school late-night drinking parties.

My Mormon friends, daily seminary classes, Sunday services, and church teachings kept me safe from drugs, alcohol, smoking, and sex.

My early religious memories included Sunday school lessons and church talks with directives and assumptions of my staying pure to be worthy of a temple marriage. Versions of the admonishments, said gently and with a smile, became more directed as we faced greater temptation as teenagers.

One particular Sunday evening, the women's group leader organized a fireside service in the church hall on Sixteenth Street, the grandest chapel in the Washington, DC, area. I knew the event's seriousness and guessed the topic, sex, even without its reference in the fireside's title. Sacred spaces in the church house didn't lend themselves to directness.

Four hundred young women mingled in the parking lot and corridors but became quiet with heads lowered, hands in our laps as we slipped into the pews. After the song and prayer, our speaker, Sister Busch, began by holding up a white rose.

"I want you to pass this rose around and look at its beauty. Touch carefully as you pass it, and then return the rose to me." Sister Busch then continued her obtusely stated dating admonishments as we passed the rose, avoiding the thorns. The last person holding the flower walked up the center aisle and handed it to Sister Busch. She reached and took the stem carefully with two fingers.

She turned toward us, paused as she looked into our eyes, and held up the rose. "Look at this rose," she continued, then reached for a second, identical rose hidden on the podium. "Look at the two roses side by side, one never touched, the other held by many. What do you see?" I laughed nervously and laced my fingers together. Others around me squirmed, embarrassed at what we knew would follow.

We stared at the two roses. Hands shot up. "One is missing a petal." Another said, "It looks limp, tired, used."

The speaker had the words she wanted and smiled. She raised her hands toward us. "Yes, the flower you touched represents you not staying pure of body before marriage. You lose the right for a temple marriage."

None of us in the room had other thoughts, if our affirmative nodding showed our feelings. The temple marriage had been my goal since childhood. My father had had two temple weddings and assumed a temple marriage for me.

"When you get married in the temple…" began many of his lectures about my future marriage plans. I believed the church teachings, including Latter-day Saints being the only true church on earth, and wanted to please my father.

My temple wedding five years later achieved this goal. Then my circumstances dramatically changed.

*

My father attempted to turn family dinners into civics discussions drawn from his congressional work. Kids yelling, a ringing phone, sentences interrupted—challenged his lectures, but he didn't give up.

Daddy sat at one end of the dining room table with his back to the living room, Mother at the opposite end near the window and backyard cherry trees. The children crowded together on each side. The kitchen doorway faced Mother's end of the table, making it handy for her to answer the kitchen phone, its long curling cord extending the phone's reach. Mother enjoyed answering the regular dinnertime calls filled with church and political gossip her friends provided. This gave us more entertainment than Daddy's lectures.

One evening, early in his first term, he cleared his throat, paused, waited for silence from the kids, which didn't come, then recounted what a friend had told him the day after the election.

Mother called out, "Who was the friend?"

"Rosalie, it doesn't matter to the story," he said gently, cutting her off. "Now let me continue. My friend looked directly at me and said, 'Brother King, now that you are elected, I hope you can forget politics and do the right thing.'"

Daddy paused for a moment, looking across the table. His low, steady voice held David Jr.'s and my attention. Frank, Steve, and Matt continued eating the cut-up chicken, oblivious to the heavy conversation at one end of the table. Baby Christine slept soundly in the bassinet behind Daddy. "Now, family," he continued, "I ask you, what is the right thing? What should I do?"

"Follow the constituents' wishes," I said. "Or follow the party? Democrats helped get you elected."

Daddy kept listening, looking toward the window, without response. He waited.

David Jr., head down: "Decide by following church teachings."

"What about constituents who aren't Mormons?" I offered. "Follow your instincts."

My thoughts and words became less sure. David Jr. became distracted by Stephen driving his toy car across the plate into his carrots.

Daddy turned to me and confessed, "Nor do I know what is best to do."

Mother replied, "Yes, you do, David. Do what gets you reelected."

This was part of a dinnertime pattern: legislative lectures, regular interruptions, phone calls, or kids yelling.

Another evening, Daddy began, "How should Congress divide up national resources when there isn't enough to go around? Who should get what and how much as we vote on the national budget?"

Mother groaned. I looked down and mumbled, "I don't know."

"Constituents continually cry out, 'Do what is morally right!'" He looked around. "Can you tell me what is morally right? Should Congress favor the poor over the rich?" he asked. "Or the more needy over the less needy?" His voice gathered strength. "Or the fishermen over the miners? Or those who voted for me over those who didn't?"

My thoughts raced to my own personal rights for college and an education—"Don't take my rights away," I blurted out, not realizing I had put myself first.

"Why should you have more rights than others?" Daddy asked. He didn't continue his lecture, but he planted the seed to question assumptions assumed sacred.

My father's dinnertime lectures changed me. I added these concerns to those of my daily events, such as getting a date, doing the dishes, or completing homework. I asked questions in civics class, read the top-line political articles in the *Washington Post* and *Evening Star*, answered questions Daddy posed—as if I, too, were a member of Congress.

The CBS top-of-the-hour headlines on WTOP radio became my ritual to track legislation Daddy cared about. To a friend in Salt Lake, I wrote, "I am lucky to live in Washington. My local news is your national news." I became a national politics junkie.

Daddy's lectures stimulated my interest in politics, helping me appreciate the complexities of melding national and local political interests. My Peace Corps policy decisions over four decades drew on these high school dinner conversations peppered with family noise and disruptive phone calls.

*

"Nana's coming this afternoon to see us," Mother told David Jr. and me one spring Saturday of my junior year. No warning.

"Dress for church," Mother instructed. "She will be here at 1:00 p.m." We hadn't seen Nana, our grandmother, in four years.

Nana arrived promptly on the hour wearing a flower-print dress, gloves, and hat, too formal for grandkids.

"How are you doing? How do you like the east?" she asked us, with no preliminary words of greeting. We sat stiffly on the matching needlepoint chairs, answering her queries in complete sentences, as if reciting a lesson to a teacher. My hands kept straightening the corduroy skirt and fiddling with my long, straight hair.

"Jody, the pink in the blouse you are wearing doesn't become you," she said once she had our school information. Her admonishments of my behavior from early childhood, mostly forgotten, now rushed back.

At what must have seemed the time to leave, Nana kissed us. "I love you both. Be good for your father and follow church teachings," and then she left. She said nothing about her family, Francine, or related aunts and uncles. She seemed to not want us in the family. Mother said nothing after she left. The Saturday continued as if she had never come.

Two decades later, Francine told me that during the visit, she had sat outside in Nana's rental car, parked around the corner, crying. "I sobbed, wishing desperately to walk up the path, ring the doorbell, look in, and see you." But Nana had been firm. "No contact." Francine had to wait six more years.

*

My father found me a summer internship in an Ohio congressman's office in the Old House Office Building (now the Cannon House Office Building). On the first day of summer, Daddy put his arm around me as we walked through the carved doors of the two-story building at the corner of Independence and New Jersey Ave.

"Welcome to the Old House Office Building, my congressional home," his voice strong, arm pointing proudly into the massive hallway. "Learn all you can this summer. You won't get this experience again."

"This hallway is as long as two football fields. Why so much space?" I exclaimed, not prepared for the massive length and height.

"I had the same question when I walked into my father's Senate offices as a kid. But I quickly got used to it. Now I feel at home," Daddy said proudly.

A door opened down the hallway, and two people emerged and walked toward us. The man wore a dark suit and black shoes, walked resolutely, his steps purposeful. Beside him, a young woman jotted notes on a card while her companion spoke. She carried files in her left hand, balancing the note card atop them while writing with her right hand. Wearing a trim medium-blue suit and high heels, she tried to both write and keep up with her companion's strides. He, taking long strides and talking, seemed not to notice her efforts.

As we passed, my father and his colleague, another congressman, exchanged greetings, no introduction of the woman. I thought, "Women don't count."

We continued walking the length of the hallway and then another before coming to my father's office.

"It's the opposite corner from the front entry, a healthy walk for both of us."

Nearing the end of the second hallway, a polished brass sign near an open door said, "John Flynt, Fourth District, Georgia."

"Go in for a moment," Daddy said, putting his hand on my back and nudging me forward. The receptionist offered us each a miniature bag of peanuts.

"Did you know Georgia is famous for peanuts?" She smiled eagerly. "Do you know what we are also famous for?" she asked as she stepped away from her desk and over to six Coca-Cola bottles across the room. "Coke's headquarters are in Georgia." Then as she moved to the back of the reception area: "Georgia can't be known as the Peach State without peaches. We have fresh peaches delivered every day Congress is in season," pointing to the basket next to her phone.

"Thank you," I said, turning to leave. "You now have a 'Come to Georgia' convert."

Thirty-five years later, I would become chief of staff to a Peace Corps director who then became a senator from Georgia: Paul Coverdell. I often visited his office three decades later. The same Georgia products greeted me. He never drank a Pepsi.

On the wall behind the receptionist in my father's office hung photos of the Wasatch front of the Rocky Mountains with the Salt Lake Mormon Temple in the foreground.

"That summarizes Utah to me, makes me want to go back soon," I said, turning toward the telephone operator. His blond hair fell over his glasses. "Are you from Utah?" I asked hesitantly, noting the blinking lights on his phones.

"Born in Salt Lake and graduated from BYU." Then he added, "Your father is good to work for."

"He is also a good father," I replied.

Daddy beamed, looked down, smiled, and then turned toward a nearby aide who called out, "Congressman, we need you!"

Behind the wall with the photo of the temple, the day's hard work began. An aide took me through my father's suite of offices. In the conference room, legal books, photos, and reminders of Utah's culture—miniature skiers, beehives, and the bright-red letter *U*—lined the shelves. The framed family photo taken at Daddy's swearing-in was centered on one shelf.

Leaving, I glanced out the window facing First Street SE. Small cramped row houses lined the block facing our four-story, block-long hulking congressional office building. Children climbed on the front stoops, occasionally looking toward my window. A girl with long white ribbons braided into her hair caught my attention. Her eyes held mine, not letting go. She didn't move. One boy's too-large T-shirt dwarfed him as he leaned against the doorway, ignored, forgotten by others. The boys jumped on the stairs and chased each other, no toys in view. They had no school supplies, and their clothes seemed wrong for school. Were they waiting for a school bus?

In the car on the way home, I asked Daddy, "Have you seen your neighbors across the street?"

"Every day I see them. I ask myself, 'What can I do as a congressman from Utah? I don't represent them.'" He stopped talking for a minute, thought, and then continued, "They don't have a representative because they live here, in Washington, DC. This city, where you, Jody, were born, is denied any official representation in Congress. It is the 'nation's capital.' These kids live across the street from congressmen who serve everyone in the country except them and their parents."

"Who speaks for them?"

"We all should, but we don't speak enough." We both stayed silent.

In 1971, these tenants were forced to leave, and their homes were demolished to make way for a new Library of Congress addition, the James Madison Memorial Building. After that year, members of Congress looked at the building's white marble exterior instead of row houses for the poor. After all, those elected officials hadn't represented the kids playing on the stoops of row houses.

The image out the window that morning burrowed into me and has returned over the years, reminding me of differences in economics, race, education, and parenting. Those children influenced my Peace Corps decision and that of my chosen profession, social work.

*

Being an aide in a congressional office became tedious. On my second day, Ted walked me to a light-brown IBM electric typewriter on the desk in a room of metal file cabinets. Local newspapers from towns in southeastern Ohio announced weddings, births, graduations, and deaths, and Ted told me, "Find those notices and use the templates I'm giving you to type letters for the congressman to sign. That includes getting their addresses from the stack of telephone books over there in the corner."

My father had once told me that the painting of the Golden Gate Bridge never ended; once completed, it was time to begin again. To me, writing constituent letters never ended; births, deaths, and weddings kept happening. Any typing mistake meant beginning the letter again. Being accurate saved time, paper, and my patience.

*

"Do you want to join me for a reception this evening?" Daddy asked at the end of my first month as an intern. He used receptions for business, never pleasure.

"Of course," came my usual reply.

As we walked through the tunnel to the Senate Reception Room in the Capitol, Daddy said, "I don't like receptions. People drink and say meaningless things." As he entered the elevator, he continued, "And everyone wants something. Receptions are to get favors and leverage committee positions. Who has fun doing that?"

"Don't you think it's a power game?" I asked.

Daddy thought a minute as raised voices drew us toward the chamber. He sighed.

"It's hard to know. I haven't learned to play. I don't like power grabs."

We picked up name tags, pasted them on our jackets and blouses, and stood at the chamber's doorway, the entrance to dark suits, unfamiliar faces, loud voices, waving hands, calls for drinks, noise, confusion.

I turned to Daddy. "Where do we begin? Who do we try to talk to?" The tightly packed crowd was mostly men. We nudged our way toward the food table, accepting greetings along the way, like "Hello, good to see you again." We became lost in the crowd.

"Be sure to watch Congressman Rich McCormick," my father whispered, picking up carrot sticks hidden among the sugary desserts. He didn't eat sugar. The carrot sticks looked as if they had attended a couple of earlier receptions, sticking limply out of a metal cup.

People jostled each other, called out names to get attention, and then formed small, huddled groups, trying to hear each other. Congressman McCormick, with his distinctive wire-rimmed glasses, commanded the attention of the largest group. Power negotiators. I watched.

Congressman McCormick had been number two in the House for nine years, rumored to be Speaker Sam Rayburn's replacement. McCormick delivered his words carefully, even among colleagues, and no one dared interrupt. His calm demeanor demanded attention, no need to move because he had the power. He touched neither hors d'oeuvres nor alcohol.

After about forty minutes, his shoulders slumped slightly. He smiled less and kept his arms still.

My father had told me earlier, "McCormick eats dinner every night alone with his wife. I don't know how he does it with his schedule, but he puts her first. I admire him for that."

Others knew McCormick's routine and began moving away. He had finished talking. Silently, he slipped away with no more hellos. The reception lost energy without his presence.

Today, how many members of Congress quietly slip away and leave in the middle of power deals to have a quiet dinner at home?

"Let's go home," Daddy said as he nudged me out.

Years later, observations of that evening haunted my internal drive to work hard. Did I even want to balance it with family?

\*

"Jody, pick up the toys, now!" Mother yelled as I walked in the front door after work, my second week of the internship. "Faster, please. Dinner is almost on the table."

The next week, at the end of the workday, Mother stood at the door, arms folded. "You don't do enough for the kids; you don't care." Her small frame belied her loud voice, her face red with frustration.

"I do care!" I cried back, wondering what mistake had brought on her anger. A great day at work and now this? My eyes grew cloudy with tears.

She continued, "You don't really love the kids. And look at me when I talk to you." Her voice now filled the living room. Daddy retreated upstairs to the bedroom and closed the door. His retreat signaled I was on my own with Mother, as usual. Wiping the tears, I waited for more words, silently, my practiced response. My speaking back would only raise her volume.

Then with a flushed face, she continued, "I stay here all day taking care of these kids while you gallivant at the Capitol acting important. Well, you're not important." She had revealed the source of her anger—jealousy of my work on the Hill. Why couldn't she be at the Capitol and I be at home? She didn't have opportunities growing up that now came so easily to me and resented what she hadn't had.

*

Mother enthusiastically attended evening congressional events with Daddy, which reduced frustration and gave her stories for friends and church groups. My father attended the events as a necessity of work. He preferred just to work. I wondered if she should have been the person in Congress.

After one particular black-tie event, she came up the basement stairs and into the living room, glowing. "Guess who I met tonight?" she called out, seeing me waiting at the kitchen door, ready to report on how the kids behaved and who called.

"Jody, Speaker Rayburn brought me raspberry crepes from the dessert table, even dodging dignitaries in the crowded room to do so. He handed me the crepes, saying, 'These are for you, Rosalie, and I want to tell you what a great job Dave is doing in Congress.' He knew my name!"

As Mother talked, Daddy walked past her and into the kitchen for a glass of water, filled it, sipped the water slowly, returned to the stairway, and started his climb to the bedroom. He turned back to us, rolled his eyes as Mother continued describing her conversations with those she had met.

"Come, Rosalie, we need to be getting our sleep." He showed little interest in sharing the chitchat. Mother kept talking to me, now her only audience. My eagerness showed on my face, and my comments about her good fortune were supportive. She needed reinforcement of value, of love, which was denied her the first two decades of her life.

As a young child, after losing both parents, she was raised by her grandfather and step-grandmother, along with their four children, Grandpa's second family. From eight years old, Mother had to milk the cow, Daisy, every morning and night, the only child to do so. She talked often to me about her thankless chore, alone, outside, in the cold Logan, Utah, winters. She hadn't been loved or thanked.

As the summer wore on, I said nothing to her about my experiences downtown and did not talk back when she yelled. Instead, I picked up toys, cut up carrots and celery for salads, and read fairy tales to Frank, Stephen, and Matt at bedtime.

Writing this memoir, I've gained clarity about my aversion to shouting and confrontations. Others have watched me turn away and otherwise avoid angry outbursts. These voices are triggers for memories of the trauma of Mother's diatribes and my helplessness to respond. They stayed with me and affected my leadership years later. I couldn't change her early life, her rejections. I had learned her story and couldn't change who she was. But her outbursts affected my lifetime behaviors.

Daddy, too, walked away when Mother yelled. He retreated to his desk, his study, his books, his outside walks. No fight, all flee. He and I remained alike.

*

"What are your college plans?" my school bus mate Linda asked as locker doors slammed shut in the WJ hallway between classes. "I think I have a lock on Cornell." We rushed to English class, bumping into others.

"Wellesley," I replied, knowing only its Boston location. We sat at our desks, opening books.

"You need great SAT scores for that school. Hope you have them." I shifted, lowering my eyes, not wanting to reveal my mediocre scores.

"Betsy's first choice is Radcliffe. Did she tell you? And Janine wants Smith."

"Great schools," I mumbled. During our high school senior year, conversations among friends focused on college applications to Ivy League schools and acceptance and rejection letters. My own chances for admission at one of these schools were low, but pretending gave me acceptance into the conversations. Never mentioned was my application to the University of Utah, my father's alma mater. To my friends, the West could have been another country.

One afternoon in early spring, Mother guided me out to the front steps and sat. "As I watch you each day, I know you probably wouldn't choose to have a big family." I tensed, body straight on the concrete step, anticipating something unpleasant. She knew I was tired of caring for kids.

"I also know you have your heart set on Wellesley."

I only nodded. "I will be okay with wherever I go," I lied.

We talked more about college and the possibilities.

"I wish I could have continued in college after my RN degree. But the hospital needed nurses." Then she lowered her voice, shifted her weight, and tapped her foot. She continued, "I think we will only be able to afford you going to the U."

She paused again, moved her weight on the step, looked across the street, and then back at me.

"I am expecting a baby in September."

I paused, trying not to look shocked.

Finally, before she guessed my ambivalence, I leaned over and hugged her tightly. "Congratulations. Great news. How much our family has grown since Stephen arrived five years ago. So full of surprises."

She loved the kids. She loved us all. But her neediness to feel important, to be accepted, got in the way.

My rejection letter from Wellesley came the following week. The University of Utah would be my home for the next four years. Christopher joined the family on September 5, 1961, the day before my leaving for Salt Lake City after almost three years in the nation's capital. In that time, I learned Utah would never be home again.

# 5

# Peace Corps Visits Alpha Chi Omega
## 1961–65

On September 6, 1961, five new students bound for Brigham Young University (BYU) and the University of Utah left Washington, DC, in a used black Cadillac pulling an overpacked trailer twenty-one hundred miles. Forty-eight hours and one accident later, the four BYU-bound colleagues dropped me off at a converted World War II hospital, my University of Utah dorm for the year.

\*

On my second day on campus, hundreds of incoming freshmen huddled near the doorway at the University of Utah Student Union at 8:00 a.m., our first day of sorority rush. "Why are you wearing bobby socks and Keds? They look weird," one girl, standing in the Union corridor looking at my feet, said. Her knee-length skirt, delicate hose covering slim legs, and pumps reminded me of a fancy dance night, not a sorority rush week.

"You aren't from here, are you? I can tell by your shoes," another rushee commented, wearing similar hose and pumps. Utah high school memories rushed back. I wanted to look like I belonged.

"I'm from Washington, DC," I said, looking directly at the two of them. I moved to hide my feet and socks behind a nearby chair. "I'm Jody King, and I used to live in Salt Lake. What's your name?" putting out my hand. They didn't recognize my daughter-of-a-congressman last name.

"I'm surprised you want to be here at the U," Sylvia commented after introducing herself.

On the first day of rush, in groups of thirty, we wound our way up the sidewalks and into five sorority houses on Alcott Street, fraternity and sorority row. Seventy sorority sisters in each house—wearing hose, pumps, and colorful skirts and tops—showed false smiles while shouting "Hello, rushees" as we entered. Behind their inauthentic enthusiasm, they watched for an unusual move or comment that meant a "black ball" vote a few days later. Their new sisters, these rushees they assessed, had to be like them. They watched us move into the living room. Their eyes began with our hair and then down to our faces and makeup, clothes, and finally, legs and shoes. I read trouble on my hosts' suspicious faces, elbow nudges, and whispers.

"She's different; she's not from here," they whispered as they saw my bulky, rolled-down bobby socks. On the second and final day of four added house visits, I walked up Alcott Street in a knee-length skirt, hose, and pumps. No more "She's not from here."

On Friday, we rushees sat nervously on folding chairs in the Union ballroom, waiting to know our fate. Chatter and fake, squeaky laughs revealed what we tried to hide: rejection. The dean passed out envelopes, words inside that would seal our college fate.

I unsealed my envelope slowly and then yelled out as I saw Alpha Chi Omega, my second choice. Social success! I had visited this house on my second day, no bobby socks. Alpha Chi, called the "Angel" sorority on campus, had the most Mormon members.

What is belonging on a campus with thirteen thousand students to an introvert? Alpha Chi became my campus family. We had each other's support in class, sports, music, and academic groups. Friends greeted me on sidewalks between classes and at snack breaks. Monday evening dinners with candles, prayers over the food, and storytelling in subdued voices beat the dorm cafeteria. New close friends grew out of our similar values and traditions. I felt their respect, and they, mine. Exchanging my bobby socks for hose and pumps on the second day of rush gave me a new life.

*

The university's rules about dress, some written, some unspoken, surprised me. I chafed at the codes, one being wearing dresses for lunch and dinner in the dining hall. Those of us living in the converted hospital trekked daily up and down hills for meals, library study, and class. Utah winters brought blustery, icy winds and snow to the city, campus, and our treks. Our legs didn't take kindly to the temperature or winds. The dress-skirt rule, designed for campus commuters, didn't acknowledge two hundred of us schlepping daily up and down the mountain.

My legs begged for pants. In December of my freshman year, I joined the campus's women's association to appeal this rule through the university hierarchy.

"Who wants to help change the rule?" I asked others as our sub-committee grew. I studied the university systems and traditions to find a method for change. After researching the code's history, number of snowfalls, and months of cold, three of us presented a case for wearing pants to the dining hall in winter. We had testimonies from students as we sat at the dean's meeting in the old, ornate, and intimidating Park Administration Building. We showed confidence we did not feel, proper deference important in Utah culture, and dressed as if for church.

"Do you want to join me on the snowy hill one early morning?" I asked the dean. "No, thank you," she replied, not tempted. Three days later the response came: request denied. We continued with cold legs under the dresses to and from the dining hall.

Although a university issue of little consequence to most women, the experience furthered my interest in decisions and influence. I failed this time but learned that showing graciousness in defeat (which I didn't feel) and respecting the outcome built goodwill among decision-makers for more significant issues. Respectful determination overcame shyness.

*

"Would you like a ride back to your dorm?" Bob Olsen asked me following a December Sunday night fireside at the church center near campus. I had never met him, but the spontaneous offer impressed me.

Six of us crunched into his car, a used, high-end, three-shades-of-tan Dodge, and introduced ourselves, our years of study, and, for the men, missions. Ten minutes later, Bob dropped me off, just ahead of the Sunday 10:00 p.m. curfew. By the next day, I had forgotten the name of the Dodge's driver.

A month later, Bob called the dorm number, asking for me. "Hi, I'm Bob Olsen. Remember, we met a month ago." I faked it, trying to place him without success.

"Sure, I remember," waiting for him to say more. He didn't, so I confessed: "Remind me again where we met."

His voice unperturbed, "I drove you to the dorm after the fireside." Then he continued, "Would you join me at the fraternity fireside this Sunday?" His fraternity, Phi Delta Kappa, only pledged returned Mormon missionaries.

"Where did you go on your mission?" I asked, assuming that as a returned missionary, he thought of finding a wife. Devout Mormon men completed a mission but then pursued marriage quickly.

We double-dated with returned missionary friends and attended Mormon fraternity parties: casual, no exclusivity, simple conversations, and little romantic energy. He had just begun a five-year architecture program following his mission to Missouri and Arkansas. Unlike my major in education and sociology, with lectures by professors talking listlessly to students who pretended to listen while doodling and reading at our desks, Bob's classes required hand-eye coordination, space visualization, color relationship intuition, and mathematical skill.

*

"Do you want to help me build a model for my class assignment?" he asked later that spring.

"Sounds fun," my favorite response when not sure of committing to something. My interest in new subjects outside of books and libraries outweighed my reluctance. I entered Bob's world, the freshmen architecture lab on center campus, a tired former World War II two-story wooden army barrack in need of paint and clean windows.

After climbing the narrow, unlit stairway, Bob and I stepped into an immense student workroom. I stopped, closed my eyes, and listened in surprise. Sounds from Prokofiev's *Romeo and Juliet* filled the room. In that music was my past: bedroom, desk, record player, Russian music, soft sounds without yelling voices.

"That's Prokofiev," I said, turning to Bob. "May I just listen?"

"Sure, but how do you know the name? A strange piece to me." He paused and then mumbled, "I didn't grow up with classical music." He remained patient, unrushed, as I listened. I turned back into the brightly lit room and toward an expansive wood-top worktable surrounded by ten guys on high stools, hunched over miniature structures—the freshmen architecture class. They worked silently, heads down. Bob introduced me. Others mumbled their greetings and kept working. Two strong lights overhead brightened the table and hands that worked with paper, cardboard, magic markers, rulers, and X-Acto knives. The table scene reminded me of a stage: the hands as actors, the models as props, the rest of the space dark.

Meticulous, repetitive technical detail is required to build replicas of architectural spaces. Like repetition gains proficiency on the piano, a building design needs practiced attention to space relationships, color palettes, environmental harmony, and patience.

"Here you go, Jody," Bob said as he reached behind him to the weed-supply table tucked under the small cracked window for a pile of miniature tumbleweed branches. "Cut them to one-and-a-half-inch-tall bushes, enough to decorate the west side of the beach house I'm designing."

These words invited me into the architecture student model building club, a group that worked into the night, listened to classical music, ate stale sandwiches and donuts, and entertained wives and girlfriends while finishing projects to be graded. Furniture measured for rooms created conversation spaces, windows angled for maximum sunlight, gardens shaped to draw visitors outside, and roofs positioned to bring harmony to the structure, built within nine- to eighteen-inch models.

"What wall colors visually expand a room?" I asked. Or "How does furniture arrangement draw people into a space and hold them?" Answers came from whoever heard the question. One evening, sitting on the stool eating pie carried out from the dining hall, I asked Bob, "How do you know what works in the spaces, the buildings? What's right?" He smiled, then frowned and shook his head as he put down the knife.

"What do you mean? It just happens." He moved, working through the question. "I keep trying, and then, voilà, I see it."

"I'm lost. How do you create? Walls are walls, and roofs are roofs. Does it matter?" I asked. Bob reached behind the table to the storage bin and pulled out a house model blueprint. He spread it in front of me, smoothing the edges.

"Even before I began architecture, I could see three-dimensional spaces when I looked at simple flat blueprints. To me, the walls visually enclose rooms and hallways and give me a feeling as I mentally walk into the space. Others tell me flat lines stay flat."

"I'm one of those flat-line people. I don't get what you see. Glad I chose to teach." Bob's talent gave us years of beautiful living spaces and my learning of the value of color and design. He taught me that well-designed visual space has as much value as words. I had only known words.

The architecture lab became a hangout, with dynamic conversations, classical music, and meticulous cutting, gluing, and admiring. Jerry, a first-year student with Bob, and his wife, Sue, joined the Peace Corps Tunisia program with us. I have used lessons from the lab experiences for fifty years to choose colors for walls, furnish a room, select clothes to wear. I learned people's comfort in being together in a space depends on a room's lighting, shadows, furniture placement, and acoustics. Before meeting Bob and others in the architecture lab, I saw space as a place for activity, not a contributor to the activity. Providing well-being for others through their surroundings is a challenge I honor fifty years later.

*

"Do you want to have a Sunday dinner with my family this weekend? We've talked about it before," Bob asked in March of my freshman year.

"Sure, your parents okay with that?"

Bob grew up on a dairy farm in Utah County. His background did not mirror mine. He had suggested his mother might be nervous to meet me, the daughter of her congressman.

"I'm just me," I explained to him. "I don't think I scare anyone."

He laughed. "No, you aren't scary. Trust me."

The family farm bordered the Utah County Airport and Utah Lake in West Provo. A short end-of-the-day walk from the farm led to sunset reds and oranges reflecting off the pristine lake surface.

"A moment of gratitude for what I have," Bob told me. Less gratifying: "I had to be up and ready for the cows at 5:00 a.m. and then after a full day, milking them again at 5:00 p.m.... every day, even Christmas." Milking defined father and son time together, family bedtimes, school routines, and church schedules. Bob fed and milked cows daily, cleaned out manure weekly, and thinned and weeded sugar beets during the hot summer season. "I hated the weeding, hands and knees in the mud, pulling out plants, and sweating.... I had to change my shirt twice a day."

"How did you do it?" I asked as we drove. "No wonder you can stay up half the night gluing buildings together. You're used to time craziness." My urban, bookish background clashed against his rural, physical environment. My family had a state and national political reputation, his family, a strong West Provo farm and church standing. These differences affected dinner conversations and church activities, how we dressed, what we read, what music we heard. It influenced my choices of schools and later professional ambition.

"My father and I had a deal," he continued during the drive as the Dodge passed the Point of the Mountain, the division between Salt Lake and Utah Counties. "I work for him without payment, and he covers everything I need—school fees, tuition, car and gas, room and board, and my mission. I'm always financially secure. It's worth weeding the summer sugar beets."

We drove down Provo West Center Street toward Utah Lake. Farms and fences replaced brick houses and cul-de-sacs as the lake became visible and the city disappeared in the background. The one-story, wood-frame, ocean-green Olsen house on Center Street hid behind an immense weeping willow tree with low branches and a tire swing.

"I have always loved the swing. It brought peace," Bob said as the car turned into the gravel driveway to the side of the house.

"I'm nervous meeting your parents," I confessed, getting out of the car slowly to postpone the inevitable introductions. "You've brought many girls home. What do they look for in a girl that you, a returned missionary, date?"

"You're fine, don't worry. I keep saying it, and you keep worrying. Just relax," Bob said as he opened the front door and shouted, "We're here." The aroma of the roast simmering in the oven greeted me as we stepped inside the living room.

"This brings back my five-year-old Sunday dinner memories," I said as I took Bob's hand and smiled. "I'm feeling better. Roasts and potatoes unite us all." Bob's parents had just returned from Sunday school. His father, Kenneth, six feet, with slicked-back medium-gray hair and false teeth that occasionally clicked when he talked, wore his blue suit saved for church functions, the pants and elbows shiny from years of use. Bob's mother, Sarah, appeared in the cotton dress I would later see often, small flower print, three-quarter-length sleeves, and tiny buttons. Dresses like Sarah's reminded me of Mormon-mother-over-forty attire—ready to run to church for Sunday teaching supplies or to greet church members and neighbors dropping over for gossip and fresh or bottled fruit. I grew up with these mothers. I didn't want to be one.

Sarah walked hesitantly across the living room over a rose-patterned carpet and reached out to me. "Welcome to our humble home for dinner," she whispered as we shook hands. She looked at her shoes, laughed nervously, stopped, and laughed again as she continued, her short, gray, soft curls catching my eye. Bob had inherited those gorgeous curls. "The roast has been in the oven for three hours. Should be about ready," she continued, looking up at me.

"I am happy to…" but paused, interrupted.

"I need to get back to cooking. Excuse me," she said, pivoted, and disappeared into the kitchen.

"I can tell she is nervous. I'm trying," I said, turning to Bob as we stood.

"She's never met a politician's daughter. She's scared she might say something wrong."

"I'm ordinary, just a student."

"You don't get it. My mom saw campaign pictures of your dad, looking all important with his smile and expensive suit. She and my father voted against him for Congressman Dawson. She's afraid you'll find out and get mad." We looked toward the kitchen door. He paused, stepped back, and continued under his breath, "She's afraid you think of us as just farmers with little money or manners."

"And what do you think?" I asked, continuing to whisper. Without waiting for an answer, I continued, "I work, always have. I'm nobody special. Our family doesn't have money."

A call from Sarah interrupted us. "Dinner's ready. Food will get cold. Time to eat."

We took steps into the kitchen, across the linoleum floor to the chrome dining set at the back of the room. The lime-colored Formica tabletop matched the five chrome chairs around the table, with their plastic seats and backs, catching the sun from the window over the sink. Ken pulled out my chair and helped me sit, the legs scraping against the floor.

"This meal looks great," I exclaimed. "And the smell of the roast makes me hungry. Thanks for the invitation."

After Bob prayed, giving extra thanks for me being at the family table, Ken picked up the steel carving knife and fork, showing the confidence of many years of practice.

"Now for the roast. Here goes," he said as the knife went through the meat without effort. He turned to me, smiling: "Jody, did Robert tell you

I grow our meat? I choose the calves, feed them special grain, and have them butchered, carved, and packaged, ready for the freezer. I can't eat anything store bought… too tough." He paused, looking at me. "Hope you like it," as he slipped a large slice of roast onto my Melmac plate, the embedded flower design faded from years of use. We passed the dishes around the table—mashed potatoes, the ample gravy boat filled to the top, home-bottled beans, and frozen homegrown corn. Small plates with Jell-O salad and a dab of mayonnaise centered on top sat above our forks.

"I love the food," I commented, eating. "I'm not sure I've had a real homegrown meal before. What a difference."

Ken talked about raising cows and the vegetable garden. Sarah talked of summer canning fresh fruit and vegetables. "Corn is the most important for freshness," she said. "Ken picks it on his way to the house. I have the water boiling. We shuck it quickly and pop it in. Three minutes later, it's ready to eat."

"You even have the water boiling? Why so fast?" I asked, knowing little about corn.

"The sugar in the corn turns to starch in a few hours. For us, used to fresh corn, it's inedible after that."

"How different this corn tastes," I continued. "I have been eating starchy corn all my life. I see what I have been missing. May I have more?"

The conversation continued—milking cows, growing grain for cows and sugar beets for the cannery, the canal system between the Provo River and the farmland farmers on the west side used for growing crops.

"We farmers and milk producers know and trust each other," Ken commented. "We couldn't survive without that trust. It's why we give the neighbors our extras when we can. We see each other at church and when we switch water sources and walk our cows." He continued, getting excited as he spoke and waving his hands between bites of food.

I kept asking questions. Ken and Sarah shared stories, talked of naming the cows, why they ate "dinner" at noon and "supper" at night, and how much milk twenty cows could produce. They laughed with each other and with Bob (whom they called Robert).

"Sarah has the best-canned peaches in Utah County," Ken said, smiling at her.

Toward the end of the afternoon, as we sat in the living room eating slices of homemade strawberry pie with fresh whipped cream, Bob stood, gathered the dessert plates, and then moved toward the kitchen with the words "Sorry all, but I guess it's time to go."

"A little longer?" I asked, still listening to why Ken became a dairy farmer. "I'm not ready. This is fun."

We hugged as we left, no hesitation finding words. "Come back soon so I can show you the cows being milked," Ken called out as we walked to the car.

"I'm ready to go back," I said to Bob on the return drive. "I love your family." Bob's family showed support for his studies, his interest in art, his conversations about traveling. I heard no words of criticism or of needing to do more. He reciprocated with his help without being asked, his time on the farm with his father, and his expression of love.

Bob was gentle, supportive, never questioning others' motives. He often told me, "You can do it, Jody. You'll ace the test. Do you want me to help you study?" With him, my fear of doing something wrong dissipated, my anxiety diminished, my mother's harsh voice faded. He and his family showed me how.

\*

My university dorm experience ended after my freshman year, when my father moved back to Salt Lake to run for the U.S. Senate. I lived at home for the next two and a half years until I married, finished college, and the family returned to Kensington, Maryland. My father's Senate campaign failed in 1962, but he returned to his House seat two years later.

\*

My home babysitting duties resumed the summer before my sophomore year—Frank, nine; Stephen, six; Matt, five; Christine, three; and Christopher, one. I didn't campaign for either Daddy's Senate or the subsequent House campaign. Instead, I managed kids many late afternoons and evenings after classes and my four-hour-a-day secretary job in the School of Journalism. The campaign pressure shortened family tempers, including my own.

"I have a big sorority event tonight," I said.

"Doesn't matter. You need to be home." Mother's tense answer ended the conversation. "You're not doing enough here," her response to most of my social requests. "You're needed at home."

"Okay," I muttered, not wanting to further upset the home atmosphere. The family gave the campaign every ounce of energy and time. "I'll do my part," I reluctantly acknowledged to both parents. I cherished my freshman year on campus, my only year of typical college life. The rest of college added more responsibilities to my plate: being home with the kids, more studying, and a paid part-time job.

\*

Sorority dinners offered needed friendship and support. As an Alpha Chi academic cheerleader, I encouraged colleagues to study and offer each other academic support. My speaking moment each Monday evening offered study tips with skits and stories about meeting the man of your dreams at the library. My sorority sisters laughed and asked for academic help. These weekly presentations, my first regular speaking opportunities, built my confidence in holding people's attention, making people think and laugh.

Later, as sorority treasurer, I collected dues and budgeted for a fundraising campaign for a house addition. The Hellenic campus leadership expressed pleasure at Alpha Chi's fiscal discipline.

By graduation, self-assurance came with my sorority and women's association leadership roles. Excellent grades had come easily. But I learned how to shake hands and talk with strangers and be trusted with commitments—and other people's money. The university gave me an important gift: self-respect.

\*

Spring of my junior year, a Monday evening sorority dinner changed my life, a random ten-minute talk from a thin, pale, university student–looking guy who appeared not to want to be at the dinner. His eyes darted across the room while we ate, looking uncomfortable as the only male with seventy women. As we finished the meal, we chattered expectantly, wondering why this casually dressed guy was there. The white dinner plates were cleared and replaced with a dessert of chocolate cake and swirls of frosting. Susan, the sorority president, stood up and clinked her glass to ensure full silence among us.

"We have a special speaker this evening," she announced, introducing Steve. He stood with the hesitancy of someone unaccustomed to being in front of a group. He began, his eyes looking toward the door, not at us.

"I am a recently returned Peace Corps Volunteer from Niger and now a Peace Corps recruiter. I became a Volunteer almost three years ago when the Peace Corps began—a scary decision. That experience changed my life."

I sat up, listening. As he began talking about farm work with three hundred villagers for two years in the Sahara Desert, his words came faster. He stood straighter, his voice stronger, his images more animated, and his passion more intense.

My last chocolate bite disappeared. No more thoughts about the cake, the seventy sorority sisters, or the exam the next day. They moved to images of farmers, strange food, and living under the stars. At that moment, without knowing why, I wanted to be a Peace Corps Volunteer.

The Monday dinner looked ordinary when Niger became possible. The urgency to escape rushed inside me, away from Salt Lake and Mormon confines, away from the noisy family, away from a predictable future without risk, wonder, or curiosity. I wanted the unknown. The speaker's stories gave words to what had been growing inside me, unaware: I'm caged. Leave.

These thoughts grew over the next few months. International issues in the news became more interesting, articles skipped over before. My trips to the airport to pick up my father now included watching planes with curiosity about where they flew next—languages, food preferences, weather, traditions. Which country? It didn't matter; any country's fine. Getting away, far away, became my dream. The church guided me and gave me beliefs and behaviors to follow but put me in a straitjacket.

My family continued to be an anchor, even with home tensions, yet I tired of caring for kids and being told to do better. The Peace Corps didn't fit into a Mormon future defined by being married by graduation, settling down, having kids, but it pushed, unacknowledged, into my plans.

\*

Bob and I continued to date my sophomore and junior years and talked casually about marriage. We formalized that conversation at a sorority traditional "pinning" ceremony for members getting engaged. This particular November Monday evening dinner, Bob gave me his fraternity pin in front of my Alpha Chi sisters and his fraternity brothers, all crowded in the sorority living room. The traditional pinning ceremony screamed,

"Marriage coming soon," and children soon after. All sisters aspired to be pinned or engaged before graduation.

"I am happy to be here with Bob this evening," I spoke up, quieting the room. "I have found my eternal companion. I am proud to have been chosen to be part of his life and lifetimes afterward." The words needed no explanation. We all knew the Mormon code words. Even while speaking, leaving Utah and the United States hung silently inside me.

The following week, Bob's parents came to Salt Lake to take us to dinner to celebrate my "being pinned." I kept the pin in my purse, unsure of wearing it.

Sarah commented after we ordered our meals. "I would love to see you with Robert's fraternity pin. We'll be lucky to have you as a daughter-in-law."

I hesitated, thought for a minute, not wanting to reach into my purse for the pin. "Not tonight. It doesn't seem quite right," I replied. Sarah nudged again, and with each nudge, my fear of what the commitment of wearing the fraternity pin meant grew. The evening ended tensely, even as Bob's parents remained gracious.

The next day, Bob and I sat together on a bench outside the architecture lab facing the mountains, wrapped in our coats against the November air. Bob said, gently but firmly, "Give me the pin back. You aren't ready to marry." He looked sad as he continued, "You embarrassed my parents last night...and you embarrassed me. I chose you, but you didn't reciprocate."

Inside me, this romance didn't feel right. I mumbled, "I'm sorry. I don't know what's happening to me." I took the pin out of the corner of my purse and gave it back, afraid to look at it.

"You're unsure. Why?" He didn't raise his voice. He lowered his head as he slipped the pin in his coat pocket, deliberately signaling finality.

"I wish I knew." I paused, trying to find something to express a certain emptiness, a quiet doubt about marrying him. "I don't have the passion. I'm not sure what I should feel." Our romance temporarily ended on that cold bench in front of the tired architecture building. Thirty years later, we learned why.

Loneliness replaced my energy for classes, sorority, and secretarial journalism department duties. Campus walks slowed, eating alone increased, encouraging words disappeared. Bob had been my cheerleader. "You will ace the test," "You look good today." He gave me confidence. He didn't criticize, belittle. He had shared activities new to me, comparing well-designed houses on the city's mountain hillsides and ushering at the Utah Symphony Orchestra concerts in the Tabernacle. He explained pioneer dwelling constructions and the fabrics that gave rooms warmth and energy.

My father chose his time reading, writing, and talking about ideas—meanings in church scripture, politics, or French cognates that had slipped into the English language. He didn't see the environment; he saw ideas. His conversations existed independently of place. Bob's conversations depended on place. Bob had been teaching me to see, to understand how my surroundings helped create my ideas, my feelings, myself. My father's demeanor, his walk, talk, and dark-blue suits said external ambition: recognition, importance. Bob's demeanor said quiet ambition: create space and design for comfort, reassurance, and artistic harmony. I had inherited my father's ambition but also wanted Bob's quieter rhythm, one with local adventure and time for environmental harmony. Were both possible?

*

In March 1964, I invented a reason to find Bob at the architecture lab, having not seen him for four months. My daily time at home with put-downs and babysitting duties, not being balanced by Bob's affirmation, left me losing confidence, sliding back toward childhood loneliness and insecurities.

"Is Bob here?" I asked Jerry as I came up the dimly lit stairway into the architectural lab.

"Sure, in the far corner at the drafting bench, sketching out a new design." He then turned into the room and shouted, "Hey, Bob! Jody's here." I cringed, shrunk, looked toward the skid-marked wooden floor, and willed myself not to turn around and leave. Bob looked up and smiled but didn't move. I walked around the familiar work table, wishing I could still be an architecture lab groupie.

Approaching him, I rushed out some words about a mutual friend and turned to leave when he called out, "Would you like lunch a little later?"

"Sure, if it's okay with you," a hesitant reply. "Student union, noon," I offered.

"See you then."

The other students watched me shuffle around stools and chairs toward the stairwell. Then they looked back at Bob. What did they say after I left?

*

"I miss our time together, what you teach me," words during the lunch that said out loud my sadness since November. Lunches, walks to the journalism department, times on the cold bench outside the lab resumed and then continued through May—the "Do we get together again?" dance.

"I want to leave Salt Lake. I'm stifled here," I said in April, drawing the words out quietly, as I knew this defied Mormon norms. I feared rejection again if Bob disapproved.

"That's fine," he responded. "I've also thought about leaving. I'm not going back to the farm."

And a few days later, "I want to leave the United States. I want to join the Peace Corps." There, spoken out loud. The Mormon admonishment to get married quickly and have kids hung silently above us as Bob stayed silent. I waited. "Have you heard of the Peace Corps?"

Bob's hands remained in his jacket, protected from the crisp spring air as we sat on the familiar bench. Looking straight at me, he said, "I'm surprised because this isn't you. Where did this idea come from?"

"I want to get on a plane and go to a place that challenges my thinking, my conversations, my daily life, and leave behind Utah's suffocation." Hidden and unspoken was my desire to find Francine, the person who had escaped two decades earlier from the church's grasp, from Salt Lake, from a suffocating marriage. I had heard she lived in Paris, an opposite life from that of Salt Lake. I needed her story to know myself.

"I can understand," he said. He shifted his body on the hard bench.

I had thrown my private, previously unspoken truth at him. I held my breath.

"I hadn't acknowledged it until now," Bob said. "I thought it wrong to think like this, so I told no one," he whispered as if still a secret he could not speak.

Bob, without words, had harbored a longing to get away, to explore different spaces, colors, thousand-year-old buildings only known in architecture books, and foods beyond beef, corn, beans, and Jell-O.

We both shared the same hidden desire to get out. That secret brought us back together. We now spoke the words Peace Corps Volunteers, maybe separately, maybe together.

*

We set our wedding date for mid-December 1964. The campaign for a third term in Congress consumed my father and the family, and school sapped my energy. The Olsen and King families expected a traditional Mormon wedding and reception—two hundred guests and bright Christmas decorations following the temple marriage and wedding breakfast at Hotel Utah, the site of my father's reception to my new mother seventeen years earlier. Wedding planning began.

The downtown building that housed my father's office had a ballroom decorated for the holiday with bows, trees, fake snow, lights, and Christmas holly. Tenants had free use of the brightly lit scenes, guaranteeing those who entered cheer and laughter. Our family needed cheer after a grueling campaign. A reception area ready for use, including finger food and sweet punch, would be easy for a stressed-out family. And finals came ahead of decorating for a wedding reception.

One evening in October, my father and I sat at the dining room table, talking about fall campaign pressures and the wedding. The space at the elegantly decorated office building should be suitable for the reception.

"No," he said firmly, now sitting straight and changing to his church-speaking lecture voice.

"But, Daddy..." I sat motionless, absorbing the word. Then with my shoulders back, I looked straight at him. "It's easy, beautiful, free. I want it."

He maintained his religious patriarchal pose as he spoke. "A wedding reception must be in a Mormon church hall to honor the sacred day of marriage." He continued, not changing his posture. "Marriage is forever, and the church is its symbol. Jody, you know this. Don't even ask."

Francine's written words were unknown to me then, her words about the daddy I recently discovered: "My emotionally astringent husband, one who invited guests on a Saturday evening to our little house on the avenues to spend two hours reading and discussing scripture."

This revealed my father's strong belief in the church's righteousness and power over individual behavior, his unmovable absolute conviction of its truth, an absoluteness that drove his wife, Francine, away.

*

As I planned the marriage, my Mormon belief remained firm but malleable to circumstances, this circumstance. With the denial of use of his office space, we planned the reception at a church recreation hall near our home. Bob didn't counter our family wishes. After all, he was a returned missionary, and his parents were devoutly religious.

My father won the election, and the family prepared to return to Kensington, Maryland, the same familiar house, schools, and chapel. The wedding reception doubled as a political occasion to thank those who helped Daddy win. However, the marriage itself, in the temple, remained a sacred event only for twenty family members eligible to enter its holy spaces.

"For the reception, we can get a blue felt background mounted on plywood, stands for flowers, and red bows," Bob said after calling supply stores located in the Yellow Pages. "These will cover up the worn brown drapes hanging in the church recreation hall. I can create Christmas at the church."

My architecturally trained fiancé turned a plain church hall into a joyful celebration of our holiday-season marriage. I watched, helped, followed his directions, awed by his visual creativity. Bob would design and decorate our living spaces for the next thirty years, with me acting as his supportive design assistant.

*

A week before the wedding, Bob rear-ended another car, totaling his trusty Dodge. The next day, we bought a used VW, using our honeymoon money, and canceled the week in Phoenix.

At dinner the next evening, my father commiserated. "Sorry about the car. You need to have a honeymoon. No one gets married without one."

"It's okay, Daddy. We can celebrate sites in the city." I didn't want to put anyone out, knowing the limits of family resources after an election.

"Here, let me give you forty dollars. That should get you away for a couple of days, maybe Zion National Park." He handed me the cash.

"Thanks. Are you sure it's okay?" still asking for assurances.

"Absolutely. You both need special time to get acquainted. We did, Mother, didn't we?"

Mother smiled, paused, and then frowned as she watched me put the bills in my purse. "Our resources are tight. Please give me back any extra money from that forty dollars you don't spend," she said.

Daddy said nothing. I touched the bills again. My shoulders sunk, my smile disappeared, the joyful moment punctured.

We took two days in Zion National Park and spent the entire forty dollars.

*

The wedding day went well. My sorority sisters, by tradition, sang to me at the reception. Utah state- and congressional-elected officials came and congratulated my father on his victory. Campaign workers introduced themselves. And kids played tag in the crowd and dressed up in the guests' hats and scarves. The punch bowl wasn't tipped over, and the finger sandwiches outlasted the guests.

*

A week after the wedding, on December 26, my parents, brothers, and sister moved back east. Bob and I found an apartment on Salt Lake's west side. We lived on little money while still in school and had weekly visits from Bob's parents, who brought milk, Ken's farm-raised beef, fresh vegetables, and occasional desserts from Sarah's kitchen.

"We can't let you go hungry," Sarah said as more food arrived. They kept our weekly food bill down to ten dollars until I graduated and began working for the welfare department while Bob finished his fifth and last year of school. Ken and Sarah's generosity and caring, given freely and without expectation, stays with me to this day. They modeled love.

# PART TWO

# *Peace Corps Volunteer*

# 6

# Goody Two-Shoes Strikes Back
## 1966

Bob and I exchanged the redbrick efficiency apartment one flight above the plumbing store for married student on-campus housing after six months. Our first apartment's address on Apricot Avenue had drawn smiles and smirks from store clerks and delivery drivers in the neighborhood. University friends politely declined invitations. "Why don't we meet on campus" became a common reply.

"We're so naive," I commented to Bob as we drove into the plumbing store's driveway. "The Red Light reputation seems known… except to us." As I got out of the car, "It's okay. The apartment's cheap at fifty dollars a month, and we can walk the four blocks to the grounds of the Capitol, celebrating spring cherry blossoms and tulips along the way." We did our walks at sunset, catching the pink clouds behind the Oquirrh Mountains and the far side of the Great Salt Lake.

Our second apartment, a third-floor walk-up on campus, included three rooms, a parking place, and a roll-out cot in the living room for my father when he flew in from Washington.

"This is fine. I don't need more," Daddy, the congressman, said as I drove him to campus from the airport in early September. "The cot's fine. I have enough blankets, and I can share the bathroom. Seeing you is important to me."

During our final year in Salt Lake, Bob spent fourteen-hour days with his architecture studies and in the lab. On weekdays, I drove across West Salt Lake as far south as the Point of the Mountain, visiting welfare recipients. And we both applied to the Peace Corps. My clients taught me about their being poor, abused, ill, and occasionally homeless. One client, a grandmother, explained being a prostitute to soldiers at Fort Douglas during the war.

"I want my daughter and grandson to have better lives than I had. Please help me," she pleaded as she sat on a stained deep-blue couch next to bunk beds in the living-dining-bed room of her three-room, three-generation apartment. At forty-eight years old, she looked a decade older with her gray hair, heavily lined face, and rounded shoulders.

I leaned in, listened carefully, watched her face as she talked. This mental imprint of her and of other clients and my finding moments of dignity in their stories opened my appreciation to individual fragileness and experiences we cannot control. Stories invite us into others' lives. Poverty in Salt Lake City had been shielded by my east-side Mormon cocoon. Prostitutes, violence against women, and homelessness were for novels, not real life. Clients' descriptions made experiences real.

\*

Bob and I applied for the Peace Corps in September 1965, his senior year. At our small kitchen table, late at night, I excitedly completed the forms, imagining myself writing on a chalkboard balanced against a chair under a tree with kids sitting around me. The Peace Corps brochure with the picture of a teacher in Africa sat nearby. It described that as a Volunteer, the teacher was part of the Peace Corps's mission and three goals, goals that would give me a lifetime purpose.

The first goal identified helping people of interested countries meet their needs. My teaching degree could be valuable, help children learn English.

The second goal, sharing my being an American with those being served, sounded easy; just be myself and learn the language and customs to make telling stories more fun.

Finally, the third goal was the most intriguing, bringing the experience home to Americans. I thought telling my family stories would be easy, though I was not sure they would listen. Unknown then, the third goal became my professional career compass.

Further instructions soon came in brown envelopes, postmarked Washington, one addressed to Bob, one to me, "Josephine King Olsen." In them were instructions for language and psychological aptitude tests, medical exams, and wisdom teeth extraction.

Twenty years later, I learned the tooth extraction requirement came from too many Volunteers being evacuated for infected wisdom teeth. Remembering my miserable time at the dentist in the spring of 1966, before my Peace Corps service, as Peace Corps chief of staff in 1989, I changed that rule: no more wisdom teeth extraction.

In the kitchen of our apartment, I held up the envelope addressed to me.

"See my name? The Peace Corps wants me."

"Why does the name matter?" Bob asked. We sat down at the table and looked at each other.

"I have my first name back. My forms are not tucked in your manila file with your name in the Washington Peace Corps office. I have my own file, my photo identification."

Bob still looked puzzled. "Why is this separation necessary? You're still you."

"No, I'm not." The sadness I felt at losing my name when I became Mrs. Robert Olsen came back. I found a couple of random envelopes sitting on the counter and pushed them toward him. "See the name on the envelopes? I've disappeared into being the 'Mrs.' of you. When we're introduced together, no one looks at me. I am just the silent 'Mrs.' I want to cry out, wave my arms, 'Here I am, I have something to say,' but I'm polite."

Bob dished out ice cream and added chocolate sauce as we continued. I sensed he wanted to show me support, try to see my point of view. But he never lost his name.

"Unlike others, I know the Peace Corps wants me for what I can do. I'm not an extension of you." After a moment, "I'm glad we're leaving Salt Lake. Here, the church, community leaders, even other married women define me. I'm seen as a housewife, a support, a cleaner and washer, and in the future, a mother. I don't need a name."

Is this why Francine left?

\*

The Peace Corps offered one architecture program in Tunisia and gave partial credit toward licensure. Professionally, Bob needed two years of practice credit before his licensing exam. Getting credit as a Peace Corps Volunteer motivated him to join the Tunisia program. And this North African country offered a couple from Utah twenty-five hundred years of architectural history—as far back as the Phoenician era through the Carthaginian, Roman, Arab, Turk, German, and French; the Mediterranean Sea along its northern and eastern border; and an unknown religion and culture.

"I love this country," I shouted out as we looked at photos in the library reference books spread out on the table. "I see myself in the Roman ceramic-tiled bathhouses next to the sea. I'm sure we'll be selected." I learned the term *Maghreb* as I studied Tunisia's neighbors, Morocco, Algeria, and Libya. Other potential Peace Corps countries faded as Tunisia's images took over my thoughts. No chalkboard under the tree.

"TUNISIA," we wrote in capital letters each time we were asked "Where do you want to go?" by Peace Corps Washington. Bob placed monthly phone calls to track the upcoming Tunisia architecture announcement. Its government offered twenty architecture slots a year to Peace Corps Volunteers.

"You got your application in early. I'm sure you'll get in."

"They'll accept us." Bob nodded and added, "This is scary."

"We're jumping off a ledge without looking down," I admitted as I walked to the sink. I hesitated a moment, then turned toward him and continued, "Staying here in Salt Lake with our friends would be easy: lawns, clotheslines, station wagons. But that's not what I want. When I get nervous about the Peace Corps, I imagine my mother and grand-mother running the vacuum cleaner every morning. That's even scarier."

Jerry Anderson, Bob's friend from the architecture lab, and his wife, Sue, applied to the same program. "Four of us there together," Jerry had said one evening in the lab as we sat on stools cutting out windows. "We'll have each other if anything happens."

On April 10, 1966, Tunisia decision day, Jerry received a telegram: "You have been selected for the architecture program in Tunisia." We got nothing.

"Congratulations, Jerry," Bob said, feigning a smile, putting out his hand as they reached for architecture supplies from the closet at the back of the lab.

The next week, Bob received a letter from the Peace Corps: "The archi-tecture program in Tunisia is full. We have assigned you a community organization project in Turkey. You can add construction drafting to your community project." My letter also arrived: "English teacher, Turkey."

"What can I say?" after reading both our letters that evening. "It isn't fair. The Andersons got it, and we didn't. We applied first." I quietly lamented the rejection, the unfairness, my overconfidence.

"As an alternative, you can stay here and vacuum carpets," Bob said helpfully.

"Okay," as I brought out Sarah's bottled peaches. "I'm flexible."

"I'm considering Turkey. I'm disappointed, but..." He left the rest unsaid. I picked up: "I got attached to Tunisia. I bet I can get attached to Turkey—same part of the world, same religion, lots of ancient ruins." Earlier that afternoon, Bob had looked up the history of architecture in Turkey in his *Sir Banister Fletcher's A History of Architecture*, the fifteen-hundred-page book we later lugged with us for two years as Volunteers.

"Yeah, Turkey can match Tunisia for architectural interest," Bob said. "Let's try to make this assignment work.... Deal?"

"Deal." My eagerness for the Peace Corps now exceeded a country preference.

"I'll have to wait another year for the licensing test, but the Peace Corps comes first," he added. "I'm tired of conforming in this city."

Our departure date for Turkey, June 15, followed Bob's graduation by a week, perfect timing.

"We accept Turkey," Bob telexed back to Washington.

Bob graduated, and we celebrated, left our student housing, and stored our furniture and a few belongings in Bob's parents' basement. To my surprise, after seeing our enthusiasm for Tunisia through the winter months, both sets of parents supported our Turkey decision.

I assured my father of staying true to my Mormon roots. "I promise we will begin a family after we get back." That clinched the deal, given my parents had no grandkids.

We camped out at Bob's brother's house in Salt Lake City, waiting for our June 15 departure. Richard, his brother, had just begun a postdoc in chemistry at the University of Utah and moved his family from Illinois to Salt Lake. The Peace Corps had Richard's address and phone number, just in case.

"Bob, the phone is for you," Richard called out on the Saturday following graduation as we moved our suitcases into his house.

"Hello," Bob answered.

"Robert, this is the Peace Corps placement officer with an emergency change of plans. We just received word the Turkey government has canceled the community organization group, your group. Officials didn't give a reason but said it was firm. Thus, we have to suspend your program in Turkey. We are sorry."

Bob put his hand over the phone's mouthpiece and repeated the conversation to me.

"What? Why didn't they know sooner? They're jerking us around. We're not yo-yos. Are they offering us anything else, or are we done?"

Back on the phone, Bob asked, "Is there another program? We're packed and ready to go." Bob sank into the chair next to the telephone and listened. He put his hand over the receiver and said, "They found an opening in India as chicken farmers. They had seen on my application that I had lived on a farm."

I called out, "Never. I will not be a chicken farmer."

"We'll get back to you in an hour. I need to talk to my wife about this," Bob told the placement officer.

An hour later, Bob called back. "We'd be happy to go to India as chicken farmers," he lied.

During that hour, I realized where we went didn't matter, what we did didn't matter, whether he did architecture didn't matter. We wanted to get out of Salt Lake, and the Peace Corps offered a two-year adventure, an experience, an unknown. We had prepared, told family and friends, and given up our wisdom teeth. I reaffirmed in that hour, looking at the phone, talking to Bob, that I had to leave my Salt Lake future and find a new one.

The next day, Richard sat with us on the couch, an atlas on his lap, as we found the region in India to be our new home.

We told both our parents about the new plans. Ken laughed, thinking of me as a chicken farmer. "You hate the smell of chicken coops," he said knowingly. Mother said, "I know how disappointed you are. I'm sorry."

"I still want to go," Bob said to Richard. "Away to someplace completely unknown."

"I don't get it.... A newly minted degree, a professional career ahead... Utah. Why don't you stay here?" Richard asked, pouring a glass of milk. "I worked for years to be here as a chemistry professor, and you walk away."

I had come into the kitchen, listening. "We don't want this Utah future now—"

"Don't leave Salt Lake; this is silly," Richard interrupted, raising his voice as he spoke and turned to me.

Bob idolized his four-year-older brother, smart, academic, and already a father of three. Bob stood silent a moment, looked at his brother, and then answered steadily, evenly, "I want a world I don't know."

I squeezed his hand.

*

Later that week, on Friday, we returned to Richard's house following Jerry and Sue's Tunisia send-off party. Their plane was to leave Sunday morning.

"Deep down, I wish we were going to Tunisia," Bob admitted as we walked in the front door. "I wish I could do architecture. I love it, but... we'll be okay."

Later, tucked into the makeshift bedroom, I heard the phone ring in the kitchen.

"Hello," Richard's voice echoed. "Jody, the phone's for you. Why a call this time of night? It's after midnight."

As I walked toward him, he put his hand over the receiver and whispered, "It's the Peace Corps."

"Jody, I know this is late, and the request is sudden, but would you still like to go to Tunisia?" the voice at the other end asked firmly, with no introduction.

"What?" I screamed. Before I could say more...

"If you and Robert can wrap up your affairs, be packed, and be at the Salt Lake airport on Sunday morning, you both can go to Tunisia. You have twenty-eight hours. Can you do it?"

I sunk into the kitchen chair, clutching the receiver. "Yes," I shouted. I mentally processed what I needed to do and said, in a calmer voice, "We can be at the airport Sunday morning." He and I walked through logistical details for getting to Providence, Rhode Island, and Brown University for training. After another moment, I said, "I'm grateful. Thank you. And by the way, why this opportunity now?"

The man on the phone laughed and then answered, "I wasn't going to say it, but you asked. Isn't your father a congressman?" I had never said anything about it.

He continued, "Your mother called this afternoon with the request. I checked the Tunisia program again and, with a recent dropout, saw that we could invite both of you. Thank your mom." I was speechless. He hung up.

The next day, I called Mother with profound thanks and continued the thanks over the years. Her one call changed my life.

*

We arrived Sunday afternoon at Brown University with eleven other couples in a class of 132 trainees, all strangers except the Andersons, shocked that we were there. Some trainees would become our best life-long friends.

The twelve couples lived on the third floor of a standard Brown dormitory. That first afternoon, Bob and I climbed the stairs and entered our assigned small dorm room, furnished with a dresser and two single beds, one at each end. We immediately pushed them together.

The trainers told us on arrival, "We reserved female bathrooms on each end of the floor for wives and the bathroom mid-hallway for husbands." That news didn't sit well with anyone.

*

All twenty-four of us crowded into the TV room that evening, sitting on worn, overstuffed couches and chairs, eyeing each other nervously. Our questions bonded us. "Where are you from?" "What school did you go to?" "How long have you been married?" "Did you also move your two single beds together in the dorm room?" Ten couples had been married a month or less.

Teke and Joey, still our close friends fifty-five years later, said, "We got married in Michigan forty-eight hours ago, had our reception, jumped into a rented car, and here we are." One couple left training early. All other couples completed training and two years as Volunteers.

Our meeting's goal that evening was to change the bathroom assignments.

"We share towels, toilet kits, toothpaste, and shampoo," Marsh, a trainee, explained. "Husbands and wives should share the same bathroom." Thirty minutes of conversation later, we switched to having four couples each to a bathroom and using it any way we wanted. The eight of us using the middle bathroom gave up modesty for expedient tooth brushing and showers. We knew when not to look.

\*

The lead language teacher announced the first Monday morning, "The English teacher trainees have to test at level two in French to become Volunteers. Architect trainees should try but don't have a language level requirement." He added, "For those few of you already fluent in French, three Arabic teachers from Tunisia will help you gain fluency in local Arabic. Good luck to everyone."

Three psychiatrist staff members joined us to counsel, assess, observe, and make suitability recommendations. They made these judgments without previous experience with the Peace Corps or time in Tunisia. This lack of experience also held true for training staff. Even so, they taught and judged a hundred twenty trainees.

My psychiatrist, Dr. Sullivan, met with me once every week, as he did with a third of the trainees. His room, a former closet, had a small desk, two wooden chairs, and one sixty-watt light bulb hanging directly above.

He questioned me about my interest in being a Volunteer and expressed no satisfaction with my responses.

"You're going because of your husband. I can tell."

"No, I want to go. I decided independently of him."

"I don't believe you."

Our conversations didn't go well. At our third meeting, looking straight at me with no smile, no detectable emotion, he revealed his judgment. "You know, if you don't pass the French exam, you will keep your husband from going to Tunisia. Bob tells me how much he wants to go. I have checked, and your language instructors tell me you are not doing well."

His words hit me hard. I flinched, then swallowed, lowered my head so he couldn't see my flushed cheeks.

"This isn't fair," I finally said. "Don't turn me against Bob. Support me, help me, don't tell me I can't do it," I continued, trying to calm down.

"I don't think you both will make it," he said without further words.

\*

Dr. Sullivan reinforced this point each time we met. My father had taught me some French growing up, I had taken two years of French in high school and thought French would come easily during training. Yet with each of Dr. Sullivan's sessions, my confidence dropped. I forgot new vocabulary, mispronounced words, misused verb tenses. I knew grammar; I read French texts but couldn't get French words out of my mouth. Failure crept in.

"You'll be okay," Bob kept saying in the evenings. "You're doing your best. We'll make it." Then the psychiatrist would push my doubts further.

As stress rose for all of us, as trainees, we became closer. Suitability, the word without clear meaning, hovered over us during language lessons and when playing volleyball. Periodically, at breakfast, a chair remained empty.

"The staff sent him home last night. He wasn't suitable enough," a fellow English teacher whispered to me. Silence at the table. Panic. During the twelve weeks, eight trainees had disappeared at night.

One suitability test required us to rank each other and draw friendship maps of other trainees. I cheated to protect as many others as possible. "I also cheated," Sue said to me. Others confessed to having lots of friends. Protect each other.

Fear of failing my French test added panic.

"I'm scared I'll let us down," I said to Bob in our room after another eight-hour language learning day. "The more I try, the worse it gets." Sadness consumed me.

"You'll pass," Bob gently assured me, arm around my shoulder. "I know you. At school you got this scared before tests, before grades came out." He paused, hugged me tighter. "And then you got As. I've learned to not worry about you."

"But this is different…"

"You always say that, and it never happens the way you fear. Stay calm."

Friendships with other trainees grew, learning to teach English as a foreign language improved my understanding of English grammar, and daily volleyball games at which I excelled affirmed my Peace Corps decision. I fought my fear and ignored the psychiatrist's scorn.

We took our language exams at the end of week twelve and would know our scores the next morning. At noon on testing day, the training director said, "We have three Tunisian language instructors flying with us to Tunisia. Could someone invite an instructor home for a week to see how Americans live?"

Bob's hand popped up. "Yes. My family lives on a farm. Should be fun for Ahmed if he wants to join me."

Bob and I were going separate ways for a week—he to Provo, Utah, me to Kensington, Maryland. "Good for you, Bob," I whispered, not thinking much about his offer.

That evening after the testing, a bar in downtown Providence offered beer, music, and long oak tables for rowdy dancing to trainees needing to release tension while awaiting the language scores and final suitability marks. Deselection awaited some of us the next day. I watched friends dance on the tables, legs and feet kicking high to the music, arms locked together with partners, heads thrown back, imitating Anthony Quinn in the last scene of *Zorba the Greek*. For a couple of hours, trainees became dancers on Greek ocean sand, and fear turned to laughter, Zorba's exuberant laughter, loud and free. We wanted to keep those moments, our last, together as trainees. Bob and I watched. We drank only water, but I lived the evening vicariously. Zorba grounded me.

We received our language scores the next morning, each in an envelope: Bob scored one out of five. Me, a one plus, short of the required two. The result said no Tunisia.

However, at breakfast, the training director had pulled Bob aside and whispered the decision: "Because you offered the invitation to Ahmed, you and Jody will go to Tunisia, regardless of language scores. Your offer was generous, and we respect you for it."

I put my head on Bob's shoulder, smiling, shaking. My body wanted to collapse as the tension bottled tightly inside for twelve weeks drifted away from the dining room and outside into the fall air. I wanted to be a Volunteer too much and had protected myself against the loss of this dream. Now I could believe.

A week later, a Pan Am flight with 110 Volunteers left John F. Kennedy International Airport in a thunderstorm bound for Lisbon and then Tunis, Tunisia. The two years that changed my life began with lightning, heavy winds, and rain visible outside the plane's windows. I didn't care. My wish for a place challenging what I knew and believed was only hours away.

*

The language and technical staff supported us, encouraged us, believed in us. Some wished they could go with us as Volunteers. However, the psychological team tried to tear us down to see who survived. Did this prepare

Volunteers for the Peace Corps experience? During its first few years, some officials thought it did. Early Peace Corps training advisors told me this years later, but they admitted no one knew. The experiment called Peace Corps was new. Members of Congress wrote to Sargent Shriver, Peace Corps founder and first director, about their fear of young Americans going overseas and representing the United States. Psychological testing placated doubters.

When I returned to the Peace Corps as a staff member ten years later, most of these methods had disappeared, and any remaining psychological tests would be gone in a year. Trainees need words of support, not fear, and should make their own decisions. In our group, the person voted by staff most likely to be the best Volunteer left Tunisia one month into his service.

# 7

# Greeting My Family in Arabic
### 1966–68

The Sousse, Tunisia, *lycée de garçons* classroom had a blackboard to my right, a desk topped with chalk and eraser in front, and forty fourteen-year-old boys sitting to my left. It was my third day in Tunisia, my first in the classroom to teach first-year English.

Fourteen-year-old boys perspire. The smell was not disturbing but strong enough to make the room feel smaller, closing in on me with each step toward the desk.

The boys' black hair contrasted with their light-colored sweaters and white collars framing their faces. Hair flopped on olive-skinned foreheads, straight locks randomly arranged and covering ears to the spot the family barber shears ended.

My walk stopped at the desk. The chalk aligned perfectly between the eraser and the desk's edge, its whiteness catching my eye. I turned around, faced the boys for the first time, searching for words mentally practiced a hundred times. No words. The event's enormity overwhelmed my practiced introduction. Forty pairs of onyx eyes gazed at me, bodies still.

Each boy looked the same and yet different. Ahmed, in front and right, poured out of his midsized desk—legs, arms, body devouring its frame. Behind him, Ali disappeared into his desk, hiding a small spare body. All waited to be disturbed by the strange English teacher.

Striped, zigzagged, and diamond-patterned sweaters showed wear from the motion of hands writing, copying, and carrying copybooks. The faded colors showed years of vigorous washboard scrubbing and rooftop clotheslines under Tunisia's intense sun. Wrinkled shirt collars poked above the ribbing and lay awkwardly against growing necks.

The sweaters caught my focus, being in this school, this country on the Mediterranean Sea. Students wore these same sweaters every school day, their individual uniforms. Over the school year, sweaters stretched as arms lengthened and chests thickened.

The boys looked at the new teacher, a young woman with short blond hair, black leather sandals, a red cotton skirt below the knees, and a long-sleeved white blouse. Facing the boys at their desks, I glanced at the door to my left, now closed, turned to the empty blackboard behind me, the chalk in my hand. A turn to the left, a walk to the door, a step outside could end this moment and my time as a Volunteer. Tempting. The students continued to stare. My feet didn't move. Instead, I said, weakly, "My name is Mrs. Olsen, and I come from the United States," in English. As first-year English students, they couldn't understand the words, but they would learn. I repeated the phrase, my voice stronger, and then asked, one by one, "What is your name?"

"My name is…" Every boy in the class responded.

"My name is…" They asked each other the same question, slowly at first, and then with added confidence. The English class had begun. Forty voices tried unfamiliar words. Repeat, repeat, establishing the language learning rhythm.

In the first weeks, I relied on hand gestures and chalkboard drawings to teach unfamiliar words and phrases, never translating from French. Looking foolish by awkwardly drawing pictures on the chalkboard or gesturing wildly brought laughter from the students. Much more fun.

The chalkboard filled with white stick figures of cups, plates, red peppers, bowls, water pitchers, rugs, donkeys, market baskets, sitting leather poufs, short-legged tables, soccer balls, street games, and children laughing, crying, running, and carrying liters of olive oil for their families. My drawings improved, my hands moved faster, and students' interpretations of the lines and circles that pretended to be objects became daily amusements. Students repeated words for the objects. Then more drawings and words.

After a couple of months, my individual words and phrases became sentences. "I take my liter bottle to the covered market to fill with olive oil every week." Or "I watched a girl hooking a prayer rug." Soon, students yelled out, "Missus, Missus, Missus," waving their arms to get my attention.

"Missus, do you like our rugs?" "Missus, do you eat Tunisian food?" Why did they ask?

"Yes, I like the Tunisian rugs. Every day I buy and eat two oranges and part of one hot red pepper. I cry when I eat the pepper."

One said, "Missus, you are wearing a Tunisian coat. Don't you wear a Western coat?"

"No I don't. This is the coat I bought in the market. I like it better." They asked about my interest in Tunisia. My responses reaffirmed a pleasure in discovering Tunisian food, objects, and arts. They brought me homegrown Tunisian olives and dates and watched me taste them, smiling with approval.

"Foreigners rarely like our olives," Ahmed said. "You're different."

The downtown *monopris* sold European household items, the patisserie sold baguettes, *pain au chocolat*, and croissants. The three French restaurants had tablecloths, wineglasses, and served steak au poivre. My French colleagues shared the best places to buy everything French.

"Jody, you can get good *pain au chocolat* at Quai de La Republic." They didn't tell me about Tunisian goods.

The students had many French teachers, the cooperants from France. Tunisia had been independent of France for nine years and still had a strong French teaching cadre in the schools. My students hadn't seen an American teacher before and initially mistook me for French, thus puzzlement with my interest in Tunisia.

"I love the rug designs." Later, "I buy beef at the market, the one with the cow's head hanging on the hook outside." The students wrinkled their noses. "I prefer my Tunisian sweater. It keeps me warmer in the classroom." Students talked eagerly about their daily lives: couscous, donkeys, and street soccer games. These conversations, in English, were new. They said, "French teachers aren't interested. You listen to our stories. You like us."

\*

My father, always the politician, insisted that learning others' names builds trust.

"When you repeat their name and remember it, when you meet

again, you show caring. I try to never forget a name." A gut punch. I could not remember any unfamiliar names.

Now five different classes of forty students each stumbled into my English classroom each weekday: two hundred boys. Each had a different Arabic name, Akeem, Hassan, Jamal, Kareem, Hafeez, Adeem.... With no Arabic language base from which to build the words, my memory for these strange sounds, already lacking skill for retaining names, failed me. Numbers were easy, always ready to be used again, but names didn't stick. Yet remembering names meant trust.

As students entered, faces and doodles on copybooks identified each of them to me. Haircuts, sweater designs, body sizes, leather sandals, and classroom-entry greetings reminded me of their personalities and learning styles. But even with effort, their names escaped me.

By early December, they had caught on. "Missus, what is my name?" a question repeated in the classroom. "Am I Ali or Mahmoud?" The trust between us slipped and, with it, the discipline. Students wanted to hear their own names and be praised by name.

The lycée had a principal and vice principal. Directeur Adjoint Maalouf, tall and heavy, strutted the hallways carrying a meter-long rod to hit students when needed. His traditional djibbah, the head-to-foot coat, swung easily around him as he executed justice.

He watched, listened, searching for unruly student outbursts, eager to return silence to classrooms. Mine became a frequent target as noise rose with students talking over each other. Student names escaped me. My voice couldn't rise over their voices, and I feared yelling, even my own. Once a week, the directeur adjoint threw open the door, stomped into the classroom, yelled in Arabic, hit a couple of students nearest the door, glared at me, and left. The students glared back at the directeur adjoint.

Then in careful English, I said, "Please sit, listen, let's be quiet together." The English lesson resumed. This ritual continued throughout the rest of the school year.

Students learned. Dates and olives arrived regularly to be eaten as students watched, visits to homes for traditional couscous came as comfort with students grew. But for those whose names I did not remember, relationships remained fragile. That failure left me sad, even today. Names still elude me.

\*

A month into my service, the plot to see Francine began. I was now of age to be able to see her. Her address, obtained quietly from my aunt in Salt Lake City, stayed safe in my wallet. In Paris, Francine lived close enough to be touched, a two-hour flight from Tunis but a lifetime away. After twenty years of silence, what had become of her?

A few days later, the Tunisian aerogram with a stamp and the address 3 rue de Philibert DeLorme, Paris, 17, France, made the connection between us.

\*

Two weeks later, her return aerogram sat in our Sousse PTT mailbox waiting to be read, the light-blue thin paper peeking out, her words inside, hopeful.

"I am skiing in Switzerland over the Christmas holidays, so I won't be in Paris, but you and Bob may use my apartment." At the bottom, she added, "I will try to come back for twenty-four hours to see you." Skiing in Switzerland. A place for rich people. I had never skied. An image grew inside me of a mother out of my reach.

"That's all I need," I told Bob. We made plans.

\*

My school teaching calendar dictated the time in Paris, ten days over Christmas and New Year's. Our accented and limited vocabulary made directions from Charles de Gaulle Airport (CDG) to her apartment challenging to the taxi driver, but at last we stood, suitcase beside us, looking up at the ten-story square, gray, imposing, post–World War II structure with Christmas lights–filled balconies opening to the city.

The concierge greeted us with only a few words, visually acknowledging our presence, given the evening lateness. The three of us and one suitcase squeezed into the mirrored elevator, small for even one person. It noisily jerked to the eighth floor and opened into a small square hall with floor-to-ceiling mirrors and three apartment doors. The one light sprang on with our movement. The concierge pointed to Francine's apartment and gave us the keys. She asked for no words, thankfully, as our French couldn't handle a conversation.

The bolt dropped as we turned the key, echoing in the hallway and beyond the door into the apartment. We opened the door and stared into the dark. The apartment, its location, how Paris people lived, how Francine lived were a mystery. We stood as if frozen, then walked into what slowly became my second home over the next forty years.

The Eiffel Tower and city lights peeked through the living room's glass French doors. My brain cautiously acknowledged what my eyes saw, the brilliant Paris skyline at night. My breathing slowed. Is this Francine's life? Will I be an unwelcome intrusion on a satisfying rhythm of her stylish daily routine?

Light switches brought the apartment to life. The balcony, with a small table, two chairs, and a well-tended planter rimming the elaborate wrought-iron railing, stretched the length of the apartment. The French doors to the balcony offered a full Paris view from both the living and bedrooms. Eight-foot-high mirrors covered two living room walls, multiplying city lights and making inside and outside feel as one, even in December. Paintings, one over three feet tall; sketches; and Asian prints hung throughout the halls, bathroom, kitchen, bedroom, study. Even the cramped bathroom had eight tall prints of Henry VIII–era nobles hanging on three sides. Dozens of glass and brass stairway dowels sat on mirrored tables, desks, and bureaus. Light, mirrors, glass, color, art stretched into fantasy. Nothing seemed real. In college, Bob had been right. Use of space is as important as words. Francine used her space as art and a warm embrace.

*

The next morning, Bob left to find a patisserie for baguettes and yogurt, giving me time to explore this visual representation of Francine's life, a movie set for *Springtime in Paris*. She left me twenty years ago, broken, and now this life in Paris. How?

After breakfast at the table under a painting of an Asian rice farmer in the small breakfast room, I explored, tiptoeing with bare feet over the Asian rug. The apartment offered few clues to her personal life: no family photos. A few Asian prints suggested international travel. The elegantly designed spaces kept others, including me, from knowing *her*.

My Peace Corps world included a Turkish toilet directly under the shower, roosters crowing at 5:00 each morning, and well water for washing clothes on the scrubboard. Francine had lush prints in her private toilette, no traffic noise eight stories below, and a washing machine. My Volunteer life seemed crude, hers elegant.

Fear of seeing her, of being rejected by her, again grew. Our clothes and suitable Volunteer lifestyle were not appropriate for studying elegant paintings. My now longer straight hair reflected antiwar protests, not high-end society. The silver cutlery, thin wineglasses, place mats matching each set of china, and luxuriously enormous bathtub renewed my childhood fears of not belonging. But curiosity kept me searching the hallway's tall Chinese chest to find her new life.

*

Francine walked into the apartment on December 27 and stayed twenty-four hours. We sat on the living room couch as she arrived, Bob in khakis and a wrinkled cotton collared shirt, me in a cotton blue dress, belted at the waist to accentuate my thin 115-pound frame. We nervously held hands.

At forty-three, Francine had the quiet beauty of a fashion model, which she had been a few years earlier. She wore a body-shaping opal-hued wool dress with off-centered white buttons lined down the front. A comb held her blond, lightly curled hair. She wore Shalimar perfume, the only perfume I wore, rarely, because of its cost. Now its fragrance permeated her apartment. My dress, hair, sturdy walking shoes seemed all wrong against her elegance.

"I am glad you found the apartment," she began. She had a warm, easy-to-listen-to voice. "Is there anything you need?"

Bob said, "We love it here. You are good at letting us use the apartment." Francine wasn't his mother, so they could talk normally to each other.

I waited and then began, "We went to Christmas Eve Mass and walked halfway across the city in the drizzle." Would she have had a car waiting for her? We sounded cheap to have walked. She smiled but said nothing.

After a moment, I asked, "Was your trip from Switzerland fine?" A dumb question.

"I took the train, a simple trip, done it many times." She walked toward the door to the hall. "Let me take a moment to settle in," and she disappeared into the brown hallway decorated with flower and landscape oil paintings.

"Bob, help me out. I'm saying stupid things. I feel small against her elegance."

"Keep going. You're doing okay," he responded.

Thousands of questions for Francine rushed forward, but I was too paralyzed to ask even one. Do her eyes see me as a straight-haired teacher in a North African country, noble in purpose but not refined?

\*

She returned to the living room. "Let's go to a restaurant for lunch. Are you both hungry?"

I said too eagerly, "Sure, sounds great," thinking sadly of our limited resources.

"I'll make a reservation. The phone's in the bedroom." A moment later, "Bonjour, Henri…" Her voice warmed the winter day, like sunlight touching a cold face. The cheerful sound would bring joy to anyone. Over the years, her *bonjour* became my favorite word.

We set out for the restaurant. The elevator hadn't expanded, still seeming too small for three. Out on the sidewalk, we felt the chilly air.

"At least it isn't Utah cold," I said. During the three-block walk toward the restaurant, our conversation could have been between a couple visiting Paris and meeting a casual friend who comments about the city. Safe. Casual.

Francine had us look back over our shoulders while saying, "My apartment building is tall, square, and gray. But my wing of the building opens over the railroad tracks, giving enough open space for a city skyline view. I knew I had to have the apartment from the moment I saw it years ago." As we walked, she added stories about the school, nursery, and flower store we passed along the sidewalk, calling out a hearty *bonjour* to most she saw.

She entered the restaurant with "Bonjour, Henri." The words remained light and generated a grand smile.

Henri said, "Bonjour, Madame Timothy, I have your favorite table ready." Linen tablecloth and napkins, two long-stemmed glasses for each of us, and a row of silver cutlery on either side of the crest-embossed plate—not a Tunisian restaurant.

"You might like the steak frites, which are so tender here." Francine described several choices, asked what we liked, and then ordered. The conversation stayed casual and safe.

After the meal, she ordered a café. "A habit," she said. "I enjoy holding the tiny cup above its small saucer and eating the wrapped chocolate on the side afterward. A perfect end to good French cuisine." She had the bill payment prearranged with Henri, no *l'addition*, no offer to pay. By habit, she put an extra French franc on the saucer. "We don't tip in Paris, but I feel better when adding an extra franc."

Francine managed the outing properly against my sense of clumsiness.

*

Back in the apartment, conversation became easier but not personal. Francine fixed another café, drank it from a French miniature coffee cup in its saucer, and suggested places to see as she gently sipped. "Do you want anything else?" she asked as she talked.

"No thank you," a joint polite reply.

"You're Mormons, is that right? I shouldn't have asked whether you wanted coffee."

She continued talking about Paris. "I never use the Metro—too dirty. I'm lucky to have a car, a garage, and a love of driving." She continued her Paris themes, suggesting, with examples, that the French were nicer than their reputation suggested.

She then said, as if an afterthought, "My daughter, Cindy, is currently a high school student here in Paris. She is skiing with me this week."

"Do I have a sister?" I asked, stunned, but I forced my voice to remain normal. My brain tumbled with images of who she might be. I tried to say something but only twisted my hands together. Thinking. Trying to find something to say. Rumors in my family suggested Francine married a military man who rose in rank to general and had a daughter, but nothing definitive. Now confirmation. But the apartment gave few clues about either her husband or Cindy.

"Of course you do. I thought Nana told you," Francine said. "I'm sorry you didn't know," profound words said so matter-of-factly. We sat silent in our thoughts, our regrets, our carefulness. After a moment, Francine picked up the conversation. "Cindy goes to a strict French Catholic school in the city and does well. She has learned Italian and Spanish in summer exchanges and is also good in Latin. We are lucky to live here." The topic ended.

Our deliberately chosen words about Paris, France, the French, the Americans, being Peace Corps Volunteers continued through the evening and the next morning. We stayed seated on the couch and the matching leather chair, looking out toward the Eiffel Tower during the afternoon and evening. The balcony offered us a few minutes of the outdoors, the crisp Paris air, and the city lights. No personal words and no emotions. Our Mormon ancestors would be proud of our properness.

Shortly before Francine left to continue her ski vacation, she said casually, "Maybe Cindy can come to Tunisia to visit while you're there. She would like to meet you."

"Absolutely," I exclaimed without thinking. "She should come."

"I'll suggest it to Cindy, maybe next year," Francine responded. Done. We said goodbye, gave each other a light hug. Proper.

Her last words were "Come again, if you can." And the visit was over. We were two people circling each other, watching, listening, assessing, wondering, but too afraid of rejection to risk moving emotionally toward the other.

I didn't say a word to my father or brother, David Jr., about my time with Francine. To keep the family tranquility, the visit remained a secret.

\*

A few months after our return to Tunisia, David Jr. joined us for a week in Sousse, having completed his French church mission.

After debarking from the plane in Tunis and seeing us among the shouting arrival crowds, he said excitedly, "The first day of my mission, bags still packed and against mission rules, I called Francine. I was now free from our parents, and I had to see her. Mission rules be damned."

David Jr. and I had carried the same secret of wanting to meet Francine from each other, driven by fear of upsetting Daddy.

As Bob, David Jr., and I drove back to Sousse, talk of Francine dominated our conversation.

"I know Daddy still loves her and Mother is jealous. But no one in the family talks, trying to erase her from our lives. They pretend she never existed." David Jr. wanted to talk, pouring out years of anger at having been shut down. He looked out to the Mediterranean Sea on our left as we drove, as if the strength to speak came from its shimmering blue waters.

"I love her," David Jr. said. "Even only seeing her briefly in Paris, I watched her poise, her smile, and listened to her voice and wanted more." He continued, "What would we have been like if she were in our lives?"

"We can't think about it," I said. "It didn't happen, and the past is gone." Silence settled in the *deux chevaux*, France's bottom-of-the-line car, as Bob maneuvered it on the single-lane road.

"But I don't know why she left," he said. "We never had that conversation. I couldn't get the courage to ask, and she never offered."

"Nor do I," I replied. "I was also afraid to ask."

During David Jr.'s week with us in Tunisia, we dug deeper into the Francine mystery. We cried for the lost time without her. On our third day together, David Jr. mentioned he had met Cindy twice, another secret he had held tight.

"She didn't know I was her brother when we met. I had to pretend to be a missionary preaching the gospel to visit the apartment." David Jr. was drinking soda in our miniature yet sunny courtyard, sitting on a bamboo chair covered by lanolin-smelling sheepskin. I sat across on one of our two wooden chairs, adjusting a pillow over the uncomfortable slats.

"Francine told me Cindy didn't know she had a brother and sister because she didn't think she, Francine, would see us again. She made me promise to say nothing to Cindy. 'I don't know what to tell Cindy all these years later,' she said, looking at me sadly. I agreed to keep quiet, even though I wanted to shout it out."

Over fifty years later, two years ago as of this writing, Cindy and I sat in her Salt Lake City living room talking of her Paris meeting with David Jr., as if a still-fresh memory.

"I was fifteen, home from school late. I walked into the apartment to see two Mormon missionaries standing by the dining room table in dark suits and white name badges. Mother [Francine] turned to me and said, 'This is David King, a son of a good friend of mine. He and his companion, Howard, came to see us.' I enjoyed looking at a handsome man."

Cindy continued, "On the subsequent visit, he and his companion gave me a church lesson. He looked serious but made it so funny. He left me with a picture of people jumping high over the coals. Even as he made me laugh, he said, 'We need to keep laughter down to sixty seconds a day.' I don't think he followed his own rule."

Cindy paused, thought, went for tea, and continued, "He seemed spiritually heavy, quiet, but had a grand sense of humor he tried to suppress. As he left after the lesson, he saw a magazine on the living room table with a model on the cover. He looked at the model, wrinkled his face, and said, 'She has all that makeup on. What if I tried to kiss her? Would I just get makeup all over my dark suit?' I kept laughing as the door closed."

Cindy finished her story with the words, "I found out a few months later he was my brother. I wanted to tell him I was happy to be his sister, but I never saw him again."

*

David Jr. toured our Tunisian city of Sousse on his own using his excellent French. We ate at three-table family kitchen restaurants at night, tears running down David Jr.'s face from the hot peppers. But he finished the full bowl of couscous and chicken each time. He knew he could succeed, even with hot peppers.

We drove back to the airport with a newfound closeness from discovering our secret Francine visits. As a family, we would heal. I hugged him and said goodbye. Even today, that memory of his tall, thin shoulders between my arms remains strong.

"I'll write," we both pledged. It never happened.

*

In March 1967, my first year, a trip to Tunis for a lecture about family planning in Tunisia changed my Peace Corps experience from being a cultural outsider teaching lycée-level English to joining the traditions of Arab family and community, learning the basics of vulnerability and trust that have remained my guide.

The day after the Tuesday evening lecture, I sat across the desk from Director Fran Macy, looking determined. "My teaching is not going well," I said. After examples of why, "May I change projects?" He sighed, another Volunteer problem to handle.

"You committed to the ministry to teach English. You can't just drop out," he said, exasperated. "We honor our agreements."

"I'll stay through the school year and offer to teach adults at night in the Bourguiba School next year, staying under the ministry." He relaxed.

"All right. And what do you really want to do? I know you—never idle. I can see in your face you have something planned."

"Teaching family planning in the maternity hospital in Sousse, a small part of a new World Bank health program." Fran scowled.

I added quickly, "I know, it's new to Tunisia. But I'll make it work. And the government's on board." My resolve held out. After a few minutes, Fran agreed to the deal.

*

Talking with village women giving birth in the maternity hospital required spoken Arabic, as most village women spoke no French nor could read and write Arabic. Determination to get out of teaching pushed me to learn the villager's language.

"A spoken language is easy to learn," a Volunteer colleague told me. "Most have about five hundred words."

"I can do that by working hard at it," I replied, laughing. The Volunteer was wrong; my language skill assessment was overly optimistic, and retrieving Arabic sounds down in my throat, impossible. But I began my language lessons.

*

The following Monday, in the lycée teacher's lounge, Mr. Mahmoud Zinelabedine, the senior Classical Arabic teacher, met me near the tea table and said in French, "I understand you are looking for an Arabic teacher. I might be helpful." Zinelabedine always filled the lounge with his powerful voice, room-expanding laugh, and a full-length, gold-embroidered white djibbah over his tall, heavy frame. Everyone knew him. Everyone respected him enough to elect him mayor of Sousse ten years later. His full, loud presence had frightened me but, from a distance, fascinated me. He commanded attention.

He reached for a small glass cup of aromatic Turkish coffee from the table and added two sugar cubes. His hand dwarfed the glass. He took a sip.

"I want to learn a little English," he added, then grinned. "Maybe the exchange of language lessons might work." Other faculty in the lounge turned to watch the conversation between two opposites, the respected Classical Arab scholar with flair and the skinny American often hovering next to the wall, silent. In the teacher's lounge, Tunisian and European teachers didn't mix.

Mahmoud had follow-up questions and then wrote a time and an address to his house. He then turned and went to class.

*

The Zinelabedines lived in a two-story whitewashed house just inside the medina and its fifteen-hundred-year-old Islamic fortresslike stone wall. The seven-minute walk from my house to his the next day involved passing market stalls of copper pans, baskets, tire tread sandals, and dried red peppers before reaching the medina gate and the Zinelabedines' door, my first experience in a Tunisian family house other than those of my students.

*

I rapped the door knocker, shaped in the hand of Fatima, similar to every door in the medina. The loud echo startled me as its sound climbed the marble stairs to the painted floor and wall tiles of the Zinelabedines' house. It seemed to echo to the other end of the medina and then was lost in the sound of the noon call to prayer.

That moment began fifteen months of the same knock, sound, loud echo, against the aqua-blue-painted door. That noon knock took me away from the market crowds—with smells of cinnamon, ground hot red peppers in burlap sacks, and deep black olives stored in clear jars—and into the Zinelabedine family's daily life.

Footsteps echoed on the inside stairs, and the door swung open. Mahmoud's booming laughing voice said "Aslemma," which means "Welcome," and then "Tafuthal," the all-purpose word that at this moment meant "Come in."

*

This began the tradition of daily noon meals with the family, Ramadan celebrations together, and Arabic lessons. Mahmoud had already described me to his wife and parents, and the dining room table had an extra place set. As we climbed the stairs to the living room, he described that day's noon meal and Suad's excitement with her father's morning food purchases. Suad, at home without her *sofsauri* (veil covering), centered the lives of her parents, husband, and two young children. Even this noon, her gentle but firm directions brought everyone to her and to the table.

From the top of the stairs, Suad said "Tafuthal" in her warm, clear voice. Her broad smile said "You are welcome here" without words. She spoke only Arabic. Having been told of my visit, Suad's parents greeted me in the small living room as they sat on the couch under the large, government-issued photo of President Habib Bourguiba. Dressed in the traditional white djibbah with gold braided trim down the front, Suad's father began with "Tafuthal" as he motioned me to sit. As we exchanged remarks in French, the grandfather paused, sat straight, and said, "I went on the hajj last year. I am now fulfilled." He described the meaning of the trip to Mecca and his adherence as a local Muslim leader, stories and meaning new to me.

Suad's mother sat still, silent, wearing a yellow nylon scarf tightly wrapped around her head. Her bright-red henna-dyed hair peeked out around her ears. She spoke only Arabic. My Arabic needed to be learned quickly to be conversant with the women in the household, a great incentive to begin.

The ritual of greetings, meals, language lessons over tea, and Turkish coffee centered my weekdays. The basic meal was couscous, the core of every Tunisian's diet, but the seasons provided variety, one month eggplant with a week overlap with zucchini. Then zucchini changed to artichoke, which changed to tomatoes. Tomatoes and oranges stayed in the markets for almost six months. Oranges turned redder each month and finally almost rivaled the tomatoes. They then disappeared as summer arrived.

Suad's father bought meat for the meals based on whatever animal had been butchered that morning. He completed his morning shopping with something sweet for dessert. My favorite was baklava dripping with honey. Every dessert dripped with honey. Food shopping ended by ten, giving Suad two hours to cook. Couscous steamers, pans, fires, tagines, olive oil, and hot peppers were the core necessities of the good meals from her well-equipped kitchen.

Our noon meal (except during the month of fast) lasted a couple of hours, six family members and me. "Take this end of the table," Mahmoud said. "You're the guest." They never asked me to change positions, even as I became part of the family.

The first day began quietly with my words carefully chosen for Mahmoud and the grandfather, the only two French speakers at the table. We all used hand gestures. But each day, a few words, stories, and common observations in Arabic became part of my new and growing vocabulary. We began leaning into each other, interrupting each other, laughing with each other as Suad went in and out of the kitchen with more surprises to eat. Even that first day, Mahmoud's booming voice and laugh as he mixed English, French, and Arabic made me laugh. Suad and her mother kept grinning. The children remained quiet.

At the end of every meal, Suad brought out coffee and tea. The quiet clatter of the cups on the silver tray, her broad smile and deep voice offering me tea as she went around the room, became a time of comfort, a time to be, and a time to do nothing except sit and talk. Just being is a grand gift and difficult for me to learn.

*

Mahmoud established the language learning routine: after the noon meal for thirty minutes, three days a week, in the study next to the dining room. I carefully wrote out in English the conversations needed for my new project. Mahmoud then translated.

"I'm teaching family planning to women in maternity hospitals and new mother clinics," I said. "My conversations are about marriage, getting pregnant, and having babies," these words I said to an Arab man in his house after a traditional meal.

Mahmoud read the carefully written phrases in English needed for my conversations with women.

He asked what a couple of words meant and then said, "The words I'm giving you are not always acceptable words. Some are street words, words women don't use. But I'm sure they know them. Given they only speak local Arabic, these are our only choices." He said these unacceptable words with the ease of a language instructor. They were swear words.

As the lessons continued, our conversations became more familial, as if we were siblings sharing family secrets. He talked more about his own sex life and those of friends in Cairo while a graduate student and before marriage. He talked of how he and Suad used natural methods to avoid pregnancy, as he feared her using pills. These Arabic exchanges in our lessons were comfortable even as the words and sounds were strange and difficult for me to pronounce, no emotional overlay they would have had if in English. Mahmoud talked about sexual traditions as he would talk to a close male friend about the price of donkeys in the market. My reactions were equally bland.

I had become a third sex, living neither male nor female Tunisian traditional roles. He brought me into his intimacies as with a close friend, telling me what he would reveal to almost no one. His ease gave me the freedom to listen without fear of unwanted advances.

Suad brought in biscuits while refreshing the coffee and tea toward the end of each lesson. She seemed at ease with these lessons as she and her husband laughed at random observations as she served. As my Arabic improved, they brought me into their stories. My confidence in conversations with village women grew with each exchange in the Zinelabedine household.

*

In July, Mahmoud excitedly told me that Suad and her parents were preparing a special meal for me later that week. Each day, the family mentioned how good this meal would be, its preparation difficulties, and how it honored me now being part of their family. They kept the meal's ingredients a secret, just smiled when asked, tempting me more as Friday grew closer. Finally, in my best school teaching skirt and blouse, I arrived at the door early and knocked aggressively. Mahmoud greeted me with his robust "Tafuthal," and Suad, in an ankle-length light-green dress, smiled broadly at the top of the stairs. The grandparents had already taken their places in the dining room, standing behind their chairs, looking eager to begin.

We all pulled out our chairs to sit as eyes turned to me. A few words of thanks from me seemed appropriate, even if raggedly spoken. The first course, *brick à l'oeuf*, tasted of tuna, spring onions, and egg and was wrapped in phyllo, all perfectly seared. Once our plates were empty, Suad stood, disappeared into the kitchen, and returned holding the expected main dish on a gleaming metal tray: half an enormous cow's head, complete with eye, ear, and tongue. All faces turned toward me, anticipating my reaction.

I looked at the head with the ear standing tall and felt sick, the nauseous smell winning at the moment. Silence in the room as my stomach calmed slightly... waiting. Words formed, poorly enunciated, missing vocabulary, but sincere.

"I'm sure it's delicious. Suad and Grandfather worked hard." All still sat silent. "But I can't eat it. It's psychological." I struggled to find Arabic words. I had no vocabulary for my thoughts. "I'm so sorry," turning away from the awful-looking head.

Silence broke as Mahmoud chuckled, then Suad laughed, then the usually silent children joined in. Laughter grew louder as they watched me mumble more words, smile, and then join them. After a few moments, Suad, still laughing, took my hand and escorted me into the kitchen, helping create a meal of beef chunks, olive oil, chickpeas, and grasslike greens. They ate the cow's head; I ate greens, everyone joking throughout the meal. We meant more to each other than this cow's head. And I took a risk, to be honest. Accepted. We trusted each other.

\*

This meal began an even closer bond among us, conversations about personal family issues, religious differences between Muslim and Mormon beliefs, my noisy lycée students. The family talked of a financially unruly uncle. We discussed why Muslims don't eat pork and why Mormons don't drink coffee or tea, why women are veiled or not, why neither of our beliefs included alcohol, why the hajj for Muslims and the temple for Mormons.

Over the next year, my own stories grew, as did their interest in a life so strange: setting bonfires after sledding down canyon roads in the winter, building forts out of tumbleweeds in the backyard, swimming in the too-salty Great Salt Lake, cooking a turkey for dozens with bread inside. They gave me their stories, the grandfather's hajj, Mahmoud's college, Suad and her mother's henna ceremonies, the proper way to steam couscous. They taught me the best times to food shop in the medina, who had the best rugs to buy and offered the best tea, and why President Bourguiba had so many houses.

\*

In June 1967, during the Six-Day War, or the Arab-Israeli War, anti-American sentiments crept into the Arabic-language newspaper Mahmoud read to me.

He laughed as he read and said, "You're fine, don't worry. We love you and the other Volunteers." But during that week, for the first time, anti-American comments dotted our conversations.

"I don't like what Americans are doing to Egypt. Your country is wrong." After another anti-American Arabic-language article, "I believe when it says half the members of Congress are gay." That week, my counterarguments didn't matter.

His fear of an Arab loss in the Six-Day War translated to anti-U.S. sentiment. We were wrong to support Israel. The Tunisian government jammed both Voice of America (VOA) and BBC that week to disallow another viewpoint. When I entered my classroom on that Wednesday, my students had written "Death to Americans" on the blackboard. They stared at me, waiting and watching. I looked at the words, looked at them, erased the words, and began class. They smiled and started the lesson.

The next week, the war was over. The Tunisian soldiers had prepared but never left the country. VOA and BBC returned, and the United States became Tunisia's ally again.

*

Bob's Peace Corps Volunteer work as a drafting teacher and architect took him to Hammam Sousse each day. The small town, five miles north of Sousse, brought him interactions in French and Arabic with teenage boys, construction workers, and engineers. Together they designed schools and hotels while discovering Tunisia's rich architectural history as far back as two-thousand-year-old Roman bathhouses and water systems. In the evenings over couscous and bread, we shared our day's adventures, as diverse as if we lived two different lives. Bob told me outdoor worker stories. I told him indoor Zinelabedine and student stories. We were both richer about Tunisian life for sharing these experiences.

*

Each day with the Zinelabedines brought us new topics, from the intricacies and traditions of hooking rugs to catching trout in high mountain streams. Mahmoud's joy in every new subject brought me closer to him and Suad. She and I had special hand motions to each other when putting something over on Mahmoud. Then we giggled together.

My noontime at the Zinelabedines became midmorning to midafternoon. Mahmoud adjusted his schedule to be home. Grandfather shopped earlier to be back home to greet me. During Ramadan, they invited me to break the fast with them each evening.

"We know you'll arrive ten minutes late, having run down the hill from class when the cannon booms, but we'll wait. You're us," Suad said. And they did, poised to begin as they heard my heavy breathing and footsteps coming up the stairs.

"What great smells," I called out, finding my traditional seat of honor. After words from Grandfather, sips of water, and one date for each person, we ate as if we hadn't eaten for fourteen hours, which we hadn't. Nightly Ramadan meals included lamb, goat, mounds of couscous, breads, *brick à l'oeuf*, olives, and honeyed sweets when tiredness overtook the festivities.

They gave me their souls, and I gave them mine, the most intense and caring friendship I've known in fifty years. Souls can bond across languages, traditions, and religions.

*

In November, two months after our arrival, my father lost the election and his seat in Congress. With a Utah Republican now in Congress, Utah took another step toward conservative politics and away from support for Medicare and Medicaid, two new federally approved health programs my father championed. However, my father's support for President Lyndon B. Johnson's agenda earned him a nomination for an ambassadorship to Madagascar, an island nation off the coast of East Africa. His fluency in French helped him earn the post.

In late spring 1967, my family passed through Tunisia on their way to the posting in Antananarivo and to what became my father's three-and-a-half-year tour as ambassador to the Republic of Madagascar. The family members were invited guests of our ambassador to Tunisia, Ambassador Russell, for two nights in the residency.

*

The ambassador, Bob, and I waited anxiously in the VIP arrival lounge, large dark leather sofas and chairs ringing the walls with small glittery Tunisian tea tables near each seating area. Servers in white embroidered djibbahs stood and greeted the arriving honored guests.

The doors to the arrival lounge opened, and into the room ran my five siblings, ages five through twelve, yelling as they entered, "I want the toilet first," "I need a drink," "Christine took my favorite book." The words tumbled out as they bumped each other for favorite sitting places and cookies from the servers, bursting the tamped-down energy from the flights to Paris and then to Tunis. Ambassador Russell stood still, stunned at the sight, possibly worrying about the state of his residence once everyone left.

"Give me hugs," I yelled out as they noticed me for the first time, turned, and ran in my direction. "You've grown," I said. Then "I don't recognize you anymore."

"You're skinny," Stephen, age ten, said to me. "I feel your bones."

Just then, my parents entered, transit papers in hand, a couple of bags over their shoulders, too precious for the luggage cart.

Mother called out, "Sit down, all of you. You need to make a good impression on Ambassador Russell." Her words meant little in the energetic, noisy chaos. She looked tired. Packing, herding kids, checking flights, getting everyone to the airport had taken its toll. She had had little help from my father.

He strode in next to her, tall, straight, wearing a suit and tie and looking ambassador-like despite the hours on the plane.

"It's a pleasure to meet you, Ambassador Russell," he said, reaching out his hand as he moved toward the ambassador.

"And to meet you, Ambassador King."

My father beamed, looking like he enjoyed the title, which took the sting out of the election loss months earlier.

He then turned and faced the chaos that was his family and said sternly, "We have twenty-two bags. I want to see them lined up here in the lounge. Stephen, Frank... lead the way to the bags." He achieved order. As if by magic, twenty-two bags appeared.

Ambassador Russell hosted us all at the residence in comfort not available to Peace Corps Volunteers: American baked goods, table linens, central heat, large bathrooms with hot and cold running water, and peanut butter. Mother loved the ambassadorial china used in the residence. The gold Department of State seal embedded in the blue-and-gold ribbon ringing the plate's edge suggested elegance.

"Will we have the same china in Madagascar?" she asked Ambassador Russell.

"Yes," he said, and then added, "My wife has already bought the china for use once we return to the States. She loves it."

My mother bought the same china after they returned and used it to host dinners for thirty years, always placing each plate with the gold seal at the top before guests came to the table, a visual statement of refinement.

\*

The promise of camel rides early the next morning brought the greatest squeals from the kids.

"Let's go now," said Matt.

"I wanna be first," Stephen replied, rushing to the car. None of us had been on a camel before, and the kids had never seen more than fairy-tale camels.

We arrived at a sectioned-off spot of desert sand just outside Tunis, where camels and their owners tempted tourists with colorful woven blankets under leather saddles squeezed between the humps. The owners looked like the extras in *Lawrence of Arabia*.

"Where can I climb up?" Frank yelled, running past the owner straight to the camel. Then he stopped. Up close, real camels smell; they have bare, large, scummy teeth; they growl; and they bite people.

"What dirty teeth," Stephen said, walking backward from the camel's face.

Mother said, "We're here. You each must at least get up on the camel. Matt, you try first."

Five kids and then two Peace Corps Volunteers, one at a time, climbed the wobbly wooden steps to the saddle while others laughed.

"I'm scared. Get me down."

"I don't like it on the camel."

"Let's go home."

The camel rides came to a quick end. Before we left, Bob and I each had our picture taken on the camel without it moving. I've never been on a camel since, nor ever want to.

*

The next day, the family returned to the airport with the same twenty-two suitcases. They waved goodbye as they began the last leg to a country that impacted them as much as Tunisia affected me.

The decades since those two days with family in Tunis had connected all of us to each other and to our rich stories about two African countries.

*

My months of local Arabic language training gave me the confidence to walk through the doors of the local maternity hospital in early July 1967 to begin my new project: talking to women about family planning.

My experience consisted of having been married for three years without becoming pregnant and conversations with Mahmoud during language lessons—confident and naive. Reality hit in the first hour.

A hundred individual four-page Ministry of Health personal information questionnaires, examples of pills and intrauterine devices (IUDs), and little brochures with the title *Etre Mama, Etre Papa* filled my straw, handmade shopping basket as I pushed open the doors. World Bank– and Ministry of Health–defined responsibilities included asking women about their backgrounds for the forms and then sharing family planning information with them at their bedsides.

Fainting at the sight of blood, getting nauseated from heavy cleaning fluid smells, and never having seen a baby born gave me pause, but only for a moment. My commitment to the powerful health ministry must be honored. The smells of disinfectant and dried blood and the sounds of women groaning as they shuffled along the corridor in labor intensified my determination. These rural Tunisian women's colorful, handwoven cloth wrapping their bodies highlighted their rural traditions, even during birth. They came on foot, delivered babies, and left within a day, new babies tucked in the same traditional wraps.

Only occasional lights hanging from the high hallway ceiling intruded on my perception of darkness, encouraged by smells, sounds, and reminders of pain. Few looked happy; instead, they gave an impression of another birth to endure. Ten rooms lined one side of the hallway, each with four metal cots with a two-inch mattress and a thin blanket folded at the bottom. A narrow, high window brought a single note of sunshine. Across the hall, two broad swinging doors hid the delivery room. These opened hourly to stretchers with mothers in labor being carried in and women with minutes-old babies walking out, wearing their same traditional wraps, now stained with blood from the birth. Peeling paint, worn floors, scratched doors, and a few metal chairs suggested an old and tired maternity hospital.

A small office occupied the space next to the delivery room. "I am Jody Olsen, a Peace Corps Volunteer," I answered to the Hungarian chief doctor, standing next to the metal cabinet inside the room and having just asked, "Why are *you* here?"

After my description, he said simply, "Just don't disturb our work… and don't come into the delivery room." The three other medical staff were also from Hungary, part of Tunisia's plea for medical support. They took their work seriously, mostly.

\*

"Do you want to join us?" the chief doctor asked me a month later. "We're having a rousing game of water balloons." Water-filled pink condoms flew up and down the hall, thrown and caught by the medical team. Drenched white coats suggested an occasional miss.

"Don't think I'll play," I replied. "Slow reflexes." But I watched and laughed with them. A dark hallway, women in labor, flying condoms, newborn babies crying had become normal.

\*

Conversations with women filled each day.

"Aslemma, congratulations on your new baby," I began most dialogues, lifting the wobbly metal chair and setting it next to the bed.

"Is it a boy or a girl?" Their faces looked puzzled at the question. A pause, then they leaned forward and smiled. They tried to understand the foreigner speaking their local language with a heavy accent while they looked at a tall, thin blonde without a head covering.

"Why do you speak our language?" "Where are you from?" "Can you stay?" Questions and answers came quickly as we squeezed hands. They had me hold their newborn infants and shared their family lives. My months of language learning now offered me intimate stories of the rural women's lives. With my speaking the local language, even haltingly, they knew my trust in them was real.

My accent occasionally brought confusion.

"I don't understand you. I don't understand French," one woman said to me in Arabic.

"I'm speaking Arabic," I replied more clearly.

Again, "I don't understand French." I tried again. After the third try, a woman to her left whispered in Arabic, "She is speaking Arabic, not French." The woman's eyes widened, looked at me, and began a torrent of words in Arabic.

Our group of four in the tiny hospital room continued stories during the afternoon. They tolerated my accented Arabic and vocabulary errors, helping with unknown words, even dirty street words. They laughed at my pronunciation of the dirtiest words: a young Western woman swearing in their language.

*

"You can decide the number of children you have," I said during conversations. "And you can choose when you want to have a child." Their faces became vague, without comprehension.

"No, no," they said. "You're talking nonsense."

"Do you have children?" they asked me after establishing I was married.

"No, I've been married three years and don't yet have children. We're waiting and planning for the right time."

"Oh," they continued, then thought for a moment, as this made little sense. "What's wrong with your husband?"

"Nothing," I replied. "This is a choice."

"Where's your husband?"

"He's working nearby."

"Send him to our husbands. They need to talk to him." The women laughed and covered their faces.

"He isn't taking care of you. They will find something for him." The comments about helping Bob continued.

"But this is our choice," I pleaded.

"No, we will help you get pregnant. You must please your family."

*

My understanding of the language didn't mean understanding Tunisian tradition. My Arabic shaped Western ideas, but the women heard North African cultures. They understood my words but not my thoughts. In villages, a woman married a husband chosen by her parents. Her husband showed his virility by producing many children, who then cared for their parents in old age. Why change it?

"He might reject me as a wife if I don't have children quickly," one woman said, summarizing the cultural disconnect. To succeed, I had to understand these women, their joys, their concerns. They couldn't understand my traditions.

Words behind words became easier to comprehend with time. We shared time together as women waited to bring babies into the world or offered newborns their first breast milk. When babies slept, we looked together at pictures in *Etre Papa, Etre Mama*. With comfort and trust, they spoke of their hidden fears.

"I get pregnant too fast" or "I have six, too many." Often, they used the words "I'm tired" or "I'm sick." Some flicked their hands toward me and away from themselves as they spoke to emphasize too many children. Underlying many comments was "I don't know how I can feed them. We have no land, no harvest, no storage."

Asking their own ages and the number and ages of children was part of the questionnaire.

"I'm twenty-five," responded a woman with four children. She looked a decade older.

"I'm twenty," from a tired mother of three. Lines around their mouths and heavily furrowed brows showed early in their lives. Breasts sagged.

"My husband wants children, many children."

With conversations about limiting family size, one woman pulled her sagging breast from under her wrap. "This is my control. I nurse as long as I can. Years, if possible." Most said the next pregnancy began once nursing ended. Others were not so lucky.

Women commented about daily unrelenting routines of carrying water from wells, cooking meals over hot charcoal kanoons, taking kids to the hammams for scrubbing, weaving scarves, and tending to their husbands.

I pulled samples of pills and IUDs from my shopping basket as conversations became more personal.

"With these pills, you can prevent getting pregnant until you and your husband want a baby," I said, showing them the round circle of white pills encased in plastic. Women looked at me, looked at the pills, looked at me again, and again at the pills. They saw individually wrapped white dots in my hand.

"What do these white dots have to do with a baby?" My words couldn't explain it. Their expressions remained blank.

Next, the IUD. This particular IUD product, from France, was a small, white, curvy, thin plastic with two thin one-inch nylon strings tied to the bottom. It resembled a child's toy in France called a *scoubidou* and had become the informal name for the IUD in Tunisia. Because of its being placed in the vagina, the new mothers had some idea of how it worked.

"Do our husbands know if we have one?" they asked.

"No," I responded. "Once the health center nurse inserts it, it's quietly there until you have it removed." The thought brought laughter... and ideas.

But even the innocent *scoubidou* fell victim to rumors spread at village wells, over kanoons, and even to me in the hospital rooms. The women giggled and blushed as the words tumbled out.

It always began, "I heard that... ," the core beginning to rumors. Then it continued, "This woman has a *scoubidou.* The man and woman are together in bed, and the man gets stuck inside, stuck on the nylon strings. Couldn't get unstuck. The woman yells to their child to get the mayor. He comes with his donkey and wagon and lifts the couple into the wagon. The donkey pulls them through the village to the hospital to be surgically unstuck. Along the road, the village laughs at them."

"The strings aren't long enough," I suggested after the giggling had diminished but knowing my words meant little. "I don't think the story is true," I finally said lamely. Another foreign idea, a strange-looking object, and an assault on the known family traditions. How could we share these opposing ideas, different traditions? We were in different worlds, even with common words.

*

Any interest in ending future pregnancies depended on the number of children and frequency of pregnancy.

"My husband doesn't understand, and I am getting thinner," one said. "Can I do it quietly? Do I have to tell him?"

The other women in the hospital room joined conversations, leaning into the discussion from their metal beds, some embarrassed, others laughing.

"Tell me more about your husband. Does he want lots of kids?" I asked, knowing my being an outsider, safe from gossip, made it easy for them to talk.

"What can you say to your husband about kids?" In this dark room with one ray of sunshine and new babies at the breast, ideas were most likely forgotten as they cared for these new lives. But maybe next year, or in five years, a spark of a memory might take hold, and a tradition might change.

Greeting new mothers each morning and holding minutes-old infants drew me to these women.

"When was he born?" "Is this your first?" "How do you feel?" opened conversations about children, caring, and loss. Nearly half the mothers had lost at least one child, unfathomable to me as the oldest of eight.

"She never gained weight" or "He just died at two" were common words of children's passing. Sorrow in their voices would then change to hope as they proudly showed me their new infant.

*

Late one afternoon, as long shadows crossed the bed, I pulled up the wobbly metal chair to sit next to a woman and her newborn twins. She still wore the same wraps from her walk to the clinic and delivery, with spots of blood from the birth. In her midtwenties, her face appeared tired as she looked down and nestled one twin in her arms. The other twin lay at the foot of the bed, loosely wrapped.

In a puzzled voice, I asked, "Why is this twin at the foot of your bed?" She looked down at the infant she held.

"May I bring her to you?" Silence. No movement. She looked past me with vacant eyes.

After a couple of minutes, she said, "She is weaker. I don't have enough milk for both." She continued her stare. "And we don't have food. I cannot take her home." Her reply was void of emotion. We continued to sit in silence.

That day, that bedside taught me how little I knew about life, death, and the fragile threads between them. And the traditions and economics that affect those threads. Who was I to judge her or anyone else?

*

My knowledge of contraception found its way into conversations on the streets and in Sousse households. I reserved my only family planning words for the rural maternity hospital women, but after a couple of months, men began introducing themselves on the streets or in shops.

"Aren't you Madame Olsen, the Peace Corps Volunteer?" one man, dressed in a Western suit speaking beautiful French, asked. "Could you tell me about contraceptives?" He paused, looked away, and then back at me, whispering, "We want no more children."

Directions to me from the Ministry of Health were clear: "You do not talk to men about family planning." But women told me men decided, and these conversations initiated by men were simply greetings and chats on the street.

These encounters repeated themselves when doing my shopping. The conversations were in French, and the men wore well-made djibbahs or Western suits. They had thought out their words and asked questions carefully. Their choosing French ensured most others in the area wouldn't understand.

"This clinic has information and contraceptives. Your wife should be comfortable talking to the staff." Their genuine *merci* and smiles radiated gratefulness.

"We are doing well enough," one man said. "We have two children, and I want to give them the best we can."

Mahmoud had said the same about himself and Suad. The differences in thinking between the rural women in the maternity hospital and these urban men were mostly based on education, economics, and experience. What were children's value to a family? The rural women's responses were steeped in hundreds of years of tradition, rarely questioned. The urban men looked to a different future they could influence. My daily conversations with the women only offered a sliver of light under the curtain of tradition for those who looked. But it began the journey.

\*

My daily activities in Sousse puzzled both men and women.

"I'm like a third gender, a person who doesn't conform to male or female roles but is welcomed by both," I commented to Bob one evening. "I overhear their comments in Arabic. I'm confusing them by walking around the markets, uncovered and alone, buying spices in bulk from the gunnysacks on the roadside, scooping out bags of couscous from bins, and filling my used liter bottle with nonexport-quality olive oil from the market keg. I don't fit anywhere."

Men and women didn't mix in public. Women rarely went out, and if so, veiled. Religious traditions discouraged men from talking to women other than those in their families. But men and women both saw me differently. Their curiosity overcame gender traditions.

A man next to me getting olive oil asked, "Why do you buy this olive oil, not the clear kind Westerners like?" His beginning a conversation with a woman in public was against tradition.

"I prefer the flavor of this olive oil." That brought smiles.

Then questions followed like "Why are you here in Sousse?" "What do you think of our food, our markets?" and "You seem to understand us."

"I am happy here. I enjoy learning, seeing, hearing, understanding." The conversations became easier as Arabic improved.

The men who offered tea or coffee as part of their selling goods invited me to share it with them. They offered me a tiny stool, hand carved, just at the doorway to the shop.

"This is how to pour it from a foot high without spilling" or "Three cubes of sugar are minimum" was how the words began. Over time and repeated doorway visits with tea, they moved on to family, children, President Bourguiba, and the medina markets. They saw me as a local person dropping by and chatting even though I was the only woman on the street.

Women congregated in lean-to kitchens or around the kanoons outside the kitchen doorway. While pots boiled, mothers and daughters sat on small stools stirring, peeling, washing, or tasting. Mostly, they talked.

Their conversations ran together randomly. "Did you get soap yesterday?" or "I worry about my son's schooling," and then giggling about sex with their husbands. Their question "Do you like sex?" acknowledged my acceptance into the group.

Being an outsider, both men and women could tell me anything. They trusted my confidence with stories only men and women each told their own gender. Listen, remain relatively silent, ask questions, be honest, honor their words. Local Arabic opened the door to their lives.

*

In the months after our trip to Paris, Francine and I wrote occasionally, guarded and careful words.

"Hope you are fine. How is your work?" No personal routines described or emotions expressed.

The following November, with little buildup, Francine wrote, "Cindy wants to come to visit over the holidays. Okay to do so? Can she bring her high school friend, Catherine?"

"I would be thrilled," I said with my usual gushiness, masking nervousness at this first meeting with my newly found sister.

Our small four-room medina house could make room for two sleeping bags on borrowed air mattresses, hardly the comfort of Paris but fine for sixteen-year-olds. Could it do as a first impression between sisters? The house had an artesian well in the outdoor center courtyard, red bricks and rough-hewn boards for bookcase shelves in the living room, Tunisian cane chairs with heavy lanolin-smelling sheepskin smoothing out the raw cane, and an unpainted wood table for our meals. Black-and-white wool Tunisian blankets warmed the bed, deep-blue patterned Tunisian *kleems* covered floors in two rooms, and red-and-orange Hammam Sousse hand-woven veils hung on the walls. These brought fresh fabric brightness and color to the basic off-white washed concrete walls. Bob easily made any rough-looking space livable.

In winter, temperatures dropped to low forties. We had no heat, only one smelly black kerosene space heater dragged from room to room with our hovering bodies within inches of its warmth. The thick walls of Tunisian houses countered summer heat and trapped winter cold.

As Cindy's visit inched toward arrival time, I asked Bob, "Is this really a good idea? What will she think of us? What will she tell Francine?" My old fears and doubts returned: rejection.

"Stop worrying. It will be fine. You have to meet your sister sometime." He moved toward the kitchen. "What about tomorrow? Should be a good time." He laughed as he spoke.

Tomorrow came. Couscous with freshly killed lamb and baklava, laid out on the table, added Tunisian smells to the medina market sounds outside the house. Six other Volunteers joined in the courtyard, sitting on borrowed market chairs and wearing Tunisian-made scarves, designs representing the villages where they taught—no pants, no jeans, ever.

"You're really meeting your sister for the first time? I want to share in this historic moment," one Volunteer said when asked to join us.

Bob, who had picked up Catherine and Cindy at the Tunis airport two hours earlier, knocked at our medina door, the hand of Fatima creating a welcoming echo in the courtyard. He and two teenagers walked in, stopped, stared at us. We stared back. Nobody moved.

Filling the silence, Bob stepped farther into the courtyard, looked straight at me, and said, "Guess which one is your sister."

I got up from the chair, buying time as I searched for a clue: hair color, size, movement. Cindy and Catherine stood straight, not giving a hint. They had planned this joke. The other Volunteers sat still, waiting.

On instinct, I pointed directly to Cindy. She rushed over, hugged tightly, and said, "You got it. I'm your sister."

"No question," I said, not honestly. She didn't look like Francine. Her medium height, broader facial features, and slightly heavier walk came from her father.

Laughter, loud voices, stories filled the courtyard space, and food served, bedroom and bathroom space noted, suitcases moved aside. Three hours later, comfort replaced shyness in our conversations, the beginnings of sharing sixteen missing years. Questions about what to see, where to go, what to eat filled spaces between occasional questions about Cindy's Catholic school, unhappiness with uniforms, and summers in Italy and Germany. Questions about her parents remained unasked.

*

Infrequently, both New Year's Day and Eid al-Fitr, the celebration at the end of Ramadan, occurred on the same day, but this was the case on January 1, 1968. To honor the occasion, we rented a Peugeot 404 for that week and drove south into the desert and to the as-yet-undiscovered site that nine years later would be used for the first *Star Wars* movie.

Two years living in Tunisia must include time in the real Sahara Desert, high sand dunes, rocky cliffs, and wadis, the vast dry riverbeds that, after a rare desert downpour, became torrents of water tearing out roadbeds and desert growth.

The four of us and one additional Volunteer, Karen, packed sleeping bags, food, and left Sousse for Nefta, four hours south on the edge of the desert.

"I can't believe I'm here. Look at me," Catherine yelled into the desert sky from the tip of the fifteen-foot dune, sun rays pounding against her face.

"You're on top of the world—or at least the top of the desert," I yelled back safely from the bottom.

The hotel clerk in Nefta drew us a scratchy map to our next planned stop, the underground Matmata tourist hotel in Tataouine, twenty-one miles farther into the desert. Nine years later, this hotel would be Luke Skywalker and his aunt and uncle's home in the opening *Star Wars* scenes.

"Someone in a Land Rover left a couple of hours ago for the same spot, so you'll probably be okay," the hotel clerk said, looking nervously at the pencil map he had just created. He didn't ask about our car.

Ragged fifty-foot rocky cliffs rose above our faintly defined gravel road, blocking the setting sun as the desert heat dropped quickly.

"The road should wind this way, not the way it appears," Bob said after having stopped the car to look at the map drawing, no distances indicated. He started again. As the evening became night, the road became rubble.

"We're lost," I said quietly, to not create panic. Bob had been dodging rocks, trying to keep to sections of the gravel.

"Looks like the last deluge wiped out what was left of the gravel roadway," Karen said from the back seat, fear in her voice.

"I don't see any road," Catherine said, beginning to cry.

"It's okay. Bob'll save us," Cindy said, using a reassuring voice while trying to hide her own fear.

Karen remained silent, staring.

"Keep moving slowly and focus on the headlights. We'll find a way," I said from the passenger seat, wishing to make it true.

With a lurch, the car stopped. The engine continued to run, and the wheels turned, but no forward movement. We felt the crunch underneath.

Catherine screamed, "We will die here!" Then she sobbed harder.

Cindy, silent, hugged her tighter. Bob sighed, shoulders fell, as he rested his head on the steering wheel, my left arm around him, squeezing tightly. Blackness defined us and the desert, except for the two headlights, pointing nowhere in particular, which Bob turned off to save the car battery.

After moments of silence, Karen's voice whispered, "We can't do anything tonight. Let's admit it."

We said nothing as we opened the car doors, groped for sleeping bags in the trunk, crawled around the car to feel for flat ground to put the bags on, and pulled leftover baguettes from backpacks. We rationed two bottles of water, filled earlier that day in Nefta. Black enveloped us as if in a tomb, leaving only our voices, which we used sparingly. I desperately held back my panic.

"We will figure this out when we wake up," I said with no other suggestion. More silence as we listened to each other pulling sleeping bags around us on the gravely desert ground.

After too much silence, I asked, "Walking south, what is on the other side of this desert, the other side of the stars we now see?" After a few guesses, I continued, "How many miles to people, to cities, to the Atlantic Ocean?"

Cindy knew. "Two thousand miles of sand, rock, and the Sahara Desert before we get to West Africa, with only stars to guide." Hardly comforting. Twelve years later, I would live in the country two thousand miles directly south of our sleeping bags: Togo.

We faded into sleep, dark, silent, alone. As the morning light appeared, we found ourselves amid scrub brush, rocks, and just a hint of a gravel road beyond the dry riverbed. We had not been spirited away to safety, and there was no sign of human life. We stirred, sat up, and climbed out of our bags, looking for the bottled water, more baguettes, and bathroom stops behind rocks and scrub brush.

As we moved, I said in my false leadership voice, "I have an idea. Bob, Karen, Cindy, you three walk toward the hotel. We don't know how far it is, but no one will find us here … and the car is going nowhere." A walk around had revealed the bad news—three flat tires on a car that sat high, centered on a rock.

No better idea emerged, so we said our goodbyes, hugged each other, and then the wandering nomads waved from the distance. Catherine still slept, so I lay back down.

*

"Aslemma," a voice sounded a few feet from my sleeping bag. The face of a shepherd stared down at me. He appeared as if he had just walked off a Christmas card with his robe and staff, curved for easy walking. Five sheep followed. His eyes looked as frightened as mine.

He asked, "Who are you?" He then stepped back, seeing me now standing, taller than him.

"I am … ," I began, searching for an explanation using the few words that might match his understanding. He had sheep to graze and no way to help, so he began walking away, saying, "A small village is five kilometers up the road. They have a telephone." His words represented a miracle, hope. Bob would find the village, make a call, and someone would save us. We would lose the car, pay for it, and be sent home for being stupid, but we would survive.

Catherine woke up frightened, yelling, "I might die," but my repeated words from the shepherd calmed her enough to bring quiet to our desperate scene. She climbed into the back seat while I sat outside, staring into the empty desert.

*

About three hours later, a faint noise from an engine made me jump. *Hope.* Over the gravel horizon, an emerging gray jeep crept slowly, slowly toward the car.

"Here I am, here I am," I shouted, waving hands, jumping and running toward the vehicle. The car continued, carefully navigating each foot forward over rocks and around boulders. Thirty feet away, it stopped, doors flew open, and Bob, Cindy, Karen, two close Volunteer friends, and a USAID driver jumped out, screaming as they ran in my direction. *What!* was all I could think.

Cindy began, speaking too fast, "We walked to a village near here and asked for a phone."

Karen interrupted, "We were told, 'It's Sunday, the phone stand is closed.' We explained our situation as best we could and were offered camels for the journey to the hotel, about twenty kilometers."

"We politely refused, thinking we could walk faster," Bob spoke over Karen.

Karen jumped back in. "We knew it would be almost a day of walking to get help. We were scared for us all, mostly you two here in the desert, almost without food or water."

"We had no choice," Cindy broke in. "We started walking silently." Their conversation had gotten faster as details tumbled out.

"An hour later," Bob picked up, "we saw a Land Rover crawl toward us, securely following the route to the village. We screamed, waved, and ran toward the car. Whomever they were had to see our desperation."

"And then Web and Diane called out to us from the Land Rover," Karen inserted. "All I could think to say was 'Why are you two here? No one comes out here; it's the desert.'"

Diane then spoke: "All I could think of to say was, 'And why are you here, walking among rocks in the desert?'"

Web and Diane filled in the details after introducing the USAID worker who owned the Land Rover. "We joined our friend here a couple of days ago to see the desert from the Algerian border and decided this morning at the last minute to drive from the Matmata hotel to this village. The hotel guide suggested it was worth a drive, even without a drivable road." The hotel guide's suggestion saved our lives.

The USAID worker commented, "You were stupid but very lucky." He could say it as often as he wanted; he saved our lives. Before moving, we stood and stared at each other, not believing this had happened, and then shouted, "We have to get to work. This car isn't going anywhere."

The Land Rover had tire pumps, and once three tires were refilled with air, the car sat higher on the rock. Seven of us pushed the back and pulled the front while Bob drove forward, nudging the car off the rock. The car moved.

After endless thank-yous and more shouts of gratitude, tears, and hugs, our group of five continued onward. We had three more days of desert, cave villages, and mountain minarets to see. A seriousness of purpose, preparation, caring replaced the casualness of the earlier days. As the trip continued, Cindy and I hugged differently.

I said, "I love you."

She said, "And I love you." The next day, she added, "Don't worry, we are fine. No one else will know about this adventure." Francine didn't know until years later.

*

I dreaded leaving Tunisia, leaving the Zinelabedines. During the almost two years together, they taught me how to cook couscous and tajine, took me to the donkey market, and taught me how to weave pile rugs. They gave me the gift of time and of themselves and, in doing so, changed my life.

On that last day, the day of goodbye, I had small gifts for everyone, but nothing adequate for the experience. Mahmoud received a small can of Metrecal, a low-calorie drink, in honor of his size. We had laughed about his size, my size, all our sizes for almost two years. He put the can in the small refrigerator to drink later. Just before my leaving, Mahmoud and Suad disappeared into the back room, then a minute later came to the door, looking at each other and chuckling. In Suad's hand was a plastic contraception pillbox, half the pills missing.

"You're using pills?" I asked too loudly.

"Thank you, Jody," Suad replied. "We're having more fun."

Getting on the plane, I knew I had at least one contraceptive customer.

Fifteen years and occasional letters later, I went back to Tunisia on Peace Corps business. Without prior notice, I returned to Sousse, knocked on the Zinelabedines' door, and heard the traditional echo. After waiting, hoping, and ready to give up, the door opened to an older, thinner, and former mayor: Mahmoud. "Tafuthal" was the most beautiful sound I had ever heard.

After an hour of conversation, tears, hugs with Mahmoud and Suad, Mahmoud stood up, saying, "I have something for you." He disappeared into the kitchen, opened the refrigerator, and returned to the dining room. He handed me the small can of Metrecal I had given him fifteen years earlier, the bottom metal ring almost rusted through. He said, "I saved it for you. I knew you would come back." I laughed, but I didn't drink it.

# PART THREE

# *Back Home*

# 8

# Tragedy and Renewal
## 1968–79

We reluctantly left Tunisia in mid-June 1968, the two-year experience complete, but hearts remaining among friends around couscous bowls or with rug merchants drinking tea. Today, I still smell cumin in the spice shop, taste strong, unrefined olive oil bought from market barrels, and feel lanolin in the sheepskin chair covers. Moments rush back unexpectedly, reminding me of the cherished place and time that continue to guide me.

*

We returned from Tunisia via Europe, two months camping by night and sightseeing by day guided by the bestseller *Europe on Five Dollars a Day*. Bob's parents and younger sister bravely joined the journey, sharing tent-raising duties and then exchanging nights sleeping in a crammed two-person VW Squareback car versus an equally space-challenged tent. We used camping sites in Denmark, Germany, Sweden, France, Switzerland, Italy, the Netherlands, and once a week in crowded local hotel rooms as a welcome respite from the campground.

The breakfasts of baguettes, yogurt, and cheese and lunches of fresh fruit and veggies earned us the right to a grand dinner each evening. The art, history, and people in each country's cities and towns amply compensated for these meager accommodations. We laughed and joked, never complained. Ken and Sarah, Bob's parents, had not been on a plane before, had only left Utah once, and knew this adventure was both their first and last. The trip was their son's thank-you to them, even on five dollars a day.

*

Pregnancies announce themselves, whether or not expected. The first of three nights in Côte d'Azur, France, in a tent-rope-to-tent-rope-crowded campground, my urge for the bathroom came once, then again. The second night, the pattern increased, forcing me to crawl out, stumble over strangers' tents along the sixty-foot path to the latrine, lighted by a partial moon. No one acknowledged my nightly ritual.

As we stuffed our belongings into the VW on the third day, Sarah whispered to me, "I think you're pregnant."

I gulped. "How do you know?"

"Your nocturnal habits give you away."

I confessed, "Yes, I could be. But I'm not sure. I don't feel different."

"I'm sure." She smiled, hugged me tight, and said, "Congratulations. It's about time."

The baguettes and yogurt tasted better that morning, and subsequently, hotel accommodations frequently replaced the tent.

*

We said goodbye in Amsterdam, Sarah confirmed her excitement for me, and Bob and I stayed a few days to ship the car back to the States. While waiting, we hovered near the hotel radio, listening to news of the Vietnam War riots in front of the Democratic Convention in Chicago on August 28, 1968. Is this America? Is this what we're going home to? Bob was to begin his master's program at Columbia University the next week, a university that had been shut down that spring by anti–Vietnam War student uprisings. Fear of returning to the States ran deep as we listened that evening.

"We have no choice," I said. "The Peace Corps is over. Europe is over. We are Americans. It's our home. We belong there."

"I won't recognize it. Think of the war, the hate, the assassinations," Bob said. "Is that my country?"

From Tunisia, we heard of Martin Luther King Jr.'s assassination just five months earlier and the riots that followed. The photos of destruction in *Time* magazine looked more like the carnage of the Six-Day War the summer before. Then in June, the assassination of Robert Kennedy.

"I'm scared. The war has made our country different. We have a language in common but little else."

Bob put his arm around me gently. "We're starting a family, returning together. We'll be okay." We both hoped.

*

With good friends in New York City, a reference letter from the World Bank doctor from my Tunisia family planning project, and lots of luck, we found an apartment and a job for me within forty-eight hours of landing at JFK International Airport. So naive. Once settled, my walk to work from 122nd and Amsterdam to St. Luke's Hospital twelve blocks south took ten minutes. My office looked over the Columbia University campus, Bob's new student home.

*

Our first morning in the apartment, Bob suggested he go out and find us breakfast. "You stay in bed; I'll bring it to you." Our bed was a foam rubber mattress on the floor, one step up from the tent.

"Thanks, I'll take advantage of my condition," I said, chuckling and feeling fine.

On his way out, Bob noticed and picked up a telegram stuck to our outside doorknob. He came back. "I bet it's saying our car is here. I'll find a phone and call the number listed."

He returned twenty minutes later, walked into the bedroom as if a ghost, his face ashen, his hands shaking, the telegram still tight in his fingers.

I screamed, "What? What's happened?"

He sat on the bed, looked directly at me. "Your brother, David Jr., is dead, killed instantly in an auto accident. Driving alone."

"*No, no, no!*" I yelled out over and over and over. "No, it's not true. No. *No.* Tell me it's not true." I kept yelling. I can't remember much. My nightgown, the sheets, wet with my crying, Bob's crying. I have to call him. No, I can't. I must call him. No, he's not there. He's not there anymore. But he's me. I'm him. We're both Francine. We have to be together.

I couldn't think. I sunk deeper, deeper, deeper into sadness, more than my body could hold. I cradled myself, trying to hug him and me together. I had no more tears, but I kept crying.

I cried out again, "I've lost my lifetime best friend, my full brother, the son of my father's lost love. I've lost part of me." More tears, until nothing left. "Francine must be told. How do I find her? Do I have her number?" I spoke irrationally. "Her heart will break. Break. She didn't even know him," my words getting lost in sobs. My need to do something, anything, overwhelmed me. Make this news go away.

"I'll call your aunt Joyce in Salt Lake. She can give her the news. Don't you do it," Bob said gently, hugging me tightly as I sat on the bed, still holding myself, not letting go.

"Daddy, Daddy," I cried out. "Has he heard? He's in Madagascar. Will he survive the news? David Jr. is Daddy's mirror, his younger self." I kept flinging out random words, no order to my thoughts.

"Your father already knows and is on his way to Salt Lake from Madagascar. Should be there tonight," Bob said. He stopped, silent, my body against him, shaking.

After a moment, "Let me get back to the pay phone to call Joyce and then the airlines." He held me again. "You need to be there to greet your father. You're his rock," saying the last few words carefully and with the strength to bring me to reality. My sorrow, my emptiness, became action.

*

Arriving at my great-aunt's house in Salt Lake that evening, where David Jr. lived while attending the U, Aunt Marge opened the door, stared at me, and broke out crying. "I've cried for twenty-four hours," she finally said. "He'd become my son, the one I never had." She sat, leaning over, silent. We stayed together on the couch, crying, crying out.

Where am I? I had been in the United States for only a week, still disoriented by people speaking English, traffic lights, fast food, and telephones in houses. I had watched New Yorkers move, eat, talk quickly. They looked and acted strange. Now here, Sugar House, Salt Lake City, Utah, holding my desolate aunt.

Aunt Marge's home had been a familiar place in a town rich with memories, but it was no longer part of me. My plane for Rhode Island and Tunisia had left two years earlier, my escape from religious heaviness and routine. Now back, my brother's dead, I'm expecting... and empty, lost, alone.

The doorbell rang. Shaking and still crying, I walked to the door, opened it. My father stood on the porch and, at only fifty, appeared as a stooped old man.

"You're here," he cried out as he pushed toward me, then arms around me. We stumbled inside. "I didn't know where you were, how to find you, if you were even in the States." His words rushed out. "I left Mauritius thirty-six hours ago, then Madagascar, then Nairobi, then New York, then here… baggage lost in Nairobi… always sitting alone on the plane… alone with terror of loss… alone. The family is still in Mauritius."

Then he collapsed into the plush living room chair and broke down, his face buried in his hands, body shaking. He sobbed, "Why David? Why not me? Why him?" over and over. He couldn't stop the sobs as he gasped for air. Thirty-six hours of being alone, holding the grief inside, twenty-one years of love for a child, his child, now gone, came out of his soul as he sat, stooped, uncontrollably crying out, screaming, shedding a lifetime of tears. Sitting on the floor, my arms wrapped around his legs, my head rested on his knees. His expressions of bottomless grief needed me there, silent, for an hour, maybe two.

Slowly, he raised his head, face wet, swollen, and red from anguish. "I'm glad you're here. I need you desperately."

"I'm here," I said. "Don't worry, I'll take care of everything, and…" I paused and smiled weakly. "You're going to be a granddad. In April."

Aunt Marge had left us, tiptoeing into the kitchen. Now she brought out bowls of homemade soup, fresh bread, and ordered, "Eat."

*

Bob flew out a day later to give needed emotional support. Always calm, he held me together.

The funeral arrangements became my responsibility, a first time to even attend one. But my father's grief had immobilized him. The city loved my father. He had been their congressman until two years earlier and was now an ambassador to Madagascar. Hundreds came to the service to share their grief and honor him. I protected him when he needed his own time and responded to painful questions from others too difficult for him to answer. He held his professional demeanor when with attendees, stoic. We said goodbye to David Jr. at the graveyard next to Daddy's parents and wept. Yet we couldn't walk away. We stood still and stared at the open grave, quietly praying for him to come back. Then we turned our eyes toward the view of the city and dragged ourselves to the car. Life had to continue.

Later, as we drove to the airport for his return to Madagascar, I said, "Bob and I decided that if we have a son, we will name him David, a gift to my brother, who helped make me who I am."

Daddy remained silent, then spoke in a whisper, "Thank you."

\*

My father wrote twenty years later in his autobiography, "David's death was the saddest and most terrifying event of my life. The impact of David's tragic death was concentrated, like a destructive laser beam, into one small moment in my long life. It was more than I could endure. I carry emotional scars to this day, which will not go away."

The emotional scars didn't go away. He lost his quick step, his spontaneous optimism. He became more religious, referring to scriptures about the hereafter and being with David Jr. He took his son's photos down in his office, rarely mentioned him. Family conversations hollowed out references to him, leaving spaces, silences where words of his family antics growing up should have been. My brothers and sister talked about David Jr., but never in Daddy's presence. His sad yet stern face gave warning.

Cindy told me, years later, about Francine receiving news of David Jr.'s death: "The word came the day we were leaving for me to go to college at Wellesley. As we packed for Frankfort to catch the military plane to the United States, Mother [Francine] received a telegram: 'David Jr. died in an accident, letter to follow.' I cried, but Mother didn't. She stayed focused on packing. She kept saying, 'We will hold it together; we need to keep going. Don't worry about me.' I cried in Frankfort for the two days; she didn't. She left her relationship with David Jr. unfinished."

Francine did not ask to attend the funeral. She had no invitation. She mourned in silence, alone. Because her husband, Tim, had asked her not to reveal her previous marriage or acknowledge the two children, none of her Paris friends knew of David Jr. To her outside world, he never existed. Deep inside, she said she mourned deeply, painfully, constantly. Forty-five years later, at ninety, she spoke his name: "Every day I miss never knowing my son."

However, in Francine's writings, her own chronicles of emotional journeys, she only wrote two sentences about David Jr.'s death: "David was killed in a car accident at twenty-one. I regret I didn't get to really know him." The deep guilt and loss never left her heart.

When Francine passed away at ninety-six in Salt Lake, Cindy sat with me on Francine's French-tanned leather couch by the bay window in the living room overlooking the city and shimmering Great Salt Lake. She revealed Francine's decades-earlier words about not being able to see David Jr. and me: "Mother told me that after the divorce, she had an agreement that once a year, David and Rosalie would ask David Jr. and Jody if they wanted to see their mother. Francine was told each year by Nana the children had said no. She thought her two children had divorced her from their lives."

I sat stunned, listening to Cindy's words. "But that's not true," I said, realizing that Francine had wanted to see me for twenty years. "My parents deceived me," I whispered, fearing to say the words. We sat still, sad at what might have been. Finally, "And then we lost David Jr. Francine never got her son back and lived life thinking she didn't deserve him. And he never knew his mother." As I sat on the couch, rubbing my hands on the familiar leather armrests, anger returned at what had happened and could have been. But I stayed still, breathing, letting it wash away. Francine, David Jr., my father, my mother, Nana, all now gone. Anger about the past had no purpose. That life is no more.

*

David Jr. lives with me, his jokes, his obscure facts, his teasing. He shares my successes, failures, risks, and stories. His unlived life is living through my own. I hope he's smiling.

My son, David, now middle-aged, is proud of his heritage. He has little resemblance to his uncle, either in looks or in temperament. But he has the name, no other similarities needed.

*

We returned to New York City after the funeral and interment; Bob began school, and I, my job, and our apartment quickly sprung to life with Thursday-night cast-off furniture Bob rummaged from Amsterdam Avenue bulk pickup. He could decorate beautifully.

Our son David was born the following April. We made the ten-minute walk from the apartment to St. Luke's Hospital between two contractions. In the delivery room, as the morning wore on and the contraction pains grew, my old fear returned. What if I don't want to care for him? Twelve early years of babies and diapers had left me numb.

One last push, and I felt David enter the world. With his first cry, my body instinctively moved toward him. As my hands touched him, my love for this new life engulfed me, a love still as pure as on April 11, 1969.

How could Francine have forsaken the instinctive mother's love for her children?

*

July, with a three-month-old, we stuffed our belongings into the VW Squareback, our previous summer's travel companion, and headed to Baltimore, two hundred miles south and the site of Bob's new job with city planning.

Our Mt. Royal Avenue apartment in the city overlooked train tracks, the Howard Street Bridge, and the still-charred buildings near the university from the MLK riots of the year before. We had no money.

Bob began his work routine; I, my stay-at-home mother routine; and for us both, the city routine. Our Peace Corps experience drifted further into history as family responsibilities and finding a permanent place to live consumed our days.

But the joys of motherhood didn't bring full happiness. David's feet kicking in his bathwater made me laugh, and his curled finger around my thumb brought a smile. He tucked himself into my arms as we both made funny sounds. Our touching skin intensified the love… and the bond. But not all the time.

I admitted to Bob, "I'm bored." He occasionally found me in tears when returning from work.

"I'm alone. I can't get out…" and more. "I have achieved what good young Mormon women want: a baby, a home, a loving husband who goes out each day and earns a reasonable salary. Why am I sad? Why doesn't the Mormon tradition make me content?" Inside, I knew the answer. It was why I left Salt Lake. I wanted more than what church teachings offered.

"You're different," Bob said. "Motherhood is a complete calling for some, maybe for most, but not for you."

"Did I wear myself out caring for my brothers and sister?" I walked across the small living room to be near Bob. "Something deeper seems wrong. For me, life isn't in these four rooms. Life's out there, in those downtown buildings poking up in the skyline. I want to be out there, wherever that is."

Bob sighed, then sat in the worn blue fabric chair that came with the apartment, looking out to the bridge, heavy with traffic, as he held David. "We'll make it work. I don't know what 'it' is, but we've been through a lot together. This is our next problem to solve."

I walked across the room, picked up David, and tickled him for a smile. Then to Bob, "You always understand. We're a different couple."

*

In September 1969, we bought a four-thousand-square-foot, sixty-year-old row house in Charles Village. It was in a city neighborhood walking distance from Johns Hopkins University and an area making a comeback from years of neglect and suburban flight. This formally elegant house had been vacant for half a decade following the death of a widow with a rumored thirty cats. One dead cat's dark outline remained stained onto the dining room oak floor. A rug solved that problem.

The first floor's twelve-foot ceilings had plaster garlands, giving the house a deceptive European feel. But its three stories lacked basics: no running water and only enough electricity to support two hot plates and two light bulbs. Three upstairs ceilings lay in pieces on the pine floors, only the construction lath remaining above our heads. Leaky roofs had taken their toll. Caked-on dirt disguised the inlaid oak floors in the formal parlor and dining rooms. But we had a bargain: ten thousand dollars, a loan from my parents. My fall first-year graduate school tuition paid for a plumber to replace the frozen pipes. With new plumbing and running water, we moved in, camped in two rooms, and began a three-year rehabilitation project, completed by hand and sweat.

Our first visitors, neighbors, said as they walked in, "You paid too much for this dump. Why buy it?"

My parents, driving thirty-five miles from Kensington, Maryland, came to inspect the results of their loan.

Mother gasped as she entered the vast hallway. "How do you take care of David in a place like this? It's filthy. It's gross."

Daddy, trying to find an upside, said, "Yes, I can see you buying this house. You were Peace Corps Volunteers. You're good at living in such places." Our Peace Corps house looked better than this fixer-upper.

Bob said, never discouraged, "Remember, I'm an architect. I promised to take care of your daughter, and I will." Three summers and thousands of labor hours later, our home was the centerfold in the *Baltimore Sun*'s Sunday magazine. That house gave us joy every day for the decade we lived in its beauty, tenderly caring for each room.

*

During our time on Calvert Street, we brought David's sister, Kirsten, home from the hospital, hosted playgroups, and exchanged babysitting duties with nearby neighbors as I juggled graduate school with motherhood and house restoration. I tested my new community organization skills as president of the Charles Village Neighborhood Association and as an advocate for additional neighborhood services. City Hall and Mayor Schaefer knew me well.

With other families, we walked up Calvert to Thirty-Third Street and then down the grassy median strip to Memorial Stadium for Orioles baseball, singing the latest hits to each other. Earl Weaver's tenure as manager brought wins, playoffs, and even a couple of World Series. David became the game's data nerd. I scraped wallpaper off walls in nine rooms at night while listening to games and hearing the nearby roaring crowds through open windows, breezes cooling the un-air-conditioned house.

Bob and I hosted dinners around our square repurposed college library table, perfect for eight-person discussions of local Democratic politics, neighborhood schools, and names of electricians and plumbers. David and Kirsten joined for the meal, sitting on stools and looking bored. Friendships deepened as children grew and houses flourished into architectural treasures. Many close friends today, four decades later, began as playgroup hosts and floor sanding partners.

*

I have always eyed earning a master's degree in social work. My year as a clinical social worker at St. Luke's Hospital confirmed the goal but with a change in emphasis to community organization and management. My graduation from the University of Maryland achieved that goal two months before Kirsten's birth. Today, she is a clinical social worker. Her training began early. We still smile about it.

Advocating for better elderly health care in the city became my passion for the next three years, then it was exchanged for my advocacy in state and national arenas as director of the Center on Aging at the University of Maryland. My studies toward a PhD in gerontology fit into the spaces between the work, commuting an hour each way between College Park and Baltimore, and family responsibilities. I slept little and saw Bob less. We handed off kids, checked schedules, attended church. Church was routine: same Sunday school lesson, same conversations about growing children, same songs. Belief fading. My frantic pace became a drug, more... more, wanting the rush of new knowledge, accomplishment, recognition. Then five years later, with the degree in hand, congressional gerontology-related hearings organized and held, courses taught, nursing home trainings done, kids in primary school, we walked away from our Baltimore life and moved to Togo, West Africa.

*

Over these ten years following David Jr.'s passing, I inched my way toward a reconciliation with Francine. The death, always unspoken except to Bob, became a heavy stone in my body, dragging me into a deep, dark room: depression hung on the edges. My twin soul would never return.

Could reuniting help? Did Francine feel the same heavy stone or something sadder? She lost David Jr. before she knew him as a son, before laughing at his funny phrases and mimes, his researched renderings about music and politics. She never held him close or at all. With a son of my own, I now understood what could be. She lost her life with her son but shouldn't also lose it with her daughter. She might learn to love me. I loved her but feared her leaving me again. I had begun tentatively healing three years earlier, but now distance kept me fearful.

We began with occasional letter writing, chatty, friend to friend, including asking if she came to the States, to DC. My parents knew nothing of this. In early letters, Francine talked about friends, restaurant luncheons, Switzerland skiing, designer dresses. Only later did I learn these dresses were from a secondhand shop. These images intimidated me. My life was overstock clothes at Shockets in Fells Point, sandwiches, and sidewalk snow shoveling.

We saw each other from our own lived experiences, strangers to the other's narratives. Neither of us took a step inward, afraid closeness would bring loss. We concealed vulnerabilities.

After two years of polite letter writing, Francine came to DC to visit her husband, Tim's, West Point military colleagues in Virginia. She invited me to join her in the hotel suite, an evening together, the two of us. Tim's friends remained out of bounds.

The next morning, as I looked into the bathroom mirror combing my hair, Francine walked in without a robe, nude from the waist up, and began applying makeup. I smiled and continued my grooming. No words exchanged.

Francine had no breast, only a foot-long scar where the breast had been, a glaring visual reminder of her cancer and mastectomy ten years earlier, a perceived vulnerability. She continued applying makeup and returned to finish dressing. Later that afternoon, as we packed up and walked to the parking lot, she said, "I've been afraid to show you my scar, fearful you would walk out of my life." She paused, tears coming, then said, "But you didn't. You're still with me. Now."

After that moment, sharing emotional scars, acceptance began. She confessed fear of being found deficient against her perceptions of my success. I confessed the same about her. Neither saw our own success, only that of the other. Her exquisite manners had frightened me; by not being able to measure up, I assumed important people, dinners, galas were integral to her life. She saw my college degrees and professional work as a reminder of her lack of training after high school. "You influence people. You make a difference," she once said. We had been judging ourselves disapprovingly against the other's success.

For the twenty years without her, I had felt sadness, regret at her leaving, not anger. People ask me, even today, why? I'm not sure. A place in me suggests knowing she left not because of malice toward me but because of her own self-contempt, inadequacy. That deep sadness of what couldn't be began to heal.

\*

On a rare, brief visit to Baltimore, Francine helped set my dining room table, found a tablecloth, then placemats, wedding silver, cutlery, china, and stemmed glasses. That cat body stain on the floor stayed hidden under the rug. Francine never knew.

"You feel accepted when you eat elegantly," she said to the four of us. "You belong." We came into the dining room, sat, admiring the still-new settings. Kirsten observed the unfolding ritual. David didn't notice. Bob brought out the first course, soup, ladled into bowls on matching small plates.

"Kirsten," Francine began, "soup is difficult to eat properly. The spoon might drip as you carry it to the mouth. Gently scrape against the side of the bowl before raising it." She demonstrated. Kirsten, aged four, stared at her. She thought a minute, put both hands around the sides of the bowl, lifted it to her mouth, and slurped it down in two gulps.

"I ate the soup," she said, smiling. No one moved. We looked at Francine. Then Francine smiled, began laughing harder, longer. She put her hands around the bowl and followed Kirsten's example. "See, Kirsten, it's okay to do it your way."

*

Years later, Francine told me why manners mattered to her and should to me. "They feel not like rules but like a secret tucked back behind daily living."

That sounded easy, but new habits take time, time for extra mentions of "Please" and "Thank you," placemats and plates under peanut butter sandwiches, best towels for guests, fresh flowers on dining tables.

"You seemed to have learned manners early," I said, "as if it were normal for everyone. How do you do it?"

"My next-door neighbors, an older childless couple, invited me to be their part-time granddaughter," Francine said. She continued the story, a story I later found written in one of her journals: "The Pattersons believed that few things could make life smoother, sweeter, and more life opening than excellent, thoughtful manners. The window to see the magic that sunshine through crystal could perform. Mrs. Patterson taught me the sensual pleasure of immersing my small hands in hot, rich, soapy water to carefully, ever so carefully, feel the shapes and textures of porcelain, softened by the soapy suds.

"I remember holding an etched goblet up to the window to see the magic that sunshine through crystal could perform. Just being trusted to handle her loved possessions as a child changed something profound in me.

"Good manners make a difference in life. Even a child's imagination couldn't have connected manners taught to a tomboy little girl in a small town to a luncheon with the Queen of England many years later. The hours I spent in that atmosphere of affection and generosity created a platform on which I have constructed much of my life."

I grew up with blue plastic tumblers, scratched Melmac plates. My father's parents' china remained hidden in a cupboard.

"You kids might break it. We'll stay with long-lasting, nonbreakable dishes," my mother told me. "Always be practical, thrifty, and efficient." Beauty didn't qualify.

Conversations with Francine about manners, beauty, continued over decades on her Paris living room leather couch, the balcony tea table overlooking Paris's skyline, and walking through nearby Parc Monceau. What I had interpreted as being aloof, distant, now I understood as her way of creating comfort for others. She created this world gently, without haste.

She told me, "What I really want is total comfort. No strain. No nervousness about being on time, staying too long, looking right enough, pleasing enough. In making this, I begin each day by having my body and face be right. The rest follows."

Francine's apartment became my occasional weekend home over years of Peace Corps travel, and her morning routine, familiar. She began each day, before entering the kitchen or living room, preparing for the day: makeup, styled hair, jewelry, linen trousers and jacket, and a silk scarf tied neatly around her neck. She said, "I look in the mirror and ask myself, 'Am I properly put together?' Only then do I make a coffee, even when alone." As we sipped our coffees from small gold-edged espresso cups overlooking the city she loved, she continued, "How can others respect you if you don't respect yourself? Self-respect transfers to support for others."

*

On one of my three-day visits to Paris, Francine eagerly approached me at the international arrival lounge of Charles de Gaulle Airport. "I have a great idea for us. Let's do Color Me Beautiful."

"What's that?" I answered hesitantly, thinking of an afternoon at the spa.

As we drove the A1 into Paris, Francine continued, "My friend Joan and I took a course to learn about skin tones and color. We look our best wearing colors suited to our particular skin."

"I'm not sure about this," I said. "One more thing to worry about when I get dressed."

Joan waited in Francine's apartment. She had color swatches laid out on the couch, scarves over chairs, and makeup palettes arranged on the side table.

"Okay," Joan said excitedly to me as I walked in. "I think we're ready."

"A little lunch first?" I asked.

After tomato sandwiches, followed by coffees in a demitasse and gossip, Joan spoke up, "Jody, I've been studying you over lunch. You're a summer. Let's begin with those colors." She could have said "You look like an alien" for what her words meant to me.

Three intense hours later, fabric swatches scattered on the floor, scarves rumpled on the sides of the couch and chairs, and Francine's shirts, blouses, and jackets jumbled on the table all represented dressing and redressing. Clothes I had packed for my onward Africa trip sat in a "you don't want to wear" pile on the chair. Makeup had been moved back to the bathroom, brushes scattered on the counter. After testing colors, trying scarves and clothes styles, Francine and Joan had declared me "Summer."

Joan said, with command, "Wear pastel blues and pinks. Stay away from bright reds, browns, yellows. Never wear black."

"Half my turtlenecks are black," I said wearily.

"Nope," Joan replied, "don't wear them."

Francine added, "You look better in bigger, fuller clothes with jackets that flair. Your small, tight-fitted, tailored shirts and jackets make you look tiny, invisible. You're bold. You're strong. Show it." She said her words clearly, smiling. "Your clothes and makeup tell others you are proud of yourself."

"I've never seen myself that way," I said meekly. "I want to conform."

"But you are bold, like a leader when you talk. Now you will look like the leader when you enter the room." Francine understood me better than I did myself.

After going into the bedroom and then returning wrapped in Francine's bathrobe, I said, "I am not sure who I am anymore. I need time out... while wearing your bathrobe."

Francine and Joan laughed. "Take your time."

I wore her bathrobe for twenty-four hours, mentally rehearsing brighter-pink lipstick, flouncier dresses, looser jackets, softer-looking hair. I put on shirts, skirts, looked in the mirror, and took them off. Sunday evening, I strode purposefully into the living room, having given a heads-up to Francine and Joan that a new Jody was belatedly emerging.

"Here I am," I said firmly, not revealing my fluttering stomach.

"You look smashing, just smashing," Joan said in her well-pronounced South African accent. "I'm pleased. I worried I might have done you in yesterday. But I knew you could do it."

"You look beautiful, larger in purpose, like the leader you are," Francine added, beaming broadly. "The scarf you now wear is yours, given with love." She stood, walked toward me, and oh-so-slightly straightened the jacket with its single button and loosely fitting pleated back. "That jacket has Jody written on it. It's yours," she said, pulling back, looking at me, and then, "I love you so much."

"Are you sure you can live without the jacket?"

"It's better on you. And I can now envision you entering a room with gentle elegance."

On leaving for the airport the next day, Francine took me via the Arche shoe shop, a high-end French brand famous for soft suede leather and bouncy soles. I walked out with a pair of Drick flats, open-toe, square-holed soft leather, and a zipper on the heel. "I'll be noticed with these shoes," I said to Francine. "If I'm going to do it, I'll go all the way." My stride improved with the bounce on my feet.

Two weeks later, returning from my travels, I wrote Francine a quick note. "Inspired by our time together. My makeup is in place, and I am getting used to it. The clothes are smashing, and I have not taken the Arche shoes off my feet. A colleague said I had been 'redone.'"

My Arche shoes disappeared into the trash ten years and a million steps later, reluctantly. My brighter, broader, bigger way of dressing still defines me today. I have become known for wearing colorful jackets.

One time, a Peace Corps staff member called out to others, "We can count on Jody always wearing something exciting." I liked it.

*

Over the years, Francine and I merged. We discovered similar hand gestures, sentence structures, head movements, and our walk.

"How do we do it?" Francine asked as someone noticed our similar laughs. "We didn't know each other."

"Magic," I said. "Something inside, unseen, holds us together."

In 1994, I wrote in a note to Francine: "Why do you understand me so well? Our brain cells seem to match each other and flow in harmony even from so many miles away. We seem to also both live with that sense of common professional decorum that makes people think we fit into situations so nicely, but quietly, we live a little closer to the edge."

I had gained a soulmate—not a mother but a twin. She anchored me, encouraged me, told jokes with me. I had lost a brother. She had lost a son. That horrific loss, unspoken, made us closer. We would not, could not, lose each other. We didn't.

Francine and Jody, 1943.

Rosalie, David Jr., David, and Jody, 1946.

Jody and Congressman David King, 1961.

Bob and Jody's wedding reception, 1964.

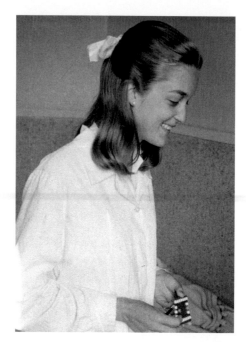

Jody as a Peace Corps Volunteer, Tunisia, 1967.

Jody's family visiting Tunisia, 1967. Bottom row: Christine, Matt, Christopher. Top row: David Jr., Frank, Jody, Rosalie, Stephen, David.

Jody and Francine at Reach to Recovery dinner, no date.

Jody and Paul Coverdell meeting a Nepalese official, 1991.

Kirsten, Jody, David, and Bob, 1990.

Jody in Mauritania, 2007.

Jody as Peace Corps director, 2018.

Jody giving Peace Corps pin to Uganda senior official, 2019.

Day "56" countdown to Biden's swearing in, 2020.

# PART FOUR

# Peace Corps Staff

# 9

# Two Cultures, Three Languages
## 1979–81

In late February 1979, a five-person College of Education dissertation faculty committee gathered in the tiny third-floor conference room on the University of Maryland campus. Their eyes fixated on the corner window where heavy clouds forewarned a looming winter snowstorm. Slumped shoulders gave away the unspoken question. "Can we get Jody through her thesis defense before the snow comes?"

I pressed my elbows close to my sides and hunched into the chair, trying not to influence the decision but wanting enough weather delay to defend my dissertation, then a flurry of flakes to rush the remaining faculty questions before a total whiteout.

I had confidence in the defense outcome—but was not sure of the process, which included explaining research methods measuring life satisfaction of older people to a group of faculty who enjoyed challenging statistical models and youth learning styles. They knew little about the elderly.

Ninety minutes later, after the committee huddled and voted, my advisor extended his hand and said, "Congratulations, Dr. Olsen." Then he added with a sly smile, "You did a great defense."

I suddenly jumped up and hugged him.

Two years sitting at a typewriter late at night were worth it to be called Dr. Olsen, at least for this moment. Snow began to fall. Within minutes, the University of Maryland Benjamin Building sat silent. That evening in Baltimore, the Olsen household celebrated.

With the PhD came job security at the university and more university research and an expanding reputation in gerontology. The Dr. Olsen hand-shake furthered this dream.

To make this degree happen over four years, my days began at 5:30 a.m. and included a short run, waking kids, driving an hour to be at work as Center on Aging director in College Park by 8:30, leaving precisely at 4:00 p.m. to pick up kids back in Baltimore, dinner, story time, and then studying until midnight. Two nights a week, courses kept me too late to come home. My faculty friend Jean gave me dinner and a bed at her house. The degree offered peace from the exhausting routine.

*

After dinner one evening in early January 1979, Bob asked, "Would you like to go back overseas? I have been thinking that I would."

"What?" I looked at him numbly. "That's not in my plan."

His deliberate words suggested days, if not weeks, of previous contemplation, then rehearsal, and then the courage to ask. His face told me his question was serious.

I had learned to stay calm at difficult moments, taking time to divide conversations into pieces, practice words in my head before answering, think deliberately toward decisions.

"What about my job, my work, my degree?" I continued, my voice rising and pleading. I thought only of my work, my future.

"Just a thought," he said, standing up from the table. Behind those three words were his months of tension trying to hold the household together and accommodating my torturous schedule and time away from home.

We had weeks of fragmented conversations sandwiched between children's bedtime stories and wearily closing down the day. We untangled the motivation behind his question. The answer would end ten years in our house, our Charles Village neighborhood, and our routine. Forty years old and bored with his architecture work, Bob wanted a fresh experience, one that would bring him closer to his earlier work as a Peace Corps Volunteer. He also wanted a closer family.

Words eventually found places to be said. Some while stacking the dishwasher, more while folding clothes, and others during typewriter breaks in the study. The reasons for Bob's question became focused and raw. As biting sentences moved between us, we both stayed calm. We cut up conversations, to be continued later, so we could stay calm. Fifteen years of marriage had perfected this technique.

"We cannot continue to be a family with your work schedule." Our conversations continued. "You're rarely home and not mentally present when you are home." He lowered his voice, spoke slowly.

"But I am present," I pretended. I tried not to look at him, fiddled with the hem of my shirt, but he spoke the truth. I had slipped away from Baltimore's crab fests, ball games, and neighborhood potlucks for Washington's politics and pizzazz and for a budding national academic reputation.

Bob had been there for me, selflessly encouraging my further education and work. He knew well his responsibilities without my appreciating what he quietly did every day to support me and the kids. He was driving kids to school, helping with homework, keeping food in the fridge, bringing up and folding laundry, scheduling activities, fixing a sixty-year-old house, and working a full-time job. My professional success depended on Bob's support. And he now suggested an end to this support.

"Why am I on this schedule? Where does it go? Where will I be in five years?" I asked myself. The answer remained in the light-blue haze of the future, over the next horizon. These were inconvenient questions that challenged me as a wife, mother, and professional. I wanted recognition. I wanted professional purpose.

After Bob's comments that particular evening after dinner, I thought for a while and finally said, "You're right. But I'm not sure how to get off the cycle of conferences, papers, students, deadlines, and commitments I have for the next couple of years."

Bob said, "Just say you're leaving for a while. Others do it."

"Not me," I said. "Don't like to let people down."

"But it's okay to let your family down?" he asked, his voice tense.

Anger welled, my body tensed. My lips tightened. He had found me out. "I thought I could do it all," I said, the truth hurting... badly.

With the passing days, the view of my father and his description of his father, my grandfather, the senator, became clear. My father, the congressman, seldom home, mentally hiding in his virtual office at one end of the dining room table when he was home, shoulders hunched over his typewriter. His body communicated, "Do not disturb." I resented his absences, his distance, but now I had become like him, detached from the family, resented by Bob.

My reactions became more defensive, short tempered: "But I wasn't out of the house that long," or "I *did* go to the store last week," or even "Don't nag me; I'm trying." My academic world began to crack.

"I'll apply for a two-year USAID contract," Bob announced in March. He chased opportunities with energy and eagerness not seen in years. His Peace Corps Volunteer experience, knowledge of French, and architecture license opened an opportunity with the housing authority in West Africa—Lomé, the capital of Togo, a small West African country sandwiched between Ghana and Benin.

"I'll ask for two years' leave of absence from the university," I finally agreed, not happily. My horizon of academic achievement moved further away, harder to see. Where was my excitement for travel from a decade ago? Or for the family? I had put self before family and couldn't admit it yet.

The kids shared their reluctance to go.

"It will be an adventure you will never forget," I said with false enthusiasm, "and you will learn French." At ages six and ten, they weren't convinced.

Our friends didn't understand why we were going to West Africa for two years. "You just finished your PhD; you are ready to teach and write," said a university colleague. "I would never agree to do this."

A neighbor asked, "Why are you leaving a neighborhood you've given so much to, one that's featured for its architecture and playgrounds in the *Baltimore Sun*." Another said, "I could never go to Africa. It won't be good for any of you, and to take your kids out of this great school… you're crazy." Bob's and my parents knew it didn't matter what they felt about this decision, so they said, "Please write."

Bob left for Togo in April. We were to follow in early July. With him away, the starkness of how he logistically and emotionally supported the family came at me hard. I now did it all: work, commute, kids, meals, while packing to leave and renting out the house. Ten years of household stuff brought smiles to the Goodwill Industries staff; doctors were kept busy with shots and exams; my two-year leave of absence from the university and a Togo gerontology research idea approved.

In late spring, my resentful tone in letters to Bob contrasted with his enthusiastic words about the work and the household in Togo. He wrote about the ocean view, a nearby waterfall, and French bread. He raved about our large house with a full-time cook and housekeeper close to a general store with needed basics.

"You'll love the colorful fabric people wear and the second-floor porch's view of the Atlantic Ocean. We're one block from the beach and only eight blocks from the kids' school."

My responses included, "The kids are sick," "The neighbors are getting a divorce," "The car broke down," and "Possible renters are scarce." My unhappiness came in descriptions of struggles. Never discouraged, Bob continued to write about delights without acknowledging the tone of my letters.

By May, exhaustion won, too tired to be angry, to resist. The kids needed me, and I hadn't been there for them. Research was timeless. Two years' leave could calm the pace of academic ambition and renew family routine.

In early June, Bob sent me a short telex: "Peace Corps country directorship open in Togo. You should apply." My only thoughts of the Peace Corps were when laughing with David and Kirsten as we looked at slides of a long-haired, neatly dressed young couple romping around Tunisian sand dunes and swimming in the Mediterranean Sea.

The memory of those words on the brown telex paper that June day remains today as strong as those of the Peace Corps recruiter's stories over sorority cake and gooey frosting over a decade earlier. My life changed again.

With my rewritten résumé in hand, I drove it and a cover letter to the Peace Corps headquarters in downtown DC the next day, no waiting for a mail delivery.

"Can you come to the Peace Corps office tomorrow?" Nancy's voice on the phone had asked me the previous day. "We are interviewing now for the Togo country director position." Nancy's husband, Dick, had set up the original Tunisian architecture program and vaguely knew me. Three interviews, a ten-day wait, and then a call with the job offer from Peace Corps Director Dick Celeste. "Welcome to the Peace Corps family."

"I am honored. The Peace Corps changed my life. I want to give back," my response to Director Celeste while sinking farther into my chair at work. A single thought screamed out, "What am I doing?" Both Togo and the position were a mystery and a sharp turn from my envisioned career. And my cherished new degree? The words of the job offer seeped in slowly, incomprehensibly. Images failed me. Togo was a forgotten dot on the African map, no headlines to draw people's attention. My leave of absence, my plan of being an expat wife to an architect in Lomé, my volunteering at the embassy and doing easy research didn't match running a three-million-dollar program with 130 Volunteers. Fear came back: failure.

*

The kids headed to Togo six weeks ahead of me, offering me time to finish work, pack out the house, and complete Peace Corps staff training.

Bob had the Togo house ready. Francine offered to entertain David and Kirsten at their stopover in Paris. "I'll buy them ice cream and keep them smiling." She was to meet them at the Charles de Gaulle Airport at 7:00 a.m. on Bastille Day, show them the Eiffel Tower, share Bastille festivities from her balcony, and return them to the airport by 10:00 p.m. Pan Am would fly them to Lomé with a short stop in Lagos, Nigeria. Flight attendants could give support. That was the plan, at least.

Ten days following the job offer, the gleaming white curve of Dulles Airport's roof floating above the trees came into view as we drove to the parking lot. David, ten, and Kirsten, six, wore fixed smiles as they got out of the car.

Walking toward the terminal, "We'll be okay," David assured me, putting his arm around Kirsten's shoulders.

"You will see Paris, your grandmother, and then Daddy," I said too many times, wanting to believe the ease of travel. David acted like a responsible big brother, a characteristic that came easily to him. Taking Kirsten's hand, he said, "I'm here. We'll stay together; hold my hand." He acted like an adult, not a ten-year-old… more adult than me.

As we prepared, we made up stories about Togo, pretending we wanted to be there.

"We will have palm trees, coconuts, and papayas in our yard; long ocean beaches for play; a hired cook and gardener; and new friends," I said, drawing from Bob's letters. "We'll learn French quickly, and some friends will speak English with an accent." Our made-up, happy images covered our anxieties: no TV, loneliness from lost friends, pale skin touched strangely by Togolese children.

"When we return, you'll have your friends again and wonderful new stories to share. It's an adventure, like *Treasure Island*." So many pretend words covering up dread.

David and Kirsten stood at the base of the stairs into the plane's cabin, the giant blue Pan Am letters across the body of the plane.

"Take good care of them. They are precious," I said to the attendant standing with them.

She smiled, "I know; I also have little ones." I gave a hug and a kiss to each as they turned to the flight attendant. Kirsten scowled; David smiled. We waved one last time as they reached the top of the stairs.

"This is the right decision," I assured myself as I turned away, knowing it wasn't true. Today, I still see my two children waving goodbye as they enter the plane without me, my arms aching for them, my heart pounding.

A call from Francine late that day confirmed a successful flight and celebration of Bastille Day, including the park picnic with thousands of flags and early evening fireworks.

Francine had told them, "The festivities have been planned for both of you to celebrate your new life in Togo." A scratchy, faraway voice came on the line the following day. "Hi, the kids are here in the house with me … so, so good to see them. We are fine. We're better than fine." Then the line cut off.

Years later, Kirsten and David told me of the memory of the flight from Paris to Lagos and onward to Lomé.

"I clung to David. I didn't want to go to sleep. What if we miss our Lomé stop, and I won't see Daddy?"

"Kirsten wanted to get off the plane in Lagos, thinking it was Lomé. She insisted, 'I will miss where I am supposed to get off.' But I knew how to keep her calm."

*

Mid-August, 10:00 p.m., my plane touched down at the Gnassingbé Eyadéma International Airport, named after the president for life. Crowds shouted from the second-floor balcony as passengers walked toward the small, floodlit, corrugated metal terminal building.

"Welcome to Togo." Faces and bodies hung over the thin railing with arms waving. The sticky heat and thick humidity hit me in the face. Then beginning to sweat, "It's nighttime. What is this?" I whispered under my breath, even a few feet from the airplane stairs. "Can I survive this over-watered hothouse?"

Bob and the kids threw their arms around me on the tarmac and walked with me to the terminal. "Mommy, did you sleep on the plane? Where did you sit? Did you eat?" She continued, "Our house has a parrot and geckos that slip on the tile floor when I chase them out of the house into the garden. The parrot doesn't talk but just screeches. We leave him on the porch."

"I missed you all," I shouted. Bob gave me a kiss. "Glad you're here. This will work for us."

The Peace Corps driver, waiting patiently outside the terminal, packed the van for our thirty-minute drive home.

"Madame, we are happy you are here as our new director. I know your family missed you." His gentle courtesy touched me. He said as we pulled out of the airport, "We'll be mostly on narrow paved and unpaved roads into the city. I hope you don't mind."

"Fine. I appreciate all you can tell me about Lomé," I responded.

"I don't think men sleep here," Bob said. "They stay up late. You'll see on our drive to the house." The driver laughed.

The airport road was lined, first intermittently, then more densely as the city approached, with corrugated tin-roofed shops, each about the size of a highway toll booth with one side open to the street.

"We can buy almost anything we want from one of these shops," Bob said, "and some items we don't want. Watch." From his tone, he wanted me to like this first drive, my first thirty minutes in Togo. He appeared hopeful we could make this two-year adventure work.

Each tin shop became an illuminated stage with props and actors against the black night sky. Flickering fluorescent tubes lit the entrance, creating dancing shadows. The driver, interested in my comments and questions, became more animated in describing what we saw. As shops became more frequent, he said, "Each sells something different, look." He pointed to knotted plastic bags of flour, sugar, and ground corn; colored cellophane-wrapped candy next to used liquor bottles filled with peanuts; cases of bright-orange Fanta next to shelves of warm cans of Togolese beer; blue and pink plastic flip-flops and matching plastic market baskets; fried plantains, hot tea, and cigarettes; and used bicycle tires.

Kirsten's voice interrupted from the back seat: "Let's stop for the bro-chettes where the smoke is swirling. I can smell the charcoal."

"You know what they are? Tomorrow."

The driver, laughing at our discoveries, continued: "I like the night-time. Me and my friends sit outside against the tin stores smoking, drinking beer, and talking late into the night." I watched the men eating brochettes over the charcoal, moving their hands and bodies, nodding as they punctuated a story, standing up, or lighting a cigarette. Their silhouettes moved gracefully against the lanterns and lights.

The driver continued, "Work keeps me busy, driving Volunteers, staff, up country, down country, around the city. I enjoy it. But these moments at night are my own."

Two evenings before, I had driven another airport highway, the Dulles Access Road in Virginia—six lanes, well lit by tall highway lamps, and well marked with white lines and posted speed limits. Beyond the dense woods lining the road were distant apartment lights from the Reston high-rises. I had safety, comfort, predictability, and on-time airport arrivals. That was no longer my reality. But the Virginia highway offered no street theater like these glimpses of buying and selling, laughter, and cigarettes, better than speed limit signs.

Before bed, even though late, the kids showed me every room in the house and the yard with coconut trees. Kirsten uncovered the parrot on the porch. "Here is Coco," she said. The parrot squawked.

*

My predecessor, much beloved by staff, had left a month earlier. Peace Corps staff waited anxiously for the new director, their boss, for the next two years. Would she be as good as Karl? I had not seen a Peace Corps country nor a Peace Corps Volunteer in eleven years, and Togo, with its dust, humidity, and tin shops, had no resemblance to Tunisia. Tunisian memories had to go. My previous work, the professional lunches and dinners, my women friends, and my comfortable Charles Village neighbors offered little to prepare me for my experiences in this isolated, hot West African country on the Atlantic Ocean. The next day, I officially began as country director.

*

My newly bought dresses for Togo accentuated my thin 115-pound slenderness. My three-inch stiletto sandals raised my height to six feet. Midmorning of my first day, the new Peace Corps trainees at the training site eagerly lined up to meet this new director, who wore a formfitting, bright-red stretch sheath dress slightly above the knees and stilettos. The shoes slapped loudly against my heels with each step. My mind had focused on what to say, not what to wear, a mistake.

I stepped forward to greet the thirty-five trainees. They stared at me as they sat tall and silent in wobbly wood chairs. The training director turned to me and said, "Welcome, Dr. Olsen. We are pleased you can be here, your first day in-country."

The trainees wore jeans, T-shirts, flip-flops, sandals, and traditional wax print cloth shirts, skirts, or dresses made by Togolese seamstresses. They kept looking at me as I groped for words to make them comfortable. Instead, I froze. Suddenly, my clothes were all wrong, looking like a cheap New York City dancer in a pine wood room in Togo with thirty-five pairs of eyes focused on me.

No words. Silence. Then I pushed my red dress and shoes out of my mind, raised my head, stood tall, and began: "I am honored to meet you all as you begin a two-year journey that will change you and this country. You will learn more from your experience than you will give."

I never asked about my impression—better not to know. The dress and shoes never again left the closet until their final trip to the local used clothing market. The next day, for my first full day at the office, a skirt, blouse, and low-heeled sandals replaced the previous day's horror outfit.

A white French colonial house with its wood paneling and second-floor wrought-iron balconies had become the Peace Corps office compound. The second-floor director's office doubled as the conference room, keeping the room busy most of the day. Red straw mats covered the tile floor, and a mammoth air conditioner noisily spewed out cold air from behind the desk. I sat six inches from the machine and thanked it every day for two years.

My first day began with a staff social hour around the conference table, coffee and tea in tiny clear glasses with two lumps of sugar, cookies, and homemade cake that smelled of fresh coconut. Most of the twenty-five-member Togolese staff, including drivers and cleaners, had devoted many years to the Peace Corps. Like me, the other three American staff had two-plus-year tours. Staff language skills varied, some fully trilingual, including a local language, French, and English. Others had difficulty moving from the local language, usually Ewe, to French, with even fewer words in English. My predecessor conducted office business in French, hopeless for me. "We will use English." Faces sagged. I said, "I'm sorry; I will try to improve my French, but it's too difficult for me now." Not a good beginning.

Staff then spoke, giving reflections and descriptions of their work for the Peace Corps, focusing on Volunteers, and speaking proudly of "their" Volunteers as stories came to life: "A new three-room school is being inaugurated next week, three hours from Lomé, and the entire village will be there. You must come. The mayor and Volunteers are proud of how hard the village worked." And "I drive everywhere to take Volunteers to their sites, even during the rainy season. One Volunteer, covered with mud, helped dig out the back wheel of the truck. The villagers had all waited, lanterns out, so we could see our way in."

The stories continued, peppered with funny Volunteer sayings or mistakes. Through their stories, they showed me why they worked for the Peace Corps; straddled two cultures and three languages; traveled extensively, including weeknights and weekends, to visit and support Volunteers; and weathered occasional misunderstandings between Volunteers and their communities. Their stories showed deep caring.

The staff watched the changes in the young Peace Corps Volunteers during their two-year tours of service. They were proud that they—from drivers to program officers—had influenced Volunteers. The staff talked about why the connection with each mattered. Volunteers were part of their family.

"Each summer, I struggle to teach French to a new group of school construction Volunteers who come without the language," a language teacher said. "Three months later, they leave my lessons for their villages with enough words to help the community build a three-room school, a first in the village. Our communities are better."

"I like your stories," I said. "You care about the Volunteers and about each other." I stopped for a moment. "Years ago, staff like you helped me as a Volunteer in Tunisia. I'm here now because they cared the way you care today."

As I took another sip of hot coffee and admired the vibrant print colors and patterns of shirts and dresses staff members wore, my words rushed out, unrehearsed. I straightened, remembering my own time in Tunisia, bright-orange veils and tea with two too many lumps of sugar.

As I spoke, my voice grew stronger. The room quieted. Thoughts, not before expressed, formed words in my head: "Peace Corps Volunteers are here in Togo for two years. They will love most of it, learn from it, and dislike some days. Most importantly, they will never, ever forget the experience. The images of their own villages, families, cassava fields become seared inside each person, shaping their lives for years to come. I know from my own experience that my Tunisian family and our daily meals, my students laughing at my spelling, the women sharing their secrets guide me now."

I paused. Where were these ideas coming from? Hands became still, dark eyes looked at me, silence except for a whispered translation by a staff member into Ewe. The cakes and candies stayed untouched on the conference table. I continued: "All of us, together, have a responsibility to give insight to each Volunteer during their time here. That richness in their language learning, classroom protocols, and community living gives them a Togolese life. Their shared ideas for new vegetables in small gardens, protecting stored maize from weevils in the dry season, or creating reading games for children who stay in the villages after the Volunteers leave. The ideas continue and become part of community life. Students take classroom stories from 'my American teacher,' as they call Volunteers, to further their education and careers. Mothers take new rehydration knowledge to save their babies' lives. Volunteers change small daily practices around them and are themselves being changed by the farmers, the mothers, and the children. They return to the United States with alternative choices and ideas for their own futures, different futures from those they had envisioned earlier. I am one of those Volunteers whose future changed. I wouldn't be here otherwise."

The air conditioner behind me struggled against the humidity, its air cooling my skin. I continued, surprised at myself. My Peace Corps self, long hidden, came back to life: "All of us make a difference to Volunteers. I listened carefully as you told your stories a few minutes ago. I heard you describe the pride in your work. You are affecting the Americans serving as Volunteers and the communities here in Togo, person by person. Togo is a stronger nation because of your work here. I am lucky to be here with you and to share your efforts these next two years." I paused and sipped my too-sweet coffee.

"Okay, enough talk. Now let's eat."

I walked around the table and shook each person's hand. The Togolese handshake includes an elbow touch and finger snap at the end. People laughed, watching me try, then took my hand, put my fingers in the snap position, and pulled. Hopeless. I never could do it. The efforts made them laugh harder.

By later that day, my hesitancy had gone. I stepped forward easily, arms outstretched, discovery at my fingertips.

"What does your name mean in Ewe, Kojo?" "Marc, how do you cook these plantains I see on the table?" Questions about the work of Peace Corps Togo could wait another day. This day built a team, a new team, a team that included me. Something happened to me, difficult to describe, but felt through the eyes of the staff who cared so deeply about their work, about the Volunteers. By the end of my first day in the office, I knew my planned academic career would not happen. This day gave me the joy and purpose academics didn't have for me. I never went back to the university.

Later in my first year in the office, I switched to accented French with poor grammar and missing nouns. "You can correct me. That's how I'll learn," I said. They did, clearly pleased with the effort.

*

Office work in the United States had a comfortable rhythm, frequent ringing phones, voices of good friends, regular mail delivery, quick and timely meetings, fall following summer. Comfort in the office depended on this regularity. Lomé offered a different rhythm, one without these cues.

My first month, Togo August heat replaced DC August heat. The noisy air conditioner mitigated the bursts of blazing sun. Summer will pass; cool air will come.

In early September, my assistant, Comfort, came into my office: "Here is the Volunteer in-service training schedule for October through January."

I said, "We have plenty of time to prepare."

A couple of weeks later, Etienne gently nudged me with the words, "You need to start approving the budget."

I said, "We have plenty of time."

The next week, he was polite but firm: "We can't begin hiring without your budget approval." The outside still offered heat, blue sky, green leaves, cotton shirts, blooming red flowers. My brain said, "August." Every day, my brain continued saying August. Trainees would not arrive until the trees had no leaves, the days were short, and we wore sweaters, a few months away. The trainees did come as scheduled, but not in the months of November, December, or March. August lingered for two years, sometimes with rain, often without, but always August.

\*

Volunteers liked to show off their projects and introduce families, village chiefs, mayors, and headmasters.

"This makes the Volunteers' work easier," Etienne told me. "They like to see the big boss come to their town. It shows caring and importance." Driving on bumpy, potholed roads with animals and villagers seeping toward the center consumed a fourth of my time as director.

School ceremonies and clinic room openings frequently anchored my visits, this time to see Kevin and his rabbit and primary school garden projects. On arrival, a banner draped across the school with one corner untethered announced, "Welcome to Aneho, Director Olsen." Children in school uniforms danced, sang, and offered fresh coconut milk to our arrival party.

"This coconut is fresh, just picked from the tree," the headmaster said as he greeted me and sliced off the top with his machete, cutting it cleanly while still holding the coconut. Fresh coconut milk substituted for undrinkable water. Women clapped and shouted, wearing multicolored print fabric with images of flowers, Togolese slogans, and President Eyadéma embedded in the print designs. The community celebrated "their" Volunteer. The headmaster, in a freshly pressed cotton agbada, greeted a limp, sticky Peace Corps country director, the result of a multihour car ride without air-conditioning.

Kevin guided me through the ceremonies and meetings. He called everyone by name, teased the kids, guided me around goats and dogs, and took me through the trees to the compound where he lived.

"My host mom worries I don't eat enough. She stuffs me," he said, introducing me.

"Mr. Kevin raises rabbits and eats *fufu* with us," the children shouted. "The sauce drips down his arm and looks funny." *Fufu*, a pounded and fermented cooked cassava eaten with fingers, looks like sticky mashed potatoes and tastes like fabric starch. Covered with fish or vegetable sauce, it was the daily Togolese family food staple. I ate it frequently. I never liked it.

"Our wonderful Volunteer gets the kids to speak up, to sing, to read out loud," the headmaster added. "He walks with the students around the village, showing new ways to protect and purify water." Kevin blushed and dropped his head, mumbling, "I don't really do that much."

Kevin lived in a single separate room within the family's compound, constructed out of mud bricks with a yellow straw roof.

He pointed inside. "See my mattress? Not too bad for one-inch foam." We walked out back with kids in tow as they talked to him in Ewe: "I have my own latrine and a bucket hooked up for showering. My family gave me the bucket idea."

"And the water?" I asked.

"Kids take turns bringing it from the well in the next village. They don't want me to have a day without water."

As we walked back to the car after formal goodbyes, Kevin turned to me and said, "I bet you already know how we live. You did it as a Volunteer."

I smiled and said, "Yes, I do," stretching the truth. My own Volunteer life of indoor plumbing, hot and cold running water, electricity, and the Mediterranean Sea remained a secret. "You are doing well," I said. "Your village loves you. Do you need anything from me?"

"No, I'm fine. But come back. The community likes to celebrate." We shook hands. My car drove away. Yes. Most Volunteers did fine.

*

Volunteers told me how they felt. No one asked me, "How are you doing?" How was I doing? Being stared at as a white woman became distracting. Being the only woman in meetings with Togo officials became tiring. I was on display, a white stranger to be gawked at, not able to disappear. No one to share concerns with except Bob, who listened but often didn't understand, his work being contained in an office with two other Americans and Togolese city planners. Where were my friends to pour concerns out to? Letters took too long, and they couldn't describe the emotions of being in an alien society. Outside of work and family meals, my loneliness remained constant, even in crowds.

*

After a few weeks in Lomé, a routine emerged: walking the six blocks between home and work twice a day, eating a lunchtime meal with the family and then a thirty-minute nap, and sharing time with Bob and the kids each evening after dinner. We had no television or phone. We filled our evenings talking, playing games, listening to the *Lord of the Rings* audiobooks and classical music on tapes, helping with homework, and writing letters.

My work became familiar and Volunteer emergencies infrequent. The cook and housekeeper took care of meals and house maintenance. Kirsten and I walked to work and school along the dirt path together most days, stopping to buy fresh, hot fried plantains at the street corner near the house. And yet I felt detached from Togo as a people, a culture, a different feeling from my passion for the program and Volunteers.

A female country director has many professional and social restrictions. My stateside routine of professional lunches, drinks after work, relaxing moments with neighbors was gone. My spontaneous phone calls and kitchen table conversations with other women were gone. In Lomé, except for Ambassador Johnson, the heads of international organizations were men. Togolese professionals in the ministries with which we worked were men. Informal leaders were men. These men went home for lunch and dinner. Phrases that had shaped my professional life, phrases like "Let's grab lunch and talk more about the proposal" or "Do you want to get together for a few minutes after work?" were against tradition and would sour my reputation. Outside my formal office meetings, no setting gave me a place to talk to Togolese colleagues. Building collegial trust requires time, stories, laughter. Without it, meetings remained formal and professionally unsatisfying.

Even being part of the American embassy community of a couple dozen Americans posed difficulties. The political officer was also a CIA officer, and the Peace Corps, by statute, could have no contact with him. We kept a distance even though our kids were the same age.

"Drop them off on the porch. I will let them in," the CIA officer's wife said as we both laughed and David and Kirsten raced inside. She then handed me a week-old *New York Times*. "This is safe for you to read, I'm sure," she said, smiling again.

The Peace Corps is an independent federal agency, not part of the Department of State, which limited my contact with the deputy chief of mission (DCM) and the ambassador to ensure Peace Corps business stayed out of official Department of State field cables.

"Anything going on in Sokodé? I'm doing a report to DC," the DCM teased.

He knew my answer, never changing: "Nothing I know." Playing monthly bridge with embassy staff, I remained careful not to mention the Peace Corps to not confuse their conversations and mine in any later government of Togo negotiations.

Pleasure with work, seeing Volunteers, and time with family came easily. But I was lonely for those informal friend conversations that kept me balanced and centered.

*

My ache for U.S. friends couldn't be solved, but my learning more about Togo could. Volunteers became my teachers.

Sarah, a Volunteer in Sokodé, eyes wide, red hair pulled back, exclaimed, "The students just sold five rabbits we raised in school to the butcher in the next village. A first." She added, "And they ask me when we can get more." While I visited her, she held up rabbits mating, a first for me. It took less than a second.

Jose, whose belt buckle gave away a fifteen-pound weight loss from a year earlier, said, "Our *fetisher* [similar to a witch doctor] came to the house and unjinxed our compound last week. My host mom had worried about spirits." He showed me the white powder and chicken feet at the compound door. He laughed. "I am beginning to believe in the *fetisher* myself." He then added, "My mom is doubling my *fufu* at dinner. I'll stay healthy." Volunteers shared their stories. I beamed like a delighted parent, but as their director, I couldn't be their friend.

In the office, Comfort showed me how to fold the traditional head wrap most women in Togo wore. When she finished, a one-by-two-meter brightly designed floral print towered eight inches above Comfort's elegant tall frame.

"You can't keep a head wrap on your head," she said bluntly but with a smile. "Your hair is too thin and straight to hold it." Our occasional office celebrations could include tastes of fermented cornmeal wrapped in palm leaves and brochettes from the corner charcoal fire pit.

"I'm working on liking the corn. I'll keep trying," I offered. The managers brought in more. They believed me. We became excellent colleagues but kept appropriate personal distances.

How do I know villagers—mothers, fathers, fears, beliefs—without the filter of others? To be a Volunteer again, even for a few hours. As November came, I asked Jamar, a language expert for the Volunteers, "Do you know a student who might accompany me to villages to interpret conversations between myself and village grandparents in Ewe? I want to talk with the grandparents about their perspectives on being elders. I did my dissertation on that subject with grandparents in Baltimore, Maryland."

An hour later, he had given me the name of a cousin, a suggestion for villages, and a promise from me to "share what I learn" with him.

"Most importantly, when you arrive at the village, find the village chief and ask permission to enter the village. He is the gatekeeper between outsiders and his charges, the villagers." Jamar continued, "This is an embedded village tradition for hundreds of years. The chief arbitrates disagreements, manages food distribution during the dry season, and ensures safety for the villagers."

The following Sunday, with me at the wheel of my VW Bug and Joseph beside me, we headed west to villages near the Ghanaian border. Joseph and I spoke French to each other, and for anyone without French, he would interpret from Ewe. Many villagers never learned French.

An hour and two bumpy roads later, Joseph pointed out the first village. "I will find the village chief and introduce him to you," he said, sliding confidently out of the passenger seat. "I'll do formalities of showing respect, and you follow me."

"Introduce me as a person living in Togo who wants to hear grandparents tell their stories. No title, no mention of the Peace Corps."

Strangers rarely came to these isolated dirt-road villages. "Madame, Madame," came shouts from children running toward me, hands reaching out, faces smiling, barking dogs trailing behind, as I climbed out of the car. To Joseph, as he returned with the chief, I said, "I have already made quite a noisy entrance. Will the chief let me stay?"

"Welcome, we rarely get visitors," began the chief. Following Joseph's lead, I bowed low, held out my hand, touched my elbow, and tried snapping my fingers as part of the greeting. I failed. The chief laughed.

Five minutes later, the chief's wife, with a grin and bow, personally brought me a chair for sitting on the porch of their mud-brick compound hut.

The chief called out into the open air of the village, "Madame wants to listen to elders tell stories. Please come and sit." Then as older villagers arrived, "As an elder, I want to go first." He never left my side. Women came out of their mud compounds, bringing coarsely woven mats, and covered the ground near the chief. They laid out their individual well-washed faded cloth (*pagnes*) to mark their spots for sitting. Women of all ages lowered themselves effortlessly to squat positions on the ground. A few men walked toward the women, holding back, standing.

"You're okay to join," I said through Joseph.

"I want to hear stories about your lives. When I lived in Baltimore, United States, I asked elders there to share their life stories. I bet some of yours are more interesting." I went slowly so Joseph could translate, wanting him to share my warmth in the request.

"No one has asked me that before," the chief said, moving his body forward to strengthen the sound of his voice.

Sitting on the wooden chair, notebook in hand, my story-guiding questions followed those used in Baltimore. How did stories from grandparents in a rural village on the Ghanaian border compare with those in suburban Baltimore?

"Tell me about growing up, your families, your schooling," I asked. Among the richness of examples came a particular common refrain.

A small man in the back, resting on his cane, spoke up: "I was just beginning school when the Germans were kicked out of Togo. The French came in. At the end of World War I."

Another said, "We had to change our school language from German to French. I didn't like it."

A woman in front, leaning on her neighbor, became animated. "And our new French teachers didn't really like us. They yelled. The German teachers were better."

"I quit school," said another woman. "It was easy to quit. The teachers didn't care." The older participants described a change to fewer classrooms; fewer, if any, books; poor attendance. In their telling, it could have been a month earlier, not sixty years. Anger remained palpable.

"The Germans planted trees in rows on the roads. This protected our village. The French stopped," said a woman rising from her *pagne*, shaking her finger. She pointed toward two roads into the village, one with tall arching beech and oak trees, one without. "See the difference?" she said.

Their stories represented the power of colonialism, wars, and the power-lessness of countries and villages caught in the middle.

Children joined the group as we shared stories, formed an outside ring of heads bobbing, voices talking and laughing. Some clapped at an answer they liked, many of the stories new to them.

I then asked three questions: "How do you want to be remembered? What are you most proud of? What makes you happy now?"

Words tumbled from two men in the back, now squatting on mats.

"Raising my chickens, the village waits for the eggs… and then the chickens."

"Sitting up all night talking when the moon is full and illuminates our houses."

A woman, leaning against her daughter's firm body, "My children, their children. They are strong."

Another added, "I give a lot to help the family. I cook, I pound, I fetch water, even though I walk slowly. I will be an ancestor this village will thank. I'm happy."

"Thank you, elders," an elder standing near the chief said, pointing toward three others in the crowd. They stood taller, even with stooped shoulders. "We're old, we're tired. We talk together, we smoke, we play Mancala. We look forward to these times."

These responses were similar to those in Baltimore. Words were different, stories were different, but their providing, having family and friends, and being remembered overlay the differences.

My village visits over the next few weeks provided similar responses. Village routines became visible. Villagers of all ages leaned into groups together, fetching water, tilling cassava fields, preparing food, and sitting outside on mats in favorite spots in animated conversation as night fell. At day's end, children kicked balls and chased each other around as men sat smoking, drinking *tchouk* (homemade beer drunk out of a calabash gourd), laughing with each other while women wove baskets and plaited hair.

Talking with older Togolese in their villages, on their mats, next to their own village chief, I found individual human complexity and depths of emotion paralleling those with whom I spoke in Baltimore. Before visiting these Togo communities, my eyes didn't see beyond the colorful yards of cloth, the mud-brick houses, the *fufu* meals: blind to their complex lives. My joy of being in Togo, and then dozens of countries I visited later, drew from their stories of lives having been lived fully, not unlike in my own hometown. But to learn this, I had to see, listen, be present, and never judge. They had trusted life stories to me. I wanted to honor that gift.

*

Six months into my tour, Bill, the new Peace Corps regional training officer, moved into the house across the street. With his arrival, Bob and I walked through the rooms of his newly rented house, stepping over boxes and rolled-up rugs.

"Where should I put this sketch of the Himalayas from my counterpart and friend in Nepal?" Bill asked. Bill had art. Bill had hand-woven Asian fabrics. Bill had hooked rugs. Bill had an individually carved panpipe flute from Peru.

I leaned in, nodded, reached for the flute, and asked, "How did you get this?"

"One of my month retreats in the Sacred Valley." Bill's thirty-eight years had been lived differently than my thirty-five years. With his slight build and flexibility, he easily jumped over boxes and moved quickly through the room spaces, trying out his collected objects on walls, floors, and tables. He, like Bob, had an eye for space, color, flair.

"Maybe this rug fits here." He talked quickly, as if we would leave before he found homes for his art.

"This Nepali head wrap scarf goes well with the *kleem* rug. Put them together in a small space," Bob offered, reaching down and picking up the scarf to match the *kleem*. During our fifteen years of marriage, Bob decorated while I watched and admired his success. His architecture degree built on an already strong instinct for use of colors, objects, and interior space.

"Here, here, and here," the two talked while reaching down to pull out objects from boxes, holding up fabric, moving frames together and apart. They could have already worked together for years. Their common sense of balance and color gave them energy to talk fast, mark up walls, unwrap specialty dishes, and hang prints. I watched hands move, arms reach, heads nod, eyes focus.

"Voilà," said Bill as his intimate living room now burst with oranges and reds. "We are done for the day."

"I am happy to continue to help," Bob offered, clapping and nodding with satisfaction. My eyes darted between the two, working closely together throughout their frenzied movements. I knew how to shout, "Gorgeous." We all have gifts. Their gift was decorating; mine, leading groups.

*

Bill became my missing close friend, the one for gossip and stories. And being silly. We asked each other for advice, mixed with laughter and his dry and sometimes raunchy humor.

An infrequent but satisfying pattern emerged. After Bob and I read bedtime stories to David and Kirsten, I kissed Bob and said, "Going to Bill's for an hour or so." I crossed the street, greeted both my and Bill's night guards, and rapped on his door knocker.

"Welcome. I have poured the sherry. Here's your glass. A toast," he offered as he ushered me into the living room and pointed to my favorite chair. I sunk into the pillows, let out a sigh, and felt my body give up its tension. "I'm staying right here," I said, sherry in hand. "The church won't know if I drink a glass of sherry. They can't find me here," I added. Another step away from church teachings.

The one glass of sherry, interspersed with evening meanderings and personal and professional conversations, continued over subsequent months. "Coming from a small California town, my Volunteer experience in Nepal opened me to the world," he said. "I discover people and their languages. I crave new experiences." He spoke French, Spanish, Nepali, Thai, and some Hindi, gathering them in his travels.

"You see each new country as a discovery. You eagerly walk into the experience, whatever it might be," I commented to Bill. "I don't. I test, I hold back, I observe before taking steps forward."

"Being gay gives me a certain freedom you don't have. I know others think, 'Oh, he's gay. That's why he said that.' But I don't care." He shrugged easily.

My conservative Mormon background framed my thinking and behavior. I tiptoed carefully into stating observations and shielded myself from experiences that suggested risk to my traditions. Invisible armor wrapped me tight against lives like Bill's. His stories remained outrageous to me, more interesting than mine.

Bill's eye for detail included people. "I'm not sure the DCM told the facts straight. Watch his eyes drop next time. And listen carefully; his voice slows." He described nonverbal minutiae that added clarity to my interactions with embassy staff. My social work background didn't match his instinct for understanding the purpose of people's movements. My own eye for detail in people improved, and with it, my trust in working with teams.

Buried in our conversations one evening months later, after sharing meals and walks with our family, Bill commented, "I see something going on with Bob that he is not facing up to. I don't think he knows what it is." He paused, then said, "I even watched last week how he lay on the beach." I asked nothing further. Our conversation moved on.

Leaving, Bill tossed out, "Your husband is quite a looker, you know." I flippantly tossed back, "He's yours when you want him." I didn't know where those words came from. I didn't want to know.

*

The phone on my desk rang. Why was the phone ringing on Sunday afternoon? I had just edited my report for Washington and prepared to walk back home. The voice on the phone cried out, "Sheila's unconscious. She drank rat poison." I heard Ted, a Volunteer in the same village, gasping for breath between words.

"Take a breath, Ted. Now tell me what happened," my voice cracking and my pulse rising.

"She's in the local clinic here in Kpalimé. They are doing what they can." Ted kept shouting out his words. "Barb had waited for her in the town center and, when she didn't come, walked over to her house and found her unresponsive. Sheila's village neighbors got her here," Ted finished his words, panting.

"Dr. Kilgauti," I said on the phone to the Peace Corps doctor, "we have a Volunteer who overdosed. Come immediately." I tried to slow myself down. Fifteen minutes later, he and the driver arrived at the office. We changed the Peace Corps passenger Peugeot 505 into an ambulance in ten minutes—seats out, stretcher in, cuff, breathing machine, other equipment gathered if needed. Dr. Kilgauti gave orders, we obeyed. Then they were off, a one-hour drive to Kpalimé.

"Ted, this is the director. Dr. Kilgauti is on his way. How's Sheila?" I asked.

Ted had been standing at the clinic telephone, waiting, and responded eagerly: "She's stirring. The nurse says it is a good sign."

"How are you and Barb doing?" I asked, afraid to breathe.

"We're scared. But we are helping the nurse. She is the only staff person here," Ted continued.

"Stay, support each other, talk to Sheila. Help her come back to consciousness," I offered, not sure it was correct.

Dr. Kilgauti called an hour later from the clinic. "Sheila is conscious but woozy. I am bringing her back to the office now."

I thought, "Think of the next steps to do... checklist, first, second, third, fourth." The Peace Corps office's ground floor housed the medical center, including a lab, exam rooms, and equipment. Another room served as an overnight retreat for ill Volunteers. The Peace Corps nurse had already prepared it for Sheila.

In Togo, we couldn't depend on outside medical care. Our office compound could become the clinic, the hospital room, the mental health center, and recovery space for Volunteers and embassy staff. We had better medical equipment and more experienced medical professionals than elsewhere in Togo. The repurposed Peugeot was our ambulance and had been bought with that in mind. Serious Volunteer medical emergencies, those not treatable in the Peace Corps medical office, required evacuation to Germany or the United States. In extreme cases, often to save a life, an air ambulance provided the transport.

The Peugeot arrived back safely. Dr. Kilgauti and the driver held Sheila under her arms and walked her to the medical office door. "Physically, she is doing a little better. I now see color in her face, and she can stand, with help. Her vital signs are good," Dr. Kilgauti explained. My hands reached out and touched the doctor and then, briefly, Sheila. No reaction.

"However, mentally, she's not well," the doctor added, saying the words carefully. "She cries out angrily and doesn't make sense." My legs sank, and I looked at my dusty feet. What's the next step in the checklist? Stay calm.

*

"You and Sheila will be on the 10:00 p.m. flight tonight to Paris," said Angele, the administrative officer, smiling as she handed me the tickets. She added, "Then twelve hours in Paris followed by the flight to DC, a long trip." Sheila's physical health had returned within two days, but her mental state remained rocky. I wrote an emergency cable, "Medevacing Sheila, prepare to meet and alert the hospital." Peace Corps headquarters approved my accompanying Sheila to DC as Dr. Kilgauti had other Volunteer health emergencies.

Three days following her attempted suicide, Sheila and I found our seats on the Air Afrique flight to Paris. The doctor had just given me a bottle of Thorazine, an antipsychotic medicine, with the instructions, "She must take a pill every two hours. Don't miss a single dose." He continued, "You must be with her all the time, even in the bathroom. Remember, she's suicidal." Sheila overheard.

"Don't tell my parents," she screamed, body stiff, hands in tight fists as the plane gathered speed on the runway. Her shouting words overrode the takeoff announcements. "Don't tell my parents," again she screamed, widening her eyes.

"I haven't and won't until you give me permission," I replied, faking calm. Useless words. Sheila didn't listen. Just focus now on getting to Paris.

"I have to go to the bathroom," her voice whispered midway to Paris. As I got up to go with her, she shouted, "Don't come with me! Don't follow me!" She woke sleeping passengers as she marched stridently along the aisle. I followed, apologizing to others and keeping a distance to respect her. This became our airplane routine.

Her every two-hour dose of Thorazine provided more drama for us both and nearby passengers.

"I will not take the pill. I don't care about the doctor," she said too loudly. Her rebuke became strident as I handed her the pill and water. Finally, minutes later, she relaxed her face, opened her hands, put the pill in her mouth, and swallowed with water. Thirty minutes before each pill, I closed my eyes, relaxed my body, and visualized the words to Sheila when opening the bottle and shaking out the next pill. Anger, sullenness, tears, resignation repeated themselves in her words, eyes, and fists each time. I'm running out of calm. Just keep counting the time to Paris.

At times during the flight, Sheila became the Volunteer I knew—green eyes vibrant, face smiling, and hands calm. "Let me tell you about my vegetable project," she offered one time. I listened. She drove the conversations, both of us trying to be oblivious to why we were in this situation. Then time for the next pill, the next trauma.

We arrived in Paris and stood in the high-domed football-sized waiting lounge at the Charles de Gaulle Airport, looking at the building-sized blackboard announcing flights. "Flight to Washington, DC, canceled," came the voice as the board shuffled the white letters from On Time to Canceled. No, I am not seeing this. This can't be happening.

I gently whispered to Sheila, "Come with me. We will change our tickets. We will fly to New York and take a separate plane to Washington, DC."

Sheila screamed, her voice echoing throughout the cavernous space, "You promised me you wouldn't tell my parents. They live in New York," shattering the hum of hundreds of passenger voices. They turned to us and stared. My body drooped, hoping to become invisible. Stay calm, stay calm. As if timed to the cancelation announcement, fifty French baggage handlers came into view. On strike, they marched straight for the center of the massive space, shouting in French while banging pans. Sheila shrieked at the commotion. She then folded her arms and legs under her body as she sank to the floor. She shook. I fell over her, hugging the quivering body tightly. We stayed in that position, oblivious to the noise, shouting, and whatever else whirled around us. The pans kept banging.

"Breathe slowly, Sheila," I said softly. Slowly, ever slowly, her body became still, her breathing normal, her voice silent.

We rose slowly, checked for cramped knees, stood, and looked at each other.

"Shall we look for something to eat?" I asked.

"Sure," she responded with a slight upturn in her smile. Just keep her calm.

"Over there, I see something with the word *manger*." As we started walking, I added, "Then I can get different tickets for flights to DC." I didn't mention New York City again.

From that moment, the trip became calmer, our conversations easier, except for the moments every two hours when the Thorazine pills appeared.

Arriving at the Washington National Airport, the ambulance driver's hand-lettered sign reading Olsen stood out among the waiting families. What a welcoming sign. I felt safe.

"We're here, over here, here," I said excitedly, wanting to keep saying the words "Here, here." Sheila cried out when told to lie down on the stretcher in the ambulance, a Washington, DC, ambulance requirement.

Two ERMs finally pulled her onto the stretcher, ready for the short drive to the hospital. Sheila knew where the ambulance was headed: the hospital psychiatric ward. Her body shook; she called out, with fear in each word, "No, I don't need the hospital. Let me out, let me out."

We arrived at the admission desk for the inpatient psychiatric unit, the hospital's top floor, and the unit Peace Corps used for medically evacuated Volunteers with acute psychiatric outbursts, a rarity. Mental health inpatients have to sign themselves in. My last step. How do I get her to sign herself in?

After twenty minutes back and forth, she arose from the seat she had shrunk into. "I will sign the paper," she said as she walked slowly and hesitantly to the receptionist.

"Thank you," I said gratefully. No more checklist steps to count. I am done.

*

I had my ticket to fly back to Togo the next evening, staying only twenty-four hours in Washington, DC. My midnight doorbell ring at my parents' house stunned them out of their sleep.

"Is it really you?" they cried. They recovered, hugged, looked at me, and then gave more hugs. "You've lost weight" were among their first words. "Unfortunately, yes," I replied. Eighteen months of chronic Giardia-like symptoms had left me ten pounds lighter and with less energy. Food, bed, sleep, and my parents' love came next.

Finding clothes to wear to the Peace Corps office consumed my early morning. Togo summer clothes wouldn't do with an outside DC temperature of twenty-eight degrees. The family clothes grab bag from years past offered a few misfitting choices, rejects from my brothers and sister.

"What are you wearing?" my desk officer asked when he saw me in a long-sleeved, large-flowered shirt, both too big and too short in the sleeves. My too-loose borrowed brown nylon pants rose two inches above my ankles. "You look a sight."

"Great greeting," I replied. We dove into our work, trainee numbers, budgets. An hour into the discussion, his desk phone rang.

"Could you send Jody to the director's office as soon as possible?" the director's assistant asked my desk officer.

Surprised, he said to me, "I didn't tell anyone you were here. This is the new director's first day in the office." A new U.S. president, Ronald Reagan, had been sworn in the month before and had selected a new Republican Peace Corps director, Loret Miller Ruppe, replacing Dick Celeste, a Democrat.

I looked down at myself, better dressed as a model for a used clothing store than for meeting Loret Ruppe, the granddaughter to the founder of Miller Brewing Company and wife of a six-term congressman, Phil Ruppe, from Upper Peninsula Michigan. After raising five daughters and helping run the Reagan-Bush campaign in Michigan, she was selected to serve under Reagan.

Her new chief of staff, David, escorted me to a seat on the couch opposite Loret's desk in the large office suite. Loret stood and walked toward me as a person confident of being in charge, even if for only a few hours. Her height, just under six feet, surprised me, as I had often been the tallest woman in a group. She had short-cropped blond hair, and her layered flowered dress flowed gently with her walk. Elegant.

"I am pleased to meet you," she began as she pulled up a chair across from me. She had a clear, strong, and yet comfortably soothing voice. Settling back onto the couch, I relaxed my hands and casually crossed my legs.

"This is my first day. Never been in this building before, never known the Peace Corps. Yet I told George Bush when he asked what I wanted to be nominated for that this is what I always wanted… to direct the Peace Corps." Loret leaned forward, eager with her words. "My sister had done years of missionary work overseas, and my mom traveled after my dad and brother were killed in the plane crash."

She paused, leaned back. She continued, "Now tell me why you love the Peace Corps. I want to know why I should honor a program President Kennedy founded."

I believed Loret wouldn't be right for the job, with no paid work experience and little knowledge of the Peace Corps. However, my misgivings about the new director and nervousness about my mismatched Salvation Army–looking clothes faded as we talked. Her easy laugh encouraged my stories, and my questions encouraged her stories.

We didn't stop until an hour later, when David said, "Loret, you need to wrap this up." We both stood, and Loret, almost without thought, reached both arms forward and gave me a gentle hug.

"Thank you," she said simply. "Have a safe flight back to Togo. You are doing important work."

A visit to Sheila before going to the airport confirmed what we feared, an acute psychotic episode possibly related to emerging schizophrenia. She now belonged to the health care professionals; she could never return to the Peace Corps.

Flying back, my thoughts turned to my conversation with Loret. She was a person I could spend time with, had the passion to treat the Peace Corps well, and wanted to learn. My time with the Peace Corps would end in a few months; the university job awaited. Loret's long-term leadership would touch those who followed me and others finishing their Peace Corps tours.

*

The sticky heat and thick humidity hit me hard as I walked from the plane to the Lomé terminal, but the words "Mommy, Mommy" from David and Kirsten assured me this was the right place to be.

"I love you all," I cried out, seeing them silhouetted against the floodlight.

"This is my favorite corner, the man selling brochettes with the cane-brimmed hat," Kirsten called out as we drove home.

"My favorite is the *pagne* stand over here. Forty different fabrics, all colors, and the owner is wearing the brightest," I replied. The journey to our house, once strange, was now normal.

*

Three weeks later, Comfort ran into my office. "The Peace Corps director's office is trying to reach you. Stay close to your phone." She shook with excitement. A Peace Corps director had never called the Togo office before.

"Jody, this is David. Remember your visit here?" The memory of my dreadful clothes returned. He talked quickly, worried about the telephone cutting out. "Loret wants to nominate you for regional director for North Africa, Near East, Asia, and the Pacific. Are you interested?" I tensed with surprise. My voice became quiet. My mind tumbled with random images. Stay calm.

After a moment, I said as if agreeing to a cup of tea, "Yes, I would be honored. Please thank Loret for her faith in me."

"Oh," he continued with a laugh, "I told her you might not have enough stamina for the job. In her office, you looked like a waif. But she convinced me." He paused.

"You will need to get political support. This is a White House–approved position," he continued. "Your father was a Republican congressman, wasn't he?" I remained silent, stunned. They would never, never know my father was a Democrat. That was a stupid thought.

With the call, my academic career became history, the Peace Corps my future.

Three days in Washington later that month garnered the necessary political support. My father, back in the family house in Kensington, had already called three Utah political friends from his own days as a congressman—President Reagan's pollster and Republican senator Jake Garn's and Republican senator Orrin Hatch's chiefs of staff. Each had agreed to write a letter of support for my candidacy, though given the different party affiliations, they would most likely blandly honor our family's Utah history but say that I do not meet White House personnel's rigorous standards for Republican political support. The letters would be ready for me to pick up at their offices.

Early the next morning, my father watched me stand motionless at the front screen door, hesitating to leave for the journey downtown to pick up the support letters. He moved to my side, then looked into my eyes and said with his low, practiced speaking voice, "When I ran for Congress, thousands of people in Utah wanted me to win. They walked streets, rang doorbells, called neighbors, stuffed and stamped envelopes from early morning until after the late evening news." He stepped closer, his voice quieter, looking into my eyes. "All these people believed in me. I had to believe in myself as much as they believed in me. I had to exert myself to my last spark of energy." He paused, his voice then more firm.

"People believe in you. Loret is the Peace Corps director. She is the vice president's personal choice, and she chose you. You must do everything…" He paused. "Everything you can today to get that support. Don't let her down."

"I'm on it." My father understood my fear, sensed my apprehension. He might have seen a self of his years earlier, a self who fought against letting his own father down. Or of David Jr., his namesake and joy for whom he had great hopes until the accident. I had to succeed for both of them. I would get the job.

My visit with Reagan's pollster produced a smile and a letter of support. "We are all in politics together," he commented. "Even as Republicans and Democrats." This letter made a support letter from Senator Garn written by his chief of staff easier. "If Dick Wirthlin does it, so do I," he said. They had been colleagues in Utah politics. Both letters were thoughtfully supporting a Utah constituent but not strong enough for the president's personnel office. My Democratic registration on a roster somewhere in Baltimore City would guarantee a no.

As Senator Hatch's chief of staff wrote out a similar support letter for the senator to sign, my last letter, the senator walked in. "What are you doing?" he asked his chief of staff. After an explanation, the senator turned to me. "What a pleasure to meet you. How is Dave?" Then he said, "For all that your father and grandfather have done for the State of Utah, the least I can do is make sure you get this job." He took the half-written draft, added several flourishes, asked that it be typed, and said, "This should do it. If not, I will call White House personnel myself to be sure."

I hesitated while his words sunk in, then said, hiding my surprise, "Thank you for believing in me and my family. It means the world to us. I will do my best job for you and for the State of Utah." I continued, "Daddy sends his wishes. He believes in you." Senator Hatch's words showed the honor that colleagues from the same state could have for each other, even crossing the aisle for each other. Senator Hatch honored his strong words of support. The personnel office approved me as regional director. In turn, I honored his commitment to do my best and then asked him to represent me twenty years later for my Senate Peace Corps deputy director hearing.

Changing my voting registration from Democrat to Republican was the most important task before returning to Togo. It had to be changed before the White House found the *D* in my records. That night, the voting registration papers lay on the dining room table as my father and I sat across from each other.

"I am letting down thirty years of Utah family political leadership," I said quietly. "Are you okay with this?"

Daddy laughed. "I'm fine. I am not going back into politics. You are the champion now. You carry on our legacy." He gave me his love and his blessings.

*

In June 1981, I reluctantly said goodbye to my two years in Togo: staff who supported and taught me; Volunteers who made differences in villages and from whom I learned patience, optimism, and how to make a trash-bag shower; and the embassy that provided in-country support with the government of Togo and with turkeys for Volunteer Thanksgiving dinners. Bob stayed for a third year. He said goodbye to David, now twelve; Kirsten, now nine; and me as we walked out to the Air Afrique flight to Paris.

In Paris, Francine's apartment became the twenty-four-hour rest stop, including watching live on a black-and-white TV screen the marriage of Princess Diana and Prince Charles, with full commentary from Francine on British royal traditions.

# 10

# Hugging a Coconut Tree
## 1981–84

"I see you! I see you!" Mother shouted above the noise in the international arrival terminal, hands waving high, as Kirsten, David, and I arrived at Dulles Airport. She spotted our wrinkled clothes and tired faces coming through the airport swinging doors, the line separating world adventures from U.S. normalcy. David and Kirsten ran to Mother with two years' worth of hugs and kisses.

"Oh my heavens, who are these two people? Can't be my grandkids. You've grown up."

"Oh, Grandma, we're your same grandkids." Kirsten laughed. We corralled suitcases and waited for Mother to bring around the family's same old station wagon to the arrivals terminal.

"Glad I'm back. Not as hot here as in Togo." Kirsten grabbed her suitcase and lifted it from the cart to the car, grunting.

Mother took I-66 and the Beltway back to the family house, only thirty minutes without much traffic.

"I remember—"

"No, I remember better—"

"What is that angled new building?" Our conversations tumbled over each other as forgotten images along the interstate rushed back.

As we pulled into the driveway of my parents' split-level house, "I remember your house. Lots of books in the basement," Kirsten said, her nine-year-old energy taking over the conversation. "Read me the special fairy-tale book. I love the princess pictures."

The familiar furniture, paintings, plastic coverings on the living room couches had not changed, but regular beds had replaced bunk beds, and miniature glass figurines sat unbothered on low coffee tables. With my brothers and sisters now in college or working, this quiet house drew me in.

"I have everything ready for you to stay here, fresh sheets and towels, and a dinner ready," Mother said as she showed each of us our rooms. "How good it is to have you home."

At breakfast, as Mother laid out bowls for our bran flakes and milk, "Sorry Bob couldn't end his contract and come home with you. Kind of hard on you, Jody, to have to do all this moving back alone."

"He'll be here for a couple of weeks to help before going back for the year. We'll make it work." Then to Kirsten, "You're getting real American cold cereal." I added, "I'm going to miss our nanny and cook. They took care of all this household stuff. I'm rusty. How do I vacuum and food shop while going to work? Well, kids, you're on your own."

"Nothing new," David said.

*

The next day, David and Kirsten exchanged their tired Togo clothes for full new wardrobes, compliments of the JCPenney department store and a checkbook. On arrival at the airport, David could have passed for a Charles Dickens character, with pants legs and sleeve hems inches above their rightful ankles and wrists. Kirsten's skirts fell well above the knees, too short for a nine-year-old.

Coming home took an adjustment. But to what home? I would see that home for the first time the next day.

*

Bob had bought a house in Silver Spring, Maryland, the year before, 1980, while two weeks in DC on a medevac with an ear infection. But I had not yet seen it. He had called me in Lomé from Washington, his static, tinny voice from across the Atlantic Ocean almost unrecognizable. We had to talk fast before losing the call.

"I put a contract on a house in Silver Spring."

"But... we didn't talk about it before you left for Washington."

"I know, but it's near DC, where we both will work. Hear me out."

"Okay. I'm listening," I said. "Talk fast and loud. I'm barely hearing you." He described the new location. I thought for a moment, listening to the static. Then realization: "That little lane you are describing. I had a friend there. Her house looked over the park." I paused. "How could you have known it's one of my favorite locations?"

As we talked about the house, catching only half the words, the noisy air conditioner behind me added distraction, but the phone line didn't cut off.

"Okay, go ahead. I know you would have anyway... I'm fine, and you have better house taste than me." The line dropped.

No second thoughts about the house, bought the next week and ready for our return to DC.

The redbrick small tudor, built in 1935, stood with eight other houses on the circular lane with miles of Sligo Creek Park as its backyard. Over the next forty years, the house has played host to hundreds of Peace Corps staff, former Volunteers, visiting and American Fulbrighters, family birthday parties, and wedding receptions for both David and Kirsten. The floor-to-ceiling glass windows in the back sunroom offer views of changing foliage, snowfalls, and the owls' annual new offspring in the backyard tree. My Sligo Creek Park walking path shares space with runners, walkers, dogs, baby strollers, and bicycles.

David and Kirsten grew up in the house, commuted by Metro to St. Anselm Abbey School (David) and Sidwell Friends School (Kirsten), and then left for college at the University of Michigan (David) and Brigham Young University (Kirsten). David and his family visit regularly from Portland, Oregon, and Kirsten and her husband now live on the house's terrace level. This enchanted house began with Bob's real estate instinct forty years ago and our belief in each other's family decisions.

*

I walked through the Peace Corps's double front doors at 806 Connecticut Avenue on my first day as regional director, President John F. Kennedy's words, "Ask not what your country can do for you, but what you can do for your country," in foot-high black letters below the two-story ornate ceiling greeting all who entered the lobby, words that inspired me to service more than a decade earlier. This building was the hub of a U.S. federal agency that looked across oceans instead of states.

Despite the office building's prime real estate across from the White

House, it did not offer luxury. Eleven stories high, its white exterior had grayed from storms, Washington dust, and car exhaust; its hallways begged for paint to cover smudges and cracks; and its carpets showed bare spots near entrances and doorways. The building was thankfully demolished when the Peace Corps moved six years later.

The eighth-floor region's opaque glass entrance door and black framed sign welcomed visitors to NANEAP: North Africa, Near East, Asia, Pacific. A new job, new staff, but still Peace Corps. Working in cubicles lining a central open space, over twenty staff members supported eighteen hundred Volunteers in seventeen countries with me as leader. They stood, smiled, and reached out their hands as I entered.

"Welcome to the best region in the Peace Corps," they called out.

"I know. It's why I'm here and nowhere else." A Tunisia desk sign to my right caught my attention. Pausing, I said to the desk officer, "This country and its people shaped me over a decade ago, giving me a passion for my work and our service."

"I'll take you into your office," Gerry, my assistant, said, coming forward from her desk near the window overlooking the White House portico. "I have fresh roses from my garden on your desk. Welcome." She showed me the office, my space for the next three years for hiring, firing, decisions about country crises, staff celebrations, and support for grieving staff and Volunteer families.

*

The region scheduled a staff meeting for 10:00 a.m., barely time to sit at my desk, put fingers on the IBM Selectric typewriter, get familiar with the office.

Gerry said, "Wheel your desk chair to the central open space. It's where we meet." Others brought chairs from cubicles, chatting and laughing while making their weekly circle. They stopped to watch me, their new director, fidgeting with my chair's location. My tailored, traditionally patterned Togo dress, pulled straight from my suitcase, caught their attention. African.

Sitting down, I said apologetically, "I'm wearing a dress from Togo, not a NANEAP country. Sorry about that." Bad beginning, remembering my Togo stiletto heels. Why do I always wear the wrong clothes?

I started over. "I'm happy to be here."

Our weekly staff meetings and office get-togethers mixed profes-sional and informal conversations as we sorted budgets, country entries, number of Volunteers, staffing, and emergencies. We celebrated the Sri Lanka new country entry, ceremonially took down the sign for South Korea as we closed our program after twenty-five years, had a moment of silence and remembrance for the Peace Corps Volunteer killed by an over-loaded truck in the Philippines, and mourned and honored a staff member who died of cancer. We celebrated weddings, new babies, the Peace Corps's overseas assignments. Each event renewed bonds of shared understand-ing of countries and of their foods and artifacts. We even gave a Ghanaian knock, a hand clap, before entering another's cubicle to respect each oth-er's privacy. Do other federal agencies work like this? Probably not. The Peace Corps has its own culture.

*

As had been a continuing pattern for decades, my home and work fused together. I brought Peace Corps stories to dinner conversations, invited staff to the house, and called countries in Asian and Pacific time zones late at night. In high school, my father put his congressional duties first; now, I had a similar pattern. Each day had new decisions, people pushing my curiosity to learn and do more. With three years left on my five-year Peace Corps employment clock mandated in legislation, time pushed me to move fast: new countries, trainings, projects. "Build a legacy before you go," I told myself. Ambition runs in the family.

"This week, I have my monthly calls with country directors in Asia, a twelve-hour time difference, my turn to be at home and they in their offices," I said as we sat down to dinner.

"Oh no, not again," Kirsten groaned. "It's always your turn. And you talk so loud, I can hear you from my bedroom."

"Sorry, I'll try better."

"You always say that, but you never do."

"I'll be with you, Kirsten," Bob added as he reached for the casserole. Bob covered for me frequently. He had just returned from Togo, a year into my regional directorship, and resumed the family nurturing.

"Thank you." I raised my eyes to him, grateful. Bob was a marvelous father, giving extra time to David and Kirsten. Without conversation, over the years, Bob and I had reversed common parenting roles. He was more attuned to David and Kirsten's schedules, meal planning, and schoolwork, whereas I was attuned to work. Unusual, but comfortable enough. He talked of satisfaction in home tasks well done, me in my work duties, home too confining. However, after Kirsten's comment, my nighttime overseas calls moved to after bedtime stories.

*

My work included travel to most countries in the region: Morocco, Tunisia, Oman, Yemen, Nepal, Sri Lanka, Malaysia, Thailand, the Philippines, Solomon Islands, Papua New Guinea, Tonga, Fiji, Western Samoa, Tuvalu, Western Samoa, and Micronesia. Travel distances to the Pacific dictated trips of two to four weeks each. Bob's international assignments continued during these years: six months in Nepal and a year part time in Jamaica. We traded suitcases in the hallway and front door, one going, one coming, just in time to exchange parental responsibilities.

"When's your next trip?" I asked Bob. With his response, I asked, "Can you adjust the time by a few days?"

"I'll make it work." Sometimes it didn't work.

"I'll ask Stephen and cross my fingers." My brother, Stephen, now twenty-four and working construction, loved the kids and became a willing part-time substitute parent and family helping hand. Although thirteen years younger, he and I laughed at our own family dysfunction and helped each other heal.

After my first trip with Stephen in charge, I walked tiredly into the house with my suitcase. Kirsten ran to me, kissed me, and then said, "Stephen let us be messy when you're gone. But he made us clean up this morning." She took me into the kitchen to show me the empty sink. "See? No dirty dishes. You should have seen it at breakfast."

"I confess, they run the house. You're not supposed to know." Stephen winked at the kids. "We have fun because we don't think about the house. But Kirsten gives away my secrets."

I looked at Stephen. "Pretend I don't know. You love the kids. That's what matters," I said as I sat on the kitchen chair, took a deep breath, and laid my head on the table. After a moment, my energy returned. "I left Suva almost two days ago, crossed the international date line, flew fourteen hours to Honolulu, airport wait, another seven to the LA airport, wait, then Dulles Airport and a taxi home. I'm tired."

"I'll fix dinner," Stephen said. "Food out of cans, but we're used to it."

We held this fragmented family routine together with makeshift meals and rotating adult supervision. "Is this working?" I asked myself but didn't want to answer. The pre-Togo work-home pattern had fallen back into place.

\*

Decades later, history confirms the strength of Loret Ruppe's eight years as the agency leader. Her respect for Volunteers and natural gift for governing with humility and grace gave us incentives to be our best, for ourselves and for her.

As a political volunteer, Loret had supported her husband's six terms in Congress, led "Bush for President" in Michigan, and then cochaired the Reagan-Bush presidential campaign in Michigan. Decades earlier, her grandfather founded Miller Beer. Her résumé said "rich," "privileged," "not one of us." We were wrong. She saved the Peace Corps in the early 1980s and became its strongest advocate for the rest of the decade.

Loret had spent over a decade in Republican politics. However, she knew instinctively that the Peace Corps had to remain nonpolitical, the *R* or *D* checked at the agency's door. Peace Corps senior leaders were political appointees, cleared through White House personnel, but no political references, policies, or activities once work began. The safety of Volunteers and our being invited by individual countries to serve depended on meeting that country's needs, not U.S. political preferences.

\*

Loret made people feel comfortable effortlessly, a model I drew on for improving my conversations at informal gatherings. However, underneath this steady demeanor, she faced job- and agency-threatening political fights initiated by a small but radical conservative wing of Reagan's White House. She knew sustaining the Peace Corps's nonpolitical work protected its very existence. Keeping it independent of political interference became her mission. And twenty-five years earlier, while still in college, she lost her father and brother in a private plane crash, a tragedy that changed the trajectory of her family's life. Loret knew how to be tough, but anxieties lurked behind, and these she shared with me.

\*

Early in her tenure, Loret invited senior staff to her home in Bethesda, Maryland, for dinner, my first time there.

"I have a reception hosted by the Yemeni ambassador that evening. May I come an hour late?" I asked, mumbling the latter phrase to hide how late I would be and certainly breaking dinner protocol.

"Fine. We'll save something for you," she said, smiling broadly.

As I drove to the Yemeni reception, I worried about not being elegant enough for the Ruppe dinner. Other invitees had been national officials, met with governors and legislators, or run businesses. My childhood fears of not being good enough slipped back into my brain. When would it disappear? Maybe never.

The hand-copied map to the Ruppe house sat open on the car seat for the thirty-minute drive from the Yemeni event in Georgetown to Bethesda. At stoplights, the overhead car light clicked on briefly, revealing the hand-scrawled turns and street names, tough to see at night. Wrong turns and difficult-to-read signs added to my anxiety, which then added to more wrong turns. I thought about being ninety minutes late and no way to call, the guests halfway through the main course, drinking carefully poured wines, and an empty chair with my name above the dinner plate. All could notice my lack of manners.

Ten minutes later, I heard, "Could someone get the door?" as I pushed the doorbell. "Come and join us," said Loret's daughter, Kathy.

My image of a formal dinner shattered the moment I stepped across the threshold. Colleagues stood in the hallway and spilled into the study and kitchen, holding drinks, talking excitedly, and wearing slacks and comfortable shoes.

"Come and tell Loret you're here," Loret's chief of staff called to me. He walked me through the crowd into the sizable kitchen that overlooked a lowered broad family room. A fire blazed, illuminating couches filled with slouching, sitting, laughing figures, some from the Peace Corps, some family, some strangers. In front of the stove stood Loret, wooden ladle in hand, stirring a mammoth pot of spaghetti sauce.

"You're just in time. Spaghetti is almost ready, bowls over here, silverware behind the pot, drinks on the bar. Make yourself at home." She went back to stirring.

"How was the Yemeni ambassador?" she asked a moment later. "Did you give him my greetings?" Even with the noise and activity around her, she remembered my earlier commitment.

With me in tow, Loret continued casual introductions. Her family and friends easily moved among the rooms, chairs, tables, and couches with spaghetti, warm bread, napkins, and wineglasses balanced on laps and side tables.

I stood chatting with her daughter and huddled laughing with colleagues near the fire. Her Upper Peninsula Michigan friends joked about Loret and Phil's hometown with the famous road sign, "End of the earth, six miles. Houghton, fifteen miles."

That evening, Loret showed that no matter one's position or resources, trust and leadership come by being true to self and respectful of others. We continued as friends during my three years as regional director and then during the subsequent decade. Later, as ambassador to Norway, she invited Bob and me to spend a week at the Oslo residence, being her same informal self.

*

My travels as regional director took me to eighteen Asian and Pacific island countries. Seventy percent of the earth's surface is water, and most seemed to be in the Pacific Ocean, at least when I traveled in low-flying airplanes from island to island for hours looking only at the aqua blue below.

The first monthlong trip began with a flight to Honolulu, then Pago Pago, and finally an eighteen-seat plane to Samoa, the island being the home to *Tales of the South Pacific* by James Michener. My days there confirmed the beauty he described and the poverty behind that beauty.

*

A bumpy fifteen-seater plane with only sea caps to watch below took me from Samoa to Tonga. The plane left Apia at 8:00 a.m. Sunday and forty-five minutes and one international dateline later arrived in Nuku'alofa, "Abode of Love," at 8:45 a.m., Monday—only forty-five minutes to observe Sunday's day of rest. Samoa and Tonga were the bookends on the world's twenty-four-hour clock.

Tonga averages heights of eight to twenty feet above sea level. I imagined touching the opposite beach across the island's width and thinking a giant wave could bury the country.

Tonga, with almost five million coconut trees, has one of the highest coconut tree densities in the world. At the time of my visit, coconuts were inextricably linked to the culture, tradition, and economy: the fruit used as a commodity and cattle fodder; the wood as a material for house construction; the leaves for network fish enclosures, mats, baskets, construction rope; and the bark as tapa cloth.

"Palm trees take six to ten years to begin producing fruit," Peter, a Tonga Volunteer, said as we walked together from the gravel road toward a group of trees near his host family's two-room house. His fast walk made my keeping up difficult. I had arrived in Nuku'alofa that morning and met Peter an hour later.

"Palm trees don't take care of themselves, even though they look self-sufficient. We have to clear the ground of underbrush and nourish the ground with fresh leaves and manure and sometimes with salt." We continued walking. "They don't look like it, but coconuts need lots of water. Island rain is critical." He picked up the freshly manured soil with his hands. "I'm not yet used to the dreadful smell of the pig manure."

"You sound like you know what you're doing." I smiled. "I'm surprised; New England is too cold for coconut."

"The Peace Corps and the farmers here teach me what to do with the trees. In conversations over cava, I help farmers think through possible tweaks for better growth and greater yields. Their goal is more coconuts. More coconuts mean more resources for the family." Peter hesitated for a moment, then looked to my left.

"Hey, Kai, come over here." His counterpart stopped digging, got up from his knees. "Meet my boss from Washington. She came all the way out to meet you and me." Peter turned to me. "Kai taught me all I know about palm-tree farming." Kai bowed slightly, his reed skirt rustling as he leaned toward me and stretched out his hand in greeting.

"We are happy Peter is here. Thank you for sending him."

"No, I am the lucky one," Peter said. "You taught me how to roast a pig the Tongan way—underground. My mom back home is ready to try it. But my new palm-tree skills won't work in Vermont."

Kai laughed. "We joke. Peter likes to joke. I laugh with Peter." He paused, thinking. "And I now see more coconuts forming by working with Peter."

I asked questions about the farming and coconut crop production. After a few moments, Kai walked closer to me, shuffling his sandals through the dried brush, and said so quietly I could barely hear, "You know the best way to get more coconuts per tree?" He paused, looked at

Peter like he wanted to give me their most intimate secret. "We hug the trees every morning. Trees are healthier when hugged."

"What, hug the trees?"

"Yup." Peter looked somber. "I didn't want to tell you that part. Didn't think you would believe me. I have science to prove it." Peter and Kai's eyes met, faces serious, then suddenly they laughed. "It's true," Peter added.

When I left their site an hour later, they still insisted that hugging the trees made a difference. I had to decide myself whether to believe them. Peter was not the first Volunteer to give me dubious information, often with small, quick smiles. As a Volunteer years earlier, I also rearranged nuggets of truth with unknowing visitors.

*

Six days later, after Tonga and then Fiji, I sat in a four-seater chartered plane headed toward Tuvalu, a three-and-a-half-hour flight through stunning white swelling cloud formations and over dozens of atolls across eight hundred miles of Pacific waters. As we approached the island country, the pilot turned to me. "Watch for the landing strip. It's as big as Tuvalu's main island on which it sits, Funafuti. You'll never see another like it."

Tuvalu, a group of eight coral atolls known earlier as the Ellis Islands, was famous as a major landing and staging site during the War of the Pacific in World War II. The airstrip, built by the Allies in 1943 for navy bombers, stretched the full width and half of the crescent-shaped Funafuti atoll, the largest of the eight. The houses of the two thousand island inhabitants crowded between the narrow strip's lagoon side, the water a few hundred feet away.

Tuvalu made international headlines in 2021, during the European Climate Summit, when Prime Minister Kausea Natano gave his speech in a business suit behind an elaborate lectern while standing in two feet of water in the lagoon. "Tuvalu is disappearing," he said, head down. That photo gained worldwide attention to the realities of rising seas.

As our plane descended, the pilot continued, "We drop down to within fifty feet of the landing strip, fly the length with engines screaming, then pull up, circle, and come in to land for real. Now watch."

"A double landing? Why?"

"The landing siren goes off three minutes before I land. Can you make out the antique red fire truck midway along the strip? With the siren, the driver climbs inside, turns on the engine, and drives up and down the edge of the strip. It's the emergency response if something goes wrong with the plane."

"Comforting," I said.

"Next, pay attention to the kids, chickens, and dogs on the landing strip. The strip is the kids' playground and the animals' grazing land with rich grass replacing the black World War II tarmac. Tiny island. No other place for kids and animals to be." I watched people and animals run off the grassy landing strip and back into the palm trees as the engine noise increased. As the plane ascended and circled, the space cleared, and the plane dropped down for a bumpy landing.

"I observe the activity carefully," the pilot commented as he turned off the engines. "I don't want to harm anything. If necessary, I will circle a second time to be sure. The strip cleared quickly this time."

"Thanks," I said to the fire truck driver as I climbed down the four metal steps from the plane's small door and greeted him as he walked toward me with a smile.

"We want all our flights and passengers to be safe. We only get a couple a week, but I drop my work in the education ministry when I hear the siren to make sure to have the fire truck ready. No accidents yet." As he spoke, he pointed to the two-story frame building yards from the landing strip with the words "Tuvalu Government Offices" neatly printed on a wood sign above the entry door.

As we spoke, the Peace Corps Volunteer couple walked toward me, sandals, summer cotton blouse, shirt, and pants.

"You're almost like God arriving. We haven't seen an American since our arrival seven months ago." Andrew reached out his hand before introducing himself and then Sylvia, his wife.

"Not quite sure how to talk to an outsider anymore."

"I'll help you out by sharing any interesting headlines in the world and then asking you questions about your experience here." Looking around the open space of the landing strip that doubled as downtown Funafuti, I said, "What's it like living here, ocean all the way to the horizon in every direction? No place here to disappear but having disappeared from the rest of global society."

"Something happens when living here," Andrew said as we strolled forward away from the lagoon. "In the first few weeks, we ached for our family, our apartment in Hagerstown, my engineering work, and news, any news from anywhere. I wanted to go home so badly."

"Then," Sylvia said, "we learned the names of our village mates, played games and read to the kids, ate taro and pig with families, learned to harvest and cook sweet potatoes with coconut, and sat with men in the afternoon making rope strands from palm leaves, gossiping about others on the island."

We detoured a few feet to look at the lagoon, its shimmering aqua water reflecting the sun.

Sylvia continued, "What told us we belonged was being invited into the nightly choral singing. Islanders have singing team competitions. The competition is fierce, practices long, and a cappella voices like choirs. While singing, we sit on benches, leaning against poles holding the thatched roof, watching flames from burning palm tree leaves in the prepared fire pit, and listening to crashing ocean waves and lagoon ripples lapping against the shores just feet away. No one lived more than a few feet from the water."

Sylvia continued, "It's magic. I sang in my small college chorus, but never well. Here, women patiently help me open my chest, push up my voice, and not be afraid of sounding out the notes."

"I'm trying to imagine your lives here," I said, thinking of my own tuneless voice. We had reached the office building and stood outside waiting until 1:00 p.m., the appointment time. "Your world is the antithesis of mine. DC has traffic, a million people, twelve-story office buildings, men in dark suits carrying briefcases looking important as they make decisions and then changing the decisions a week later." We stared out at the lagoon again as I continued. "Are people in DC satisfied? For whom do they really make a difference? Who really knows?"

Sylvia joined in: "Andrew and I see tiny differences here, a child learning to read, a new catchment tank for rainwater, a villager gaining courage to go to New Zealand for school. Makes us feel good."

Sylvia and Andrew walked me around the center of the lagoon side of the island.

"You don't see pigs here. Pigs are kept on the far edge of the crescent where no one lives as the land there is only a few yards wide. Pigs are kept away because they attract flies, and the island is too small to share with flies. A new group of women each month paddle small boats to the island's edge and take care of the pigs. Downtown Funafuti has no pigs and no flies."

*

Prime Minister Tomasi Puapua came to the two–guest room hotel that evening to treat me to dinner as a welcome to Tuvalu: roasted chicken, seaweed salad, and well-seasoned taro root.

After dinner, we moved outside and sat on the three-foot-high rock wall dividing the hotel from the lagoon, dangling our feet in the gentle, lapping Pacific waves. The air didn't move.

"I was a surgeon in New Zealand," he commented as we settled as best we could on the hard rock of the wall. "I grew up here, got my medical degree in Fiji, went to New Zealand, had a good career, and then the Tuvalu Parliament asked me to come back as prime minister. I now spend most of my time here, but do go back to New Zealand occasionally."

"How did you adjust to the change?"

"I feel I am two different people, the leader of Tuvalu when here talking with coconut and vegetable farmers and an ordinary professional in Wellington, New Zealand." He moved his body to get more comfortable and looked out into the lagoon. "Look out over the water. The two hotel floodlights catch the lagoon ripples and reach outward before disappearing into the ocean blackness that stretches hundreds if not a thousand miles before land. Listen to the silence, only faint laps of the waves, barely heard. It's lonely here, if I think of my work in a hospital, in Wellington, with daily rushing people."

The prime minister's assistant brought out tea. We drank, still dangling our feet in the water.

"But here is a nation of lives lived and traditions maintained from before time. People's lives here teach us about friendship, love, humility so easily forgotten in the maze of big city survival. This land helped give victory at the end of World War II. I know it will continue to have an important place in the world." He stopped a minute, kicking the water with his feet, taking a sip of tea, and moved his body again. "I'm lucky to lead this nation. We have a small, quiet, but important place in the world." I sat silently, absorbing his words, the faint aroma of coconut oil, and the nighttime, so distant from what is thought important and yet filled with humanness that matters.

During my years with the Peace Corps, I have met many heads of state in countries across the world. Prime Minister Puapua of a nation of eight thousand people taught me that evening about the power of individual humility and leadership.

*

Before leaving Tuvalu, I flew to three additional island atolls, each with fewer than a thousand inhabitants. A Volunteer couple living on each island taught young children English and helped construct and then adapt the new water catchment tanks for community use.

Volunteers on each island stood waiting on the beach, toes buried in the white sand, watching my seaplane land. They handed me fresh coconut milk and a hibiscus.

"We haven't seen anyone off the island for months except the boat captain and the pilot. We're starved for American conversation," the first of the three couples said in greeting.

During the next few hours, they offered me a tour of the island (a fifteen-minute walk), homegrown tea drunk with the mayor, palm wine collected and fermented by a tapper from the cut flower sap of palm trees, fresh water from the newly constructed tank, and a choir practicing British hymns.

"We're not doing competitive singing tonight," Arthur said after our tour and community visits. "You'll miss a real treat. But last week the ocean side team played the lagoon side team in cricket, and the lagoon team still insists the other team cheated. The two sides are not yet talking or singing."

"What, on a one-square-mile island with only seven hundred people? You can't walk five feet without bumping into someone."

"Welcome to the world in miniature, a pocket version of my community interactions as an engineer in Providence, Rhode Island. This island is like a college course in human behavior when people can't get away from each other. They tell us how strange we are to them. But beneath our strange accents, we're not. They laugh with us and then gossip about each other. We're safe because we are both insiders and outsiders."

*

Friends say first experiences remain most memorable. They force new synaptic journeys inside the brain, pushing against ruts of daily routines. The Pacific Islands did that to me, changing assumptions of normal space and time and interactions with others. The island spaces were smaller than Rhode Island, some only slightly larger than the Mall of America, and surrounded by lagoons and oceans and no other land seen on the horizon. Societies on these islands have flourished since "before time," with little if any outside communication, houses without walls, and rainwater and coconut trees to meet most of their needs. This experience challenged my sense of need and what brings a daily smile or laugh.

Among the twenty countries visited as regional director, the Pacific Island nations taught me the most about humility, of being in communities isolated in a vast ocean, surviving and thriving when each person is responsible for the group's survival.

*

Postcards represented the only communication with my family during the month in the South Pacific, a strange thought today knowing the availability of instant communication. Today, my family could have shared the pigs squealing or even talked with the prime minister as his feet made ripples in the lagoon. But instead, they saw nothing except a few photos taken with two rolls of precious film on a throwaway camera and developed into prints a week after my return. David's and Kirsten's memories are only of an absent mother coming back with strange handmade gifts and dirty laundry. For David, thirteen, and Kirsten, ten, they saw my absences instead of my work.

"David and Kirsten missed you," Bob said as we drove up I-66 from the Dulles Airport. "Spend extra time with them this next week. All is fine at home, except you've been gone."

"I'm glad to be missed, but it hurts," feeling conflict between being gone and celebrating the trip's memories.

"I know it hurts, but it's true: too much traveling. Just make it up to them."

"I'm driven, but I'm lucky to have you. How do you put up with me?" He smiled. "It's okay."

*

My first day back in the office began with questions from the Pacific desk teams as I walked through the doors.

"What was your favorite site?"

"What's it like to sit in an economy plane seat for forty-eight hours?"

"Did you really meet Bloody Mary?"

My Volunteers and staff stories at the staff meeting gave value to the desk staff's hard work. They worked across time zones and scratchy telephone conversations to find lost emergency medical supplies, support in-country staff members handling Volunteer and staff emotional breakdowns, and calm family members waiting for Volunteer letters gone astray or never written.

*

"You have a meeting with Loret this afternoon," Gerry told me as my papers, notebooks, bags from the trip landed with a thud on my desk. "She wants trip details. And by the way, I brought you more flowers from my garden."

"What a great welcome."

My feared jet lag took hold as Loret greeted me at her office door wearing a two-piece bias-cut silk dress that moved gently as she walked. My body said "Five a.m.," my legs said "Sit down," and my eyes said "Close."

"I brought you something," I said as I held out a miniature perfectly painted Samoan fishing boat made from pounded tree bark. Even the two tiny seats and four oars were exact replicas.

"I missed seeing your hand gestures, always moving with the rhythm of your words," she said, taking the boat. "Easy to remember your ideas because you mime your thoughts." I hadn't realized how often my hands caught the attention of others. My mind needs my hands to express words, even decades later while doing Zoom calls.

"Now, how was the trip?" She arranged the red-and-orange Malawi fabric pillow behind her back. During the conversation, she didn't ask her usual questions and observations that showed curiosity. Something seemed wrong.

After a few minutes, she sighed, dropped her head slightly, and let her arms rest on the sides of the chair, hands hanging down.

"Sorry, I'm distracted," she said. "It's been a tough week," sighing as she spoke.

"I'm listening." Her sentence told me she trusted me with agency issues.

"The neoconservatives, the Far Right in President Reagan's administration, hate the Peace Corps." She said it quietly, without emotion. She knew President Reagan supported the Peace Corps, and she didn't want to imply disrespect toward him.

I sat, silent. Then "How do you know?" sitting even straighter, anger rising toward those invisible people opposing us. "They're wrong." My anger pushed out the words. "If they could just see the Volunteers," I said unhelpfully.

"They have power." Her voice turned harsher, her face tightened. "They are crafting a bill in Congress to put the Peace Corps back under the ACTION agency. This would throw away our independence only achieved a couple of years ago under President Carter."

"Once under ACTION," she began, hesitated, then continued, "the administration can eliminate the name Peace Corps, reduce the number of countries and Volunteers, and let it wither away, like they tried under Nixon. I've not been here even a year and am already passionate about saving this agency, even against parts of my own party. This agency saves the world. I have to fight some of my own government colleagues who want to do this." As she spoke, she shook her head, tightened her hands, and sat straighter. "Will you support me?"

"That's an easy answer—of course I will," showing volume in my voice.

She shifted slightly. "It's getting personal. They say I don't support the president, that I'm a fraud... but they're lying." The sunlight caught tears in her eyes. She raised her hands and covered her face for a moment. "But I won't give up. We'll win this." She had so few people with whom she could speak honestly. Her words, day and evening, were those of the Peace Corps director, never those of a private person. This moment replicated my own experience of loneliness forty years later as Peace Corps director under President Donald Trump. I knew to trust no one and to share feelings with only my daughter, Kirsten.

The conversation with Loret showed the isolation of leadership, of not having a personal self that could speak out, and of having every word measured against contrasting and deeply believed political points of view.

"The opposition forgets I know almost every member of Congress. I hosted, entertained, supported functions for Phil during his twelve years as a congressional representative. I helped him through legislation strategies, visited staff offices, and met socially with congressmen's wives." She stopped, stared out the window at the White House across Lafayette Park. Then with growing power in her voice, she said, "I'm taking advantage of this knowledge. Now."

She did. She found an ally in Congressman Jim Leach (R-Iowa), who supported the Peace Corps based on his own commitment to volunteerism and international service. He prepared a small team to meet one by one with members or their staff about the Peace Corps's independence. Loret said nothing publicly. She gave those opposing the Peace Corps no quotes to use against her. Those opposed to her leadership continued to attack her personally, thinking they had the upper hand. But she stayed one step ahead.

Both Peace Corps and ACTION shared the same office building, ACTION on the lower floors, the Peace Corps above them. Staff from both agencies watched the two directors going in and out of the grand lobby with Kennedy's famous words above the windows. Their personality differences, shown in faces and hand gestures, were a metaphor for the Peace Corps/ACTION legislative fight.

The new director of ACTION walked through the front door to the elevator before 8:00 a.m. without a smile or nod to others in the lobby. As he stepped inside, he rarely acknowledged either the elevator operator or others inside its lighted cubicle.

Loret arrived in the lobby waving, smiling, and talking to those she saw. "Taking time with people who serve Volunteers is as important as anything I do for the Peace Corps," she told me later.

Leaders influence their agencies with gestures as well as words. Others watch and respond. Staff members laughed and talked in the Peace Corps hallways. They kept their heads down and walked quietly in ACTION hallways. The differences continued as they exited elevators, bought sandwiches at the deli next door, or ate lunch in either Lafayette or Farragut Park.

One sentence in the original Peace Corps legislation provided our win. This sentence forbade anyone with a background in U.S. intelligence activities to serve in the Peace Corps as either staff or Volunteer. The legislative writers understood that such a background put Volunteers and the agency itself at risk in other countries.

A month into the legislative fight and with significant research, the director of ACTION's intelligence background during the Vietnam War became public. Thus, he could not lead the Peace Corps, even within the ACTION agency. The fight ended. The Peace Corps stayed independent. Loret won.

\*

The Far Right continued its Peace Corps animosity even as Loret showed goodwill. The group didn't trust Peace Corps Volunteers or the agency's mission, a relic from Nixon's Vietnam view of the Peace Corps: draft dodgers, peaceniks, anti-Americans. Not true, but the image held.

Male Volunteers got neither deferment nor credit for alternative service during the Vietnam War. When I was a Volunteer in Tunisia, we talked about who might be drafted out of service or afterward. Fear hung silently behind our local bantering. It became real when my Volunteer teaching colleague Gary's draft board ordered him into the army and on a plane to Vietnam two months after he completed three years of Peace Corps service. His life ended with a Vietcong bomb four weeks later, a useless death after his service to his country as a Volunteer.

Now ten years and more after the war, the neocon group continued its work against both the Peace Corps's goals and Loret, whom they blamed for their legislative loss. Ed, her deputy director, represented the group's furthering efforts to diminish the agency.

Fifty feet separated his office from Loret's, and a five-foot partition divided their two secretaries. Despite the partition, overheard information flowed from secretary to secretary and into Ed's office.

"Why does Ed want to be here?" Loret asked during one of our director's office closed-door conversations. "He rants, he explodes at slights, he scowls. He won't talk to me when I ask him questions." She paused, looking exasperated. "And he's in charge when I travel. Think of the orders he can give when I'm overseas and can't communicate." She ordered coffee and stood for a moment.

"We work hard, we care, and then I see his smirks at the pain he gives me. I want to smack him, but I keep smiling. He hovers near when I'm in conversations, gleaning bad news tidbits for that reporter at the *Washington Times*, who then publishes the gossip."

Loret fought for us but got little political support. She fought the White House political battles herself, not risking conversations with other senior staff. Because of our growing time together, she knew me to be safe.

*

A few months later, Loret called me in again. "I need to get staff ready for another article by *that* reporter, George, coming out tomorrow in the *Washington Times*. It's a bad one. And as usual with his reporting, completely misstated.

"Seems the *Washington Times* devotes an article a month to supposed misdoings here at Peace Corps, blown out of proportion or completely wrong. Makes us look like a clown show.

"Ed got information about my letting go a senior staff person last week—for cause, by the way—and got him together with the reporter for an interview. Anger and misstatements are detailed and generalized. So discouraging."

We weathered this article and many others produced by the *Times* reporter. But it ground down leadership. Being second-guessed and then misrepresented by those wanting the Peace Corps's leadership to fail made decisions difficult. Loret showed commitment to our work and mission, stayed steady with Congress and the White House, and stepped forward to defend the Volunteers serving around the world whenever challenged.

But in her office, shoulders dropped, speech hesitant, movement slow as she described the impact of the attacks. Through it, she never wavered. Overseas, Volunteers and staff remained oblivious to the Washington drama. Members of Congress and senators continued to send letters of support to their constituents serving as Volunteers. They knew firsthand from their stories the impact made.

*

My five-year term limit with the Peace Corps came after three years as regional director in the summer of 1984. The legislative mandate that limited consecutive years of service spared no one. This had been my dream job; no other would equal it, and there was no thought of a return to the agency.

Five years and two weeks later, the legally required time away, I returned to the Peace Corps as chief of staff.

Loret completed eight years of agency leadership under President

Reagan, double that of any other Peace Corps director before or since. A year later, President George H. W. Bush named her ambassador to Norway, where she completed a successful three-year tour. She died of cancer at age sixty, seven years after leaving the Peace Corps. I still grieve her passing.

*

Loret was a mentor, a friend, and demonstrated that humility and respect strengthen leadership's power. She gave me the courage to fight for the Peace Corps's core values and goals even as agency responsibilities necessarily adapted to national and global events. Her devotedness gave me strength as I was later challenged by Peace Corps evacuations, civil unrest, and the political challenges facing a nonpolitical agency. My passion has always remained with the image of each Volunteer, each community, and the interaction that makes a difference to both, sometimes for decades.

# 11

# And the Wall Came Tumbling Down
## 1989–92

Wanting to change people's lives drove my Peace Corps post–regional director job search. I relished stories of strangers becoming families, foreigners becoming colleagues, and new ideas becoming joint projects. Being the vice president of Youth for Understanding (YFU), a high school exchange program, gave me the chance to experience students living with families in other countries and building lifetime relationships that follow.

\*

The Peace Corps showed me how host families in other countries saw and adjusted to Americans. YFU opened my perspectives to the reverse: how American families became hosts to European, Asian, and Latin American students. The experiences required the family and Volunteer/student to be vulnerable and honest and allowed each to trust and accept the differences in the other. At YFU, we asked American families to give of themselves. We asked the same of Peace Corps host families.

\*

During my five years with YFU, I drove Kirsten, now a teenager, to school each morning. Both Sidwell Friends and the YFU offices shared neighborhood space with hundred-year-old stately houses and imposing oak and maple trees in the northwest section of Washington, DC. With regular hours and a predictable work routine, we protected our twenty minutes of drive time.

Kirsten wore tight pants and baggy, mismatched tops and shaved the left side of her head, showing five earrings lined along her earlobe.

"You look sloppy. Is this what you want?"

"I don't care. Let me be."

I watched other students gathering near the school entrance looking like Kirsten: baggy and shaggy.

"Okay, I get it. I'll stay quiet."

"Good. I won't change." I kept my feelings to myself. Kirsten did well at school despite her dress. Fortunately, she changed pants for a skirt for church and counted church friends as her strongest. My continued church attendance was largely to support her own commitment, which she has maintained to today. But she kept the five earrings in her left ear for another few years.

*

George H. W. Bush succeeded President Reagan and, with the election, nominated a new Peace Corps director. Six months later, I could legally return, as I had been gone five years.

I missed the Volunteers, languages too difficult to learn, *fufu* and cous-cous meals, songs sung in perfect harmony, diseases that kept us thin, textiles woven with the woof held between the weaver's toes, three-day weddings, braying donkeys at dawn, Volunteers teaching under baobab trees while kids sat on mats, or host families surprising a Volunteer on their birthday.

In Togo, one Volunteer argued with me about whether introducing a more sturdy pig into his village would be too much change for the village; another taught the chemistry of oxygen displacement in a village lycée by creating a chalk drawing of a full-sized lion in a giant beaker on the black-board; and another showed her family from Chicago full command of an obscure language during their visit to her village. I missed the dedication of host-country staff in Thailand willing to drive nonstop for twenty-four hours on muddy roads to reach and support a Volunteer whose grand-mother had just died and of a physician health minister in Côte d'Ivoire telling me it was a Volunteer teacher who had had the patience to learn that his ten-year-old self only needed glasses to excel in class. The Peace Corps held my heart.

*

Two months after telling the White House of my interest in returning to a senior position, I sat on a deep-red fabric couch against the back wall of the new Peace Corps director's office, nervous. My gold-themed silk Hermès scarf, a gift from Francine, over a yellow suit with a knee-length pencil skirt shouted, "I want to impress." Paul Coverdell, the new director designee, faced me. He sat on a matching red cushioned chair, his back straight as his hands moved in sync with his words. A white cup of coffee on a matching saucer sat on the table between us. He reached for it as he paused for words, the cup being a prop for thinking. He rarely drank the coffee, letting it sit, cold, in the cup. We didn't know that day, but our seating positions, the cold coffee, and our similar hand movements became a daily ritual for the next two and a half years.

My frumpy but cherished "806 building" across from the White House had been torn down, and the new Peace Corps's office building looked out over a bank and George Washington University.

After perfunctory introductions, Paul began crisply, "You were one of three people White House personnel noted as having strong Peace Corps experience, which I value in a chief of staff." He paused, took a sip of coffee. "I will select one of you."

As a friend of the new president, Paul had framed Bush's successful "Southern Strategy," key to the president's election. He had given his farewell speech to the Georgia Senate two days before we met, having been Republican minority leader there for twenty-five years. This was his first day at the Peace Corps.

Paul was fifty years old, slightly built, five-foot-eight, and balding. His wire glasses and high-pitched voice defied the stereotype of a successful politician, but his even, quiet, and methodically delivered words and stories held people's attention.

"It was really tough to leave Georgia. I love Atlanta and Georgia politics. But I wanted to learn about national politics here in Washington." He expressed trepidation about adjusting to a national political culture. He learned well, as four years later, he returned to Washington, DC, as a U.S. senator.

He continued, "I'm intrigued by the Peace Corps, the Volunteers. I turned down an offer to head the Small Business Administration for the Peace Corps to learn how Volunteers survive and thrive." These words returned a year later when, as the two of us sat on a plane on the Seoul airport tarmac, cold, blistery rain hitting the window, he told me of being a GI stationed in Korea.

"I was the only American in a rural village, living in a corrugated tin building with no heat and a leaky roof. Every day, I worked on small army projects, watching the cold water drip, sometimes off icicles. I never got warm. But I knew I would go home. My coworkers knew they would not. I learned about caring, and I learned about my privilege. I serve today because of that cold winter in Korea."

Was it my words? My determination? My scarf? The next day, he offered me the chief of staff position. The twenty-five pages of White House forms were already in hand.

\*

July 5, 1989, 8:30 a.m., Paul's ten-person senior staff team walked into the eighth-floor conference room, my first moment as chief of staff.

As we sat, Paul spoke without introducing me. "The first Peace Corps Volunteers to China are in training here in DC. They depart next week. China wants us in Chengdu Province to teach English. Both ambassadors want it." He stopped, stood, looked at the group, held his cup of cold coffee, waited a moment.

"The Tiananmen Square uprising ended on June 4 with violence and hundreds of deaths. Since then, the administration and Congress have asked me if it is wise to send Volunteers to China next week as its violent response still resonates around the world. I told them the Peace Corps is nonpolitical, but either a yes or a no gives a political message. Which should it be?" Paul stopped, stood, picked up his coffee cup, turned to me.

"What do you think, Jody? You know the Peace Corps. You know politics. Give us advice."

"We should cancel this group of Volunteers," I said without hesitation. The team gasped. No one moved or spoke. Those were my first words as chief of staff.

"I think you're right," Paul said after a moment. At 9:00 a.m., we called the trainees with the devastating news. The decision made headlines.

The Peace Corps China program began anew three years later under Elaine Chao's Peace Corps leadership. In 2019, the program celebrated twenty-five years of community partnership, the service of three thousand Volunteers, and personal friendships. COVID-19 brought it to a close in January 2020.

*

An hour later that morning, still numb from the earlier decision, the senior staff assembled near the window in the director's office. Sunshine lifted spirits. They watched as I raised my hand and repeated the U.S. government oath Paul had taken two months earlier, the same oath every new Peace Corps Volunteer takes when beginning service overseas on behalf of the U.S. government.

My new colleagues in the room applauded. Paul Coverdell welcomed me. Then his desk phone rang. Directors' desk phones rarely ring.

He walked across the room, picked up the receiver, "Hello." Then silence as Paul listened. His right hand, holding the receiver, tensed. After a moment, "I just swore her in. She's already here." He paused, listening. Then "You said I could choose whom I wanted." Another pause. "Thank you. I appreciate your confidence in me."

He walked back to the group, smiled, and said, "The White House just said you didn't politically clear. No campaign support. You heard how I responded." He stretched out his hand to me. "Welcome. I'm happy we will work together."

I shook his hand tightly. I had scraped through a political process again.

My two and a half years as chief of staff included visiting fifty countries, negotiating twenty-five new country entries, managing emergency exits from ten countries, and supporting a tireless leader. The breakup of the Soviet Union changed the world. And it changed the Peace Corps. I helped lead the change.

*

One early morning the next week, Molly, Paul's personal assistant, rushed into the director's office. "American ambassador to Hungary, Mark Palmer, is on the phone. Should I pass him to you?"

"What would he want?" I asked, sitting on the couch reading through staff notes. "We have nothing to do with Hungary."

"We might," Paul said as he picked up the call.

He talked excitedly with the ambassador as he looked at me silently staring at him. I thought, "Peace Corps doesn't belong in Europe."

"The ambassador has invited us to explore the Peace Corps in Hungary. I said yes."

I blurted out without thinking, "We can't go there."

"This is a new era and a new Peace Corps." He sat, holding his coffee cup, and said, "You've committed to me. Be with me on this."

I panicked inside. Hungary didn't fit into the Peace Corps's traditions, spirit, and three goals. President Kennedy didn't have this in mind when he said, "Ask not…" We went to poor countries, giving technical support, sharing ourselves as individual Volunteers, learning about host communities, bringing knowledge home. If we considered European countries, Congress could reduce our budget. Staff and well-organized returned Volunteer communities would lobby Congress against the decision. And they did.

By the summer of 1989, Hungary had pulled away from the Soviet Union, declared itself the Republic of Hungary on October 23. But this was not in the Peace Corps's world. Paul Coverdell lived in a bigger world, one that didn't follow the Peace Corps's traditions. With the ambassador's call, Paul saw individual American Volunteers in communities and schools of a country where citizens had been taught to hate Americans. Peace Corps traditions did not tether him.

"They will see us as we really are, how we think, how we talk, how we treat each other," he said quietly but firmly. We would not persuade him otherwise. By late that afternoon, a new job for me emerged: defending a decision to staff, thousands of returned Peace Corps Volunteers (RPCVs), and some members of Congress who were themselves RPCVs, a decision I opposed but could not admit. Paul believed in our going to Hungary. As the day ended, he looked for a smile, a word of concurrence from me. None came.

By the next morning, my brain had somersaulted toward a new perspective and became ready to say with commitment to anyone challenging the decision, "Yes, our agency can do this."

Staff members stood at my door, angry. "Stop him from doing this."

"We're doing this," I said without emotion.

But how?

Kennedy's original words represented the globe. The use of the terms *third-world countries* and *developing countries* was not in the original 1961 legislation. They had crept into the Peace Corps's vocabulary over the twenty-five years and became truth. Hungary didn't meet this made-up truth. Hungary could incorporate the three Peace Corps goals anchored in the original legislation. It could honor Kennedy's vision.

The negative reaction from both staff and returned Volunteers throughout the United States exceeded our initial fears. Hostility came by phone, letters, and calls to Congress. I led the response, listening to and countering words against a Peace Corps Hungary program from thousands of Peace Corps believers. No one knew what I thought. Silence. I was good at silence.

In late July 1989, the director of congressional relations gave Paul a memo summarizing congressional staff reaction. It confirmed our fears. She, too, had told me of her opposition to the decision and hoped to influence the director.

The congressional memo said, "This is moving beyond the Peace Corps's mandate and scope. Where will you go next? Poland? Is this a convenient public relations tool for the president's trip?"

Through the negative noise, Paul said to me, "You can handle the RPCV community. It's why you're here. And once Volunteers are in Hungarian communities, they can tell the story." He had it right. His belief gave him courage to take risks, to defy tradition. He taught me the courage I needed to run the agency years later.

On July 14, 1989, Paul sent a memo to all Peace Corps staff, only a week after the ambassador's call: "On Wednesday, July 12, President George Bush told the people of Hungary that 'as long as governments ease the way, people can do the rest.' That was an exciting, thought-provoking prelude to the announcement that the Peace Corps Volunteers will go to Hungary to teach English.... This will be the first time our Volunteers have been welcomed into an Eastern Bloc nation.... This program is entirely consistent with the three goals of the Peace Corps... and that the pursuit of peace is a goal that has no geographic or political boundaries."

The reaction by staff and Peace Corps's stakeholders to the announcement came swiftly: angry, fearful, and questioning political motives. Peace Corps should remain nonpolitical. By the next June, hundreds of these same staff made it happen. The new Volunteers themselves told their own stories, similar to those from more traditional Peace Corps countries. European countries would, over time, join the traditional countries.

\*

We flew to Budapest, Hungary, in October 1989 to attend a Peace Corps English training conference, an early step toward our entry.

"This region is changing by the day," Ambassador Palmer said as he escorted us into the city. "The East German general secretary is rumored to be on his way out. The fall of the Berlin Wall can't be far behind." He continued as the ambassador's bulletproof car drove toward our hotel, "Movements ending communism here in central and eastern Europe are palpable on streets, in government meetings, with my Hungarian embassy staff. The Hungarian education ministry wants English, business, and Americans in the communities. They have no fear of Volunteers living with families."

"No fear of us living with Hungarians in communities?" I asked, believing the years of communism had left an anti-American mark.

"You'll see tomorrow," the ambassador said. "Don't take my word for it." As we drove, we stared at lights, cars, buildings, people waiting for buses as the evening descended. Normal. But in Hungary? In Hungary?

The minister of foreign affairs welcomed us to his office the next morning. "We need you; we need your English, as we are now looking west to Europe and the opportunities for business, trade, and commerce."

Paul said, his voice strong with purpose, "We can help make that happen, school by school, family by family. I commit to your purpose." Ambassador Palmer beamed. I took notes.

The next day we drove to a high school outside Budapest, two stories of sturdy red brick without distinguishing features, surrounded by rows of groomed bushes. This school could have been anywhere.

The large door opened to a petite woman, hesitantly reaching out to Americans with American English. As she shook our hands, she looked down, stayed silent, then after a moment, "Welcome. I am in charge of the English department here at the school." She continued, choosing her words carefully, slowly, "I have never spoken with native English speakers before, ever. I'm afraid I'm not good at the language. Please forgive me."

Rushing forward, I put out my hand. "Your American English is excellent. I don't hear an accent."

Startled, she stepped back. "Are you sure? I've been afraid to meet, thinking you would judge me harshly." Her eyes brightened, her shoulders straight.

I continued, "I'm in awe of your linguistic skill. You will be an excellent guide for us."

*

Warsaw came next, a surprise visit requested by the education ministry. Poland had begun transitioning to a new democratic government after years of communism and uprisings.

We arrived in Warsaw at 5:30 p.m., October 16, 1989, the sun already setting. News of the imminent resignation of President Erich Honecker in East Germany made news in the airport. People along the roadway stayed close to radios, their faces anxious.

Ambassador Davis greeted us and said, "The deputy minister of education wants to meet you in an hour. He's staying late in his office to do so." We drove into the city, the ambassador's voice describing our journey. "You see, the Germans bombed 85 percent of Warsaw in 1944, destroying a society, a country. The Soviet Union then replaced bombed-out buildings with gray fortress-looking buildings lining downtown streets block by block. You can count the fragile metal balconies clinging to the sides and shapeless chimneys on top. No interest in beauty."

Ambassador Davis continued, "By coincidence, the deputy minister's office is in one of the 15 percent of buildings the Germans left standing. At 25 Szucha Avenue, this imposing structure housed the German Gestapo and today is the Museum of Struggle and Martyrdom."

As we arrived and stepped onto the pavement, the ambassador pointed to the sign at the door's grand entrance: "The only authentic place of Nazi torture in Warsaw." "During the Second World War, it was an interrogation center where Polish prisoners were horrendously tortured. The museum houses ten actual imprisonment cells where doomed detainees were tortured, killed, and their bodies then stored. I'm surprised the Ministry of Education has its offices here."

We studied the sign. Here... Torture... Death... Remembrance. Paul hesitated before entering this place of World War II evil.

We stepped inside. Rainy and dark outside, light and elegant inside. A sign pointed down the stairs to the basement cells and museum. A large crystal chandelier lit the carved-mahogany foyer, and a lush red carpet extended to a broad stairway of the same carved wood leading to the next floor. We walked along the carpet and up the stairs, our foot sounds absorbed in the surrounding lushness. At the top of the stairs, the carpet disappeared, and the hallway became narrower. A cluster of light bulbs replaced the chandelier. We kept walking up another set of stairs, into a narrower hall, and then finally into a small room: one light bulb, a plain wood desk, three metal chairs facing the desk, and no windows.

Deputy Minister Tadeusz Diem put his pen down, closed his notebook, and stood up to greet us, his chair scraping the floor.

"Welcome to my office. I'm sorry about how it looks, but we are new here. As you know, our government is only a few months old and still finding its way in this new democratic environment."

The chairs were hard as we sat. Images of Nazis, bombings, tortured men, marching German and Soviet soldiers were present with us. Countered by soft-spoken Deputy Minister Diem, he offered greetings and then, sitting tall as he began, made his appeal. This bare room with one light and one man making a request for the Peace Corps reminded me of Kennedy's words and the Peace Corps's beginning.

Deputy Minister Diem said, "We want Volunteers to teach English in teacher training centers throughout the country. We have thousands of teachers who speak Russian, Poland's second language, but we now want to shift to English and retrain our teachers in this global language of business and trade. Our young people have opportunities unavailable to them before, but they need English to reach beyond our borders to the West. You can give us English, the tool we need to thrive."

His words mirrored those of the foreign minister in Hungary the day before. By accident of birth, I grew up with this tool, English, sought by countries in central and eastern Europe, a tool Americans take for granted and could now easily share.

"Ambassador Davis called me a few days ago," Diem said, "telling me what Peace Corps Volunteers offer. His call answered a dream I had about bringing English to Poland. And now you are here. Thank you."

"We can send you English educators," Paul said, "about sixty by next summer."

I gulped while writing the words. No way can we have a program here in eight months. We will disappoint the ministry. Vice Minister Diem had just described his hope for a new national English education model based on the work of our Volunteers.

Diem continued, "These last couple of months, several representatives from organizations offering aid have sat where you are now sitting.

They looked eager and made promises. I haven't heard from any of these organizations since. I now look at you, Director Coverdell. Will you also disappoint? Is your word good?"

"Our word is good. We will have the sixty Volunteers ready to begin the next school year. You can count on us," Paul said, his words carefully spoken and firm. The commitment made, the effort must succeed.

"Thank you. I want to believe you." He stopped, stood up, reached across the desk, and shook Paul's hand. "I will hope." He sat again, looked at his hands, thought a minute, then raised his head to look at Paul directly. "I apologize for asking this question, but the minister insisted I do." Paul leaned forward.

"Are you with the CIA?" Both Paul and I let out our breaths, leaned back, and smiled. A simple question.

Paul said confidently, "No, we can assure you. And your question is normal for people who don't know us. Our legislation prohibits—and let me say again, *prohibits*—any interaction with intelligence agencies, including the CIA."

"I thought so. My minister will be pleased."

After chatting about Poland's history and hope for the future, we stood and shook hands again, ready to leave.

The deputy minister stood straight, cleared his throat, then seemed to hesitate. "Don't remember us Poles as you see us today. This is not who we are. We are better than this. You will see the real Poland when you return with Volunteers next summer."

Paul and I walked back down the hall, down the stairs, the red carpet, and to the car without exchanging a word.

"Do you think we can do this?" I then asked. "Peace Corps has never done it this fast since 1961. I'm worried."

"We promised. We will. I won't let Diem down." We completed our visit and left the following day for Manila, the Philippines. As we arrived at this island nation's airport twelve hours later, the announcement of Honecker leaving blared on the TV screens. East Germany was to cease as a country.

*

Eighteen months later, in June 1991, Paul and I returned to Poland to see the office, staff, and the new American Volunteers, the third group being sworn in. Just before our arrival, Ambassador Davis had sent a four-paragraph cable to the Department of State, which included the following message: "Quite simply, the Peace Corps operation has been the jewel in our crown, the cutting edge of the overall U.S. contribution to this country's progress toward an open society and an open economy.... The Peace Corps was here the firstest with the mostest. The programs have been specifically tailored to the development priorities, which we share with the authorities in the new Poland. The English-language teachers will help open a door not just to the Western civilization and culture from which Poland has been isolated these many years but to the world economy."

On this first day in Warsaw of our second trip, we sat in the large, well-furnished office of the Polish minister of education. Ambassador Davis, the Peace Corps country director for Poland, Deputy Minister Diem, and notetakers and interpreters joined us as we faced the minister with the flags and plaques of authority behind his desk. Sixty people had just completed their first year of service as education Volunteers, thirty business Volunteers had arrived six months earlier, and a new group had begun training near Warsaw.

The ambassador, the minister, and Paul exchanged pleasantries and talked briefly about Poland's progress in reframing educational subjects to match Poland's turn to the West and democracy. He began talking about English's importance to the country.

"Mr. Minister, Ambassador, Director Coverdell," the deputy minister said loudly, "may I have your attention?" As he called out, he waved both his hands and stood up, facing the group. The minister looked at him, surprised and silent. Deputy Minister Diem then walked across the room to a wall-sized map of Poland.

He said, standing proudly and pointing to the map, "Here is a new regional English training center. Here is one over here, and one here, and then another over here." He continued pointing to specific spots on the map until he had identified thirteen centers scattered throughout the country. "I am proud of these centers, only a few months old, and all are teaching English. This is happening because of the Peace Corps Volunteers serving in every center. They live with families, they share stories, they motivate our teachers, even after being here one year." The deputy minister then turned back to the group and pointed to Paul Coverdell.

"Do you remember eighteen months ago when you came to my small, windowless office?" Paul affirmed with his nod. "I was relatively new, I was fearful of what needed to be accomplished, I was afraid to ask for help. Paul, with your visit that late afternoon and your affirmation that together we could begin centers throughout the country, I felt hope for our future. Your commitment, your assuring words that day, gave me the courage I needed to establish these centers. We are celebrating here today because of your courage that day." He paused. "Thank you, Director Coverdell. Thank you." He then returned to his chair. The room remained silent. I looked at Paul, a man who always maintained an inscrutable face, and saw his tears. I felt mine. For the only time in our time working together, Paul couldn't find words.

Paul believed in what the Peace Corps could do, but during those early days, others of us did not. His courage to believe in the Peace Corps's response to this historical moment in eastern Europe changed countries and changed the Peace Corps. That moment strengthened my resolve to stretch beyond what could be possible, a drive I have drawn on for decades and, importantly, when I was Peace Corps director during the COVID-19 pandemic three decades later.

*

We returned from our visits to Hungary, Poland, and the Philippines to news of interest in the Peace Corps by three other nations in central and eastern Europe.

"We can't do all this work this fast," agency staff said to me quietly in stairways, hallways, and restrooms, but never in my office—too close to the director's. Some gripped my arm hard, showing aggravation.

"Paul wants this, but he's wrong. We don't belong in Europe. We're needed more elsewhere. Please make him understand. He trusts you." No one could know my personal feelings, cautiously accepting.

My answers, gently given, included, "I understand your fear of failing," "I know this looks political coming under President Bush," or "I also sense your fear Americans might see the Peace Corps as just another foreign policy boondoggle by the Republicans." These words represented my understanding of their feelings. Acknowledgment precedes change, even for me.

I described my growing passion for these new programs, drawing examples from our visits. "These are the words of the deputy minister,"

I said, describing in detail our meeting and the follow-up support. "The English teacher in Hungary excitedly told us of their needs, their hopes." With each telling, my belief strengthened. Peace Corps's legislated mission of "World Peace and Friendship" included Europe. Countries were finding their own way in 1989, 1990, 1991, and 1992 as the Soviet Union fell. American Volunteers had much to give, learn, and bring home.

"We will not pull a single Volunteer from any other country. I promise you," Paul said as he listened to what others said. "We honor our commitments, including on the African continent." He knew the agency's attitude, had heard from Congress and the press. With each negative word, his resolve grew to move quickly into these new countries.

May 29, 1990, a *Washington Post* op-ed piece by a Peace Corps staff member from the 1960s discussed what many former Volunteers and staff had said to me by phone, letter, and in RPCV gatherings: "The Peace Corps, which has arguably been the United States' best foreign policy initiative in the last half of this century, was ill served by ... recent decisions of Director Paul Coverdell, ... which betrayed that he and the Bush administration do not understand much about the genesis of the Peace Corps's political strategy abroad.... Peace Corps was conceived as a way for the idealism and skills of U.S. citizens to help countries with severe development needs."

Stories from my travels of why eastern European nations asked for the Peace Corps specifically were met with "You have given away your idealism for politics. You're selling out." Their words stung. Is it idealism, or is it protecting tradition, forged in the 1960s?

"We are maintaining the Peace Corps's three goals in these countries. Volunteers live with families in small communities, learn the language, share themselves, learn from their hosts, and bring their experiences home." Their angry words continued. Tradition dies hard.

"And Kennedy's goal says, 'To help the people of interested countries in meeting their need for trained men and women.' It says nothing about poor countries," I repeated.

"But," came the responses, "we must serve in poor countries; they need us more."

I fought with myself about past and future, about tradition and opportunity, and about enhancing or possibly destroying a global bright star of the Kennedy era. Paul saw enhancement. Others saw destruction.

Paul's decision would not change. I used RPCVs' own traditionalist words to cut through their anger.

I asked the question of others, "Should we judge the development value of a country that asks for Volunteers? Our mission is to respond to country requests, not our own judgment of who we think needs us." These words broke through my ambivalence. As a Volunteer, I didn't judge. Why should I now?

Over the next five years, Czechoslovakia (later the Czech Republic and Slovakia), Bulgaria, Romania, Albania, the three Baltic nations, the three Caucus nations, three of the five nations of central Asia, Ukraine, and Russia itself all requested Volunteers. For many of these countries, the Peace Corps's presence lasted less than ten years. For others such as Ukraine, Armenia, Georgia, Albania, Kyrgyzstan, the relationship lasts to this day.

To this initial group of countries over the decades has been added Bosnia, North Macedonia, Moldova, and Montenegro. Since 1990, Volunteers have served and returned to tell their Peace Corps stories, similar to those from other regions of the world. American and host-country staff have established and honored Peace Corps training and programming traditions, and senior officials have praised the organization and their own Volunteer teachers and community workers.

The prime minister of North Macedonia told me in 2019, "I worked with three community advisor Volunteers when a city mayor. I strengthened management skills and am still personal friends with them today."

As I write this, Ukraine is defending itself against the Russian invasion. The 3,500 Volunteers, having served over a twenty-eight-year period, have given Ukrainian families, schools, and communities strength in their own development and contributed to the intensity of the defense of their country, its language, and its own rich history and traditions.

\*

After our return from Hungary and Poland in the late fall of 1989, against the avalanche of criticism, Peace Corps Europe had to succeed. Paul outlined his directive: "Sixty Volunteers each in Hungary and Poland in June 1990." Forty years of Communist systems, lies about the United States, and Cold War nonfraternization policies that deepened fears of Western antisocial thinking challenged in-country decisions we made. We had systems for new country entries, but not in societies whose daily activities had been ordered by dictatorial leadership.

We had to find office space for thirty employees, hire host-country staff, meet U.S. legal management and banking standards, and do it in half the time. Paul's promise to Deputy Minister Diem in Poland pushed us harder through the skeptics.

"No banks, no wire transfers, no checking accounts," the agency's administrative officer, Janice, said matter-of-factly of the in-country fiscal situation.

"Okay, I'll carry fifty thousand dollars cash strapped to my body," John replied as he prepared an early visit.

"I didn't hear a word you said," Janice replied as cash appeared. We tried not to do that again. I'll never know.

Tim, the new Poland country director, called the first week in February to report on getting an office. "What is the guarantee that this lease will be honored as written?" he asked.

"I don't know," the agent said. "The office owner, whoever he is, can do what he wants."

"Doesn't Peace Corps have legal rights for what it pays for?" Tim asked.

"No" was the impassioned reply.

"Pay him and hope," I told Tim.

"Our new hires don't understand vacation and sick days," Tim said in a subsequent phone call. "They don't understand what an eight-hour workday is. They come to work, or they don't. Work does not relate to being paid." We changed that routine.

*

A year later, in an in-service training class in Warsaw, Polish business Volunteers described their experiences to me.

One Volunteer, an experienced business manager in the United States, said, "I just assumed the systems needed for businesses to succeed were part of every community. I never thought about deeds, taxes, zoning laws, county record offices. They all worked in the United States. I took them for granted."

The Volunteer continued, "We have no such system in my town.

For decades, the central government in Warsaw made the decisions. The mayor told me he only carried out the central party's wishes. Just this year, he got permission to make his own decisions. 'What do I do?' the mayor asked me."

The Volunteer said, smiling, "I have switched from small business to small town infrastructure building expert. The mayor and I work well together." He stopped a moment, thinking. "I didn't know this is what I would find here as a Volunteer. I know I'm making a difference to my town's future." He paused, smiled, opened his hands. "And I love it, every day."

*

Recruiting new Volunteers for this region of the world posed challenges. Our recruitment stories, public service announcement videos, brochures, created expectations for Africa, Asia, Central and South America. Volunteer hopes for future stories for their children included mud huts, students under baobab trees, wells, and animal carts. Small Soviet-style gray school buildings with Hungarian names drew less interest. This country was part of the Soviet anti-American sentiment. Should Americans believe our new Peace Corps ads?

Creating recruitment materials challenged us to create visuals of families, community centers, and classrooms that drew Americans into trusting this new and strange Peace Corps opportunity.

"What draws a person in? What makes a person want to commit to two years with a four-hundred-dollar-a-month stipend?" I challenged the communications team. Stories of personal connections across decades of political divide didn't photograph as well as thatched roofs and colorfully designed cloth. We included newer messages of community and school partnerships in our Peace Corps service messages, a subtle shift that became and remains central in recruitment messaging today.

With Paul's firm hand in the background, we pushed the agency forward.

"My grandmother will not let me go from where she escaped after her father and mother were killed," one college student said to me firmly. "But I wish I could go. Maybe I could bring peace to my family." More often, "I have encouragement to go back to the old country, to the language my mother barely remembers." The recruitment interest increased as the list of potential former Soviet countries grew.

"I don't care which country I go to, I want to learn more about the stories from this region, this time in history," one recruit wrote, which summarized the feelings we heard. New Volunteers didn't know the Peace Corps traditions.

For the difficulties of building new programs in a region Peace Corps knew little about, those joining had the faith and flexibility to adapt to unforeseen challenges, including our own preparation shortcomings. These new Volunteers learned to speak difficult languages untaught before by the Peace Corps while realizing, day by day, that their challenges as Volunteers were in overcoming differences between societies that had learned to hate each other and the other's way of life. Their experience challenged Volunteers as profoundly as the logistical limitations of other Peace Corps countries. Local project counterparts and families became welcoming in-country hosts to the strange Americans whom they had been told to hate.

*

Our official trips to Czechoslovakia, Bulgaria, and Romania in 1990 reflected similar stories of countries testing new freedoms of expression and governance wrapped in their own individual languages and cultures. Both Poland and Czechoslovakia had risen against the Soviet system, Poland through the nine-year antiauthoritarian social movement Solidarity, began in 1980, and the Czechoslovakian through the Velvet Revolution, began in November 1989. Václav Havel, the just-elected interim president and leader of the Velvet Revolution, spoke to the U.S. Congress in March 1990 and welcomed the Peace Corps to his country. Paul and I flew to Prague in late May for the signing of the Peace Corps agreement with the government of Czechoslovakia.

The city's lampposts, walls, fences still sported the tricolor signs of the revolution that had begun only six months earlier. The U.S. newspapers and television headlined these moments with pictures alongside the fall of the Berlin Wall in Germany.

"Do you think I could take one of these signs off the wall?" I asked Paul as I touched a symbol of citizen bravery loosely connected to a gray concrete wall.

"I suggest not," he said. "We are here as guests." Even today, I wish to have a piece of the sign to remind me of the energy on people's faces walking that day, in their smiles to each other, feeling free.

The ambassador, Shirley Temple Black, had partnered with the Foreign Ministry for a Peace Corps signing in the palace, the most elaborate signing venue seen in my six decades of Peace Corps service.

As we drove to the palace, Ambassador Black said to Paul, "President Havel told me it was only the United States that had kept the door open and given support and encouragement for his efforts to gain freedom for the country." She continued, "He honors this opportunity to bring in Americans to live side by side with families here as we strengthen our English-language programs."

Our country's agreement-signing counterpart, the foreign minister, talked about his years in Washington, DC, as a Czech journalist and then brought back home to be a boiler stoker. The Communist leaders feared his knowledge and language. As he told his story, he said, "The Communists pretended to pay us, and we pretended to work." A familiar story.

\*

Bulgaria, the eastern European country in the Soviet orbit since the beginning of the century, eagerly signaled its interest in the Peace Corps before its next-door neighbor, Romania. Paul and I traveled to Bulgaria's capital, Sofia, three times in eighteen months, watching it shed its Communist symbols. Our hotel faced the two-story statue of Lenin, standing at one end of the four-lane multiblock "Yellow Brick Road," as Bulgarians call it today, lined with massive columned buildings housing the Communist Central Party.

On our second visit to Sofia a few months later, Lenin had been smeared with red paint, and many hammer-and-sickle reliefs had been chiseled beyond recognition. For our third and final visit to Sofia in the summer of 1991, the partially demolished Lenin statue lay flat on the roadway, the Communist headquarters main office building down the bright-yellow road had been burned.

"No respect for the previous government," I said to Paul, eyeing the collective damage. "I can feel their anger as they chiseled out the hammer and sickle on the building's third-floor exterior."

During our three visits, we watched people walking on the nearby streets, waiting for buses, lining up for limited goods.

On the first trip, "I see no smiles," I said to Paul. "And their shoulders look heavy."

"You're right," he said after studying the faces of those jostling each other for a place on the nearby bus. "Their heads stay down. No eye contact. And they keep their arms close to their sides. I feel sad watching them."

We watched a different Sofia on our third trip. They wore similar clothes, got on the same buses, and continued to walk to nearby stores now filled with stacks of goods replacing empty shelves.

"They're smiling," Paul said, studying the crowds. "They appear to look at each other. Their heads turn to others, not away."

"And they talk. They use their hands, they move their bodies, they walk with lighter steps," I said.

Those we met in former Soviet countries during the first months of independence talked of a fear that drove decisions, actions, a painful contrast to my trusting people and daily routines taken for granted in the United States.

"I've been told what to do: just follow. Don't discuss. Don't think about what I'm told," one Bulgarian official said. "Would leaders punish me for making a decision, for talking to the wrong person? It's easier to follow silently." They talked about oppressiveness, the fear shown in the stooped shoulders of those silently walking on the streets.

*

The first Bulgarian Volunteer training program in the summer of 1991 brought Paul and me back for our third visit. Housed in a former Communist retreat house, Volunteers and staff shared their meals at carved oak tables with red velvet cushioned chairs. The opulence of the secret retreat centers, unknown to most Bulgarians and counter to Communist propaganda, contrasted dramatically with Peace Corps training sites around the world. The Peace Corps believed training centers should be in simple, minimally resourced settings and offer experiences similar to that of Volunteer communities where they served. With the Bulgarian Communist government now gone, this site had not yet found a new purpose. The government offered it free to the Peace Corps for the summer.

A grand chandelier lit the dining room, with its one-story rock fireplace and mantle.

"The Communists treated themselves well," I commented to Ambassador Sol Polansky.

He laughed and replied, "This is only one of many such opulent places." Ambassador Polansky had been a quiet figure to opposition leaders as they took early steps toward independence following the Hungarian and Polish leads.

"Thank you, Paul," he said, now facing the director who watched Volunteers bringing their plates of food to the table. "I promised these new leaders our government's support, and the Peace Corps came through. Look at these new Volunteers." He turned; watched them bring their plates of Shopska salad, Bulgarian kebab, and rice to the table; and with a smile, walked over and eagerly shook each Volunteer's hand.

*

Outside on the roadside near the training staff tent sat four Bulgarian-language teachers laughing as they wrote the next day's lessons in spiral notebooks.

"We seem to only keep a day ahead. Volunteers learn so quickly," one said as I introduced myself and sat beside them.

"You probably know that you're key to their success. I hope you're enjoying the Volunteers."

"Absolutely." More smiles.

After a few moments as they tried hopelessly to teach me new Bulgarian words, I asked, "How do you find working for the Peace Corps? Probably different for you. Americanisms might seem strange."

"We've never experienced this before. You all care about the work… the Volunteers… and us language teachers."

"What do you mean?"

"We were afraid of each other, of everyone." The other three instructors jumped in.

"I didn't trust anyone, did my work alone, kept it hidden. I knew someone would steal it."

"Peace Corps hired us from the teacher training school. We didn't know each other. Strangers." They moved their arms to punctuate words, heads high.

Another cut in, voice excited, "The training director told us we had to work together, 'Work as a team. You can do that.' 'No, I wouldn't,' I thought. 'Never.' The other teachers will tell me I'm wrong. Do me in."

Still another voice said, "The training director told us our contracts depended on working together. Teaching conversations depended on teams. He didn't understand our Bulgarian Communist culture."

Another, "We stared at each other, stayed silent, then reluctantly shared our names. We had a deadline to begin teaching, just a few days away, and couldn't keep staring fearfully at each other. We began, almost whispering, 'What are the first twenty words a Volunteer should know?' Suggestions. More words. A smile. More words. And look at us now, a month later."

"We're different people, friends. It feels good."

With the conversation and the laughter that morning, I had hope each day Bulgarians added more smiles and straighter shoulders.

*

Our trip to Romania in the fall of 1990 offered a different view of the results of absolute totalitarian leadership. Nicolae Ceaușescu had been the Communist Party leader since 1967, and his regime, with a growing cult of personality, became known as the most repressive of the Eastern Bloc. During his last years of power, he ordered rationing of food, water, oil, electricity, and even medicine. The First Lady, Elena Ceaușescu, had begun a program dictating the number of calories to be consumed depending on the worker's tasks. Under her edict, construction workers could eat a third more than teachers.

In the 1970s, Ceaușescu ordered the Romanian population to grow. He outlawed and rigidly enforced all abortion and contraception and publicly rewarded women with over five children. Women began abandoning children in the countryside, the orphans then housed in orphanages without proper food, clothing, or adult interaction.

After a national uprising began on December 22, 1989, Nicolae and Elena tried to flee but were held, tried for treason the morning of December 25, and executed later that day. Of the countries in the Eastern Bloc, only Romania ended its Communist rule violently.

We focused our first Peace Corps projects on orphanages, the children abandoned by families who couldn't feed them. The orphan tragedy had made international news, made worse by HIV breaking out among the children from unsterilized needles and unsafe blood, most of whom would die.

We entered an orphanage in Bucharest, a supposed showcase for visitors. Everywhere, there were white bare spaces with little furniture. Hallways stretched for blocks, visually broken by closed wooden doors disappearing in the hall's emptiness. A few children played in the corridors, a ball, a rope, a few blocks their only toys. I wanted to scream with the pain I felt for the children. They could not grow emotionally. They needed adults to touch, kiss, talk to, love.

The orphanage director walked us through hallways, dining halls, and a few rooms with cribs for young children, alone, no stimulation. These spaces brought back my memories as a four-year-old spending a week in a children's home filled with beds, no toys, and the hard, hot concrete outside. That experience lasted one week, and it still haunts me. These children might grow up here, scarred for life.

We returned to the main lobby, a large circular space devoid of furniture. The walls were white, plain: no photos, posters, color, stimulation. As a mother, I ached.

"Please excuse our empty walls," the orphanage director said as if reading my mind. He swept his arms around, pointing out the space. "We used to have lots of photos of our leaders covering the walls and rooms, but we took down the references the day after they were killed." He walked closer to us, lowering his voice. "Their regime finally ended, thankfully."

He continued to look at us, stood still as if talking to himself. "We don't know yet what to put on the walls. What if I choose wrong? Make a mistake?" He stepped back. No place to sit. "I can't get used to being able to choose." As he spoke, Paul and I looked around again and saw the walls with new meaning, with hope for the children. I pictured photos of the Ceaușescus glaring down into this sad space, devoid of love. These walls had now become a time-out, waiting for a different story to be told.

After a moment, the director continued, watching our eyes follow the whiteness down endless hallways, "These walls are like our minds. We have emptied the past decades of tyranny, trying to flush away the images." He tapped his fingers to his head. "But we don't know what to put in our minds. Who will we become? Our minds are now blank, sitting between a terrible past and an unknown future. We need you to help us know what to put in our minds."

Paul responded, as he had done country by country, "We won't let you down." And we didn't.

*

The six countries I visited between 1989 and 1991 felt heavy, sad, colorless. Buildings looked gray. Clothes appeared worn. Conversations were low, voiced with little emotion. Market shelves had few goods.

But the faces of those with whom we negotiated about Volunteers coming to their countries became animated as we talked of new curriculum, new languages, and travel to the West. The education officials practiced making decisions and sharing ideas without saying, "I'll have to go to my boss," the code for Communist control. Even as they talked, some hesitancy in sentences and pauses between ideas reflected the uncertainty of their new authority.

"I'm still not sure I can decide this," one official said. "I know I can because my old bosses are gone, but I still look behind me."

Today, I recall that time thirty-five years ago, the countries, the moments when Communist controls fell, and wonder the extent of influence Communist leaders had on the eighty million people under their ideological authority. My experience was only a moment in history as new national leaders threw off centralized, stifling, interconnected governments drawing orders from Moscow. They tested new Western-styled decentralized governments after forty-five years of forced control. Each country, save Romania, did it within weeks and without bloodshed. Each country we visited wanted our trust and our Volunteers, unthinkable before June 1989. My support for democratic principles, responding to the will of citizens, and trust in systems that support these ideas strengthened my political resolve after having personally seen the destruction of the human spirit and human life that tyrannies brought.

These experiences, thirty years before my own three years as Peace Corps director, stayed core to my beliefs and guided me through painful decisions brought under the Trump administration. I had seen fledgling democracies and would do my best to protect our own.

*

As Hungary, Poland, Czechoslovakia, Bulgaria, and Romania moved from Soviet Communism to new democracies in 1989 and early 1990, Albania, across the Adriatic Sea from Italy, clung to its strict Communist regime under the iron hand of Communist dictator Enver Hoxha and then, after 1985, Ramiz Tafe Alia. Alia seemed secure, and Albania remained a nameless space on the Peace Corps European map, impenetrable to change even as its regional neighbors moved toward internal decentralization. Alia tried to reform while maintaining power but failed and, on April 30, 1992, resigned. Albanians could now emerge from forty years of hermetic living. Chris Hill, an RPCV and the new chargé d'affaires, invited Paul to visit Albania to explore a Peace Corps program.

Albania had no cars, and the new U.S. embassy staff comprised two people working in a room on the third floor of Tirana's only hotel. Chargé Hill had said we had to negotiate our own logistics. He had no staff. Thus, Michael, training officer in Peace Corps Poland, came the 750 miles to Tirana to set up meetings for Paul and me, find an interpreter, and be ready to greet us at the airport. Hours before we left Washington, he cabled us, "You will be welcome here."

The Albanian embassy representative in Washington, DC, had never issued visas to Americans, as we were not allowed in Albania. Now the new Albania was less than a month old.

"You don't need visas," he said. "We now want Americans to come to our country and will make it easy to do so." The blank visa pages in our passports made me nervous.

"Okay. I'll take your word," I said.

"Good luck. I hope you travel safely," the representative said and then hung up.

Within a week, Paul and I sat in the Rome airport at noon, waiting for our one-hour Romanian airline flight to Tirana, Albania. Just before boarding, I heard an announcement: "Mrs. Olsen, please check with the gate agent."

"I bet they're giving us an upgrade. They probably looked at our hectic travel schedule and wanted to be kind," I said to Paul as I rose from the seat. Always the optimist. I walked through the crowd to the agent, screening passengers.

"You can't get on the flight. You don't have a visa," the agent said bluntly. This large, unsmiling man in a blue uniform gave me the news with a firm voice that defied contrary points of view.

"We have to be in Albania. We're meeting with the prime minister." I spoke out, stunned at the news. "We must be on that plane. We must." I lost professional decorum as my voice grew louder.

The agent remained unmoved. "You cannot get on the plane without a visa," he repeated in his same firm voice. My anger rose with my fear of not getting on the plane.

"We *must* get on the plane!" I shouted. The agent had planted his feet, stared, and did not move. Panic and helplessness.

Directly behind me, another American screamed at the agent, "I will get on this flight. You can't stop me." The agent remained unmoved.

"Last week we let an American on the Tirana flight without a visa, and the Albanian authorities sent him back at the Romanian airline's expense. I will not let that happen again. You cannot get on the flight. Period."

We both stood staring at the agent, a new silent friendship emerging between us, this slightly older American in a business suit and me. The agent called the others to board. He lost interest in us. Paul stayed sitting in his chair, waving to me, thinking we were fine. I had no guts to tell the truth. I was responsible for getting us on the plane.

The American told me he was a Serbian-Albanian-American businessman, fluent in Albanian and Italian. "I *will* get on this plane," he said to me forcefully. He turned to the Romanian airline agent. "What if I call the Albanian ambassador to Italy here in Rome and get his permission to get on the plane? Will that do?"

The agent hesitated. "I need to talk to the ambassador myself and hear his words before I let you on. I know that won't happen."

"I can call the ambassador, describe the situation to him in Albanian, and then let you speak to him in Italian. Does that work?" my new friend asked.

"Okay. But I bet he isn't in his office. This is the noon hour," the agent said, turning back to his announcements. My business friend turned to me, winked, and walked purposefully down the hall looking for a pay phone, hoping to find one within the sight of the agent. I shadowed him, only a foot behind and with the same determined stride. Strange. Peace Corps's Albanian future was in this Serbian-Albanian-American businessman's hands.

Luck changed. He found an Italian pay phone, a Roman telephone book, the listing for the Albanian embassy, and the voice of the ambassador after dialing the listed number. The first heated and then calm conversation in Albanian commenced.

"Go get the agent. The ambassador will speak to him in Italian." I ran, bumping into people, until face-to-face, breathless, in front of the agent.

Ten minutes later, Paul, the good Samaritan businessman, and I took our seats, ready for takeoff. I sweated and breathed hard. Paul smiled and only said, "That was close."

*

As our plane taxied to the tin-roofed airport, we saw Michael waving both arms high above his head in front of the car with its Peace Corps sticker written in Polish. He had maneuvered the car to the edge of the tarmac, ready to scoop us up and into vehicle-free Tirana. I waved back.

As the plane came to rest, four uniformed soldiers holding rifles pointing down stood at the bottom of the plane's stairway.

"Everyone stay seated while the soldiers come aboard. They need to check papers before anyone leaves the plane."

"They look frightening," I said to Paul as I played out scenarios in my head about what might happen. Nothing good. They strode up the stairs and into the center aisle, pointing guns at the passengers and demanding to see passports. Sitting at the rear, I hoped they would be tired of their tasks before getting to us. Mike kept waving, only yards from the plane, but with uniforms, guns, and passports without visas between us. The soldiers crept through the cabin, studying every document, never speaking or smiling. One soldier took our two passports, Paul's being diplomatic, and pointed guns at us. This soldier passed them to another soldier, who studied the dozen visas and stamps from previous travel. He looked at the word *diplomat*, handed them back, and nudged his gun with the gesture that we could go.

Jumping up before the soldier could change his mind, I turned to Paul. "Is Albania ready for us?"

He always appeared calm and assumed I would solve whatever problem presented itself. He got up and smiled. "Let's get started."

Driving into the city on an empty road, we confirmed the rumor about no cars. As we pulled up to Tirana's only hotel, four shiny red pocket-sized cars lined up in front of the modest doorway, having been delivered two days earlier, the first private-use cars for the city and probably the country.

Michael escorted us up three steps into the five-story gray hotel, torn drapes over the windows in the small lobby, all rooms in desperate need of paint. Businessmen crammed into the lobby, shouting into bricklike phones wired to their briefcases. They sat on tippy metal chairs, balancing papers on their knees and struggling to write as they shouted into the phones.

"The country opened for business a week ago. Businessmen from all over Europe responded, each trying to outdo others with a contract for banks, cars, and restaurants. It's a free-for-all," Michael said as we moved to the check-in desk.

We climbed the stairs and walked down the dimly lit, gray hallway to our rooms on the third floor. We passed room 302, the USAID office; 303, the residence of the U.S. embassy's top official; 304, the embassy office, each a converted bedroom. Our two rooms were farther down the worn, carpeted path. U.S. diplomacy had arrived in Albania two weeks earlier.

"I eat C rations dropped off by American troops returning from the Gulf War. Food is unavailable to buy," Hill said as he welcomed us to the converted bedroom, now serving as an embassy.

That night, we looked out our windows into the town square. Families filled the brightly lit tree-lined park and strolled idly around the avenues enclosing the central space. They looked happy, laughing as kids ran through their legs and onto the grass and talking as they walked. They carried no bags or purses, and children had no bikes or scooters. No vendors sold food or trinkets. No cars or motorcycles competed for space. They had the warm spring evening, conversations, and the center promenade for walking, a Tirana tradition.

The next morning, our interpreter said, "We buy and sell nothing. Even glass is unobtainable. Our windows are random sizes of broken glass pieces."

*

Former president Alia's compound on the edge of Tirana had opened to the public a week earlier. During his dictatorship, he told the nation he lived as they did: sparse surroundings, rationed commodities, limited transportation. Yet his and his family's residences were walled off from public view. The nation had to trust his word.

With the compound now open, curiosity about the truth brought Tirana city residents to the residences, having walked substantial distances to view the houses. The crowded double line snaked along the house and garden pathways, looking at the truth behind Alia's words. We walked with them, blending into the files of people, watching their faces. Alia had lied. The crowd gasped as the well-kept homes stretched before them, revealing his celebration of good living and disdain for them.

To me, the compound looked like a traditional upper-middle-income housing complex in the United States: sturdy two-story brick, multibed-room houses surrounded by tall trees, well-kept grass, and flowers in bloom. However, to those walking through the grounds, living in two-room walk-up apartments without amenities and having to accept gov-ernment rations, this represented what they had been denied in order to create a perfect socialist state.

The image of the faces at the moment a society discovers its leader lied to them angers me these years later. Democracy depends on truth. Always.

*

We met with the new ministers of foreign affairs and education, the for-mer appearing uncomfortable in his new role and his new suit. He looked to be in his thirties, small, his coat sleeves extending over his hands and his suit trouser cuffs hiding his shoes.

"I've been minister for two weeks, and I'm not sure what to do." He stared at us like a child discovering a new toy. "I don't know what I should ask for," he said, following our introductions and pleasantries about the beauty of Albania. "We need everything. What can you give to us?" he blurted out, arms moving faster.

The minister of education, who had served under the previous regime, expressed eagerness to bring English into the schools and Albania closer to the West.

"Albania should be part of Europe, and English will help. Alia did not allow English in the country, a result of his fear of losing power. The Volunteers can help us with the language we need." We talked further, then stood up to shake hands and say farewell.

The minister paused. "Maybe you don't realize, but we have to destroy all our textbooks. They are full of lies. They praise a rule, a society, based on fraud. Can you help us get all-new books with new ideas?" We stopped, stunned.

"All books?" Paul asked with disbelief.

"All books," the minister repeated. Paul referred the minister to USAID.

"We can teach and will use whatever you give us."

*

Nine months after our visit, the Albanian foreign minister with whom we met strode into my office in Washington, hand out in greeting. "Good to see you again," he said with confidence, using his heavily accented English. He looked healthy, having gained a few additional pounds, and his new suit fit perfectly. An hour later, in Director Coverdell's office, the Albanian foreign minister and Paul signed the Albanian country agreement. Peace Corps Volunteers could begin.

In 2019, Albania celebrated twenty-seven years of Peace Corps with a bell-ringing ceremony for the thirty-five Volunteers completing two years of service and for a newly arrived Volunteer group. Over eight hundred Volunteers had served. As Peace Corps director, my arrival for the ceremony included a crowded highway from the new airport to the fifteen-room Peace Corps office in Tirana, a city filled with buses, traffic jams, commercial businesses, restaurants, and a dozen skyscrapers. The hotel from my visit in 1992 was enclosed by a barbed wire fence and hidden by tall weeds, awaiting its next life. Several first-class hotels had replaced it. The city square still hosted walkers, now with strollers, bikes, and backpacks.

The Peace Corps staff laughed at my descriptions of my 1992 visit. "It's not possible," the younger staff members said. Older staff said, "Yes, it is. We've come a long way."

*

My time as chief of staff, from 1989 to 1992, offered a plethora of additional adventures, in part because outcomes from the Soviet Union breakup rippled throughout the world.

We were among the first international organizations invited into Namibia, Southern Africa, as it obtained independence from South Africa in March 1990. Paul and I met the new and popularly elected president, Sam Nujoma, in his palace, a sprawling two-story house with a yard and a white fence, not unlike many U.S. homes.

"The president has little protection," Paul said as we accompanied the ambassador to the meeting. "I see only a few guards or soldiers. He seems to respect the Namibian people after three decades of his being a rebel and fighter trying to gain freedom for his country."

We returned over a year later and met with the minister of education to get a perspective on the new Peace Corps education program.

After we introduced ourselves in his modest ministerial office, I asked casually, "Have you seen any impact from the work of the Volunteers? They've now been teaching and living here almost a year." He thought for a moment.

I continued, "Are they meeting your expectations as you adapt the national English program?" I thought of them introducing new teaching techniques or helping rewrite curriculum components. These were skilled education Volunteers.

He smiled and then responded. His answer stunned me.

"Yes, I see a difference, but not the one I expected." He reached over his desk for a local language book prepared by the Peace Corps and held it up proudly. "Your Volunteers came here to teach with us. To do so, they learned our tribal languages, even though difficult. They speak these local languages with their counterparts, with host families, and in the community." I waited, wondering what difference that made. He continued, "We had never seen white people speak our languages before. By learning our languages, you give us dignity and respect. You honor us. This is the best gift you can give."

Our lives, our skills, our interactions depend on mutual respect. His answer reminded me why Volunteers share themselves as much as they share their skills.

\*

January 13, 1991, our regional manager got a call from the White House National Security Council (NSC) with the terse words, "Get the Volunteers out of Morocco, Tunisia, Yemen, Mauritania, Tanzania, and Pakistan within forty-eight hours. You have no appeal. Just do it." This had not happened before in the Peace Corps. We had our own authority to make these decisions, and the NSC had never challenged that authority.

With anger, I called Paul in Atlanta, repeating the order. "They can't do that. We make our own decisions."

Paul took a moment before responding, "I will double-check these orders, but I think I know why. Set up evacuation procedures." He couldn't say more.

We set up a twenty-four-hour hotline for each of the six countries. The country directors tracked down by phone and cabled over five hundred Volunteers—not only those in the individual countries but also those vacationing in Algeria, Israel, Egypt, Syria, Nepal, India, and Sri Lanka.

Our travel team begged airlines to give us emergency tickets from over a dozen countries to Europe and then the United States. Angry words at having to leave sites, families, work, with no explanation why, flooded to our frustrated staff trying to manage this evacuation from Washington, DC, and the affected capital cities.

I couldn't express unhappiness with the decision to anyone, just held it deep inside. My words during those forty-eight hours were "We have to trust the White House, no other choice." Without sleep, I worked the phones and wrote cables helping others find flights, lost Volunteers, personal items left at site, and gathering places for end-of-service debriefs for each country. Miserable. Volunteer safety came ahead of our feelings about a decision we didn't understand.

Seventy-two hours later, the answer came: the U.S. military led a coalition air and ground war against Iraq and its military incursion into Kuwait. The NSC feared that once the United States attacked Iraq, that country or its neighbors could push back against our programs in Muslim countries. It didn't happen, which made the evacuation decision and the lives disrupted seem purposeless. But we didn't know and couldn't risk it. The war ended in less than a month, and the six countries invited us back. Half of the Volunteers returned to their sites.

To say thank you to the six nations for trusting our leaving and return, Paul and I traveled to Pakistan, Yemen, Tunisia, and Morocco in four days from wheels up to wheels down. Paul said as I rushed to get tickets and appointments, "We abruptly left. We had no given reason. We disrupted schools, health clinics, children's centers. But they welcomed us back. I must thank them for their belief in us, quickly."

We only slept on airplanes, no hotel rooms. We showered and changed clothes in the ambassadors' residences.

"You're crazy to do this without sleep. I wouldn't do it," said three ambassadors.

"Why not?" Paul replied. Paul never slowed down. Sleep wasted time.

Prime Minister Azzeddine Laraki of Morocco greeted us in his palace, the last of our four thank-you visits. He talked warmly about the Peace Corps's history in Morocco, almost back to 1961, and commented that the Volunteers were always welcome. He said toward the end of our short meeting, "I know the three goals of the Peace Corps and have seen hundreds of Volunteers." He then recited them perfectly and smiled.

\*

Paul resigned the directorship in September 1991 to run for the U.S. Senate from Georgia. Elaine Chao became director, and I continued as her chief of staff until the administration changed from President Bush to President Clinton a year later. She successfully furthered the work begun in 1989 to bring the Peace Corps to the Caucasus, Baltic nations, Ukraine, and even China.

Paul won the election and successfully served as U.S. senator from Georgia for eight years, rapidly rising in the leadership ranks until, tragically, a stroke took his life at age sixty-one. The Senate could be different today if he had lived.

\*

All my professional work since that time of global realignment, nationhood reawakening, and renewed respect for individual dignity has drawn on the profound experiences shown me by those with the courage to fight for these beliefs. I've needed and used their stories. The United States needs their stories now.

## PART FIVE

# *Falling Apart*

# 12

# I Knew before You Told Me
## 1992–94

While celebrating Peace Corps's global new frontiers as chief of staff, my marriage descended toward dissolution with denial, then bewilderment, anger, and finally, a judge's gavel. With it, my active church membership ended.

For our twenty-year wedding anniversary, Bob and I celebrated at La Ferme Restaurant, Chevy Chase, Maryland. We laughed as we looked back on our lives together: walking on Tunisian beaches late at night; playing bridge in Luxembourg Gardens, Paris, with the kids for six hours; or driving as a family across the country, playing word games. As we celebrated that evening, the marriage looked good.

Often on Saturday evenings, both in Baltimore and Washington houses, Bob and I enjoyed dinners with other couples and friends around the square solid oak dining room table. David and Kirsten came in and out, hovering when conversations turned to politics. We discussed mortgage rates and commuting routes while Bob and I leaned gently toward each other with our eyes reflecting burning candles on the table center. We conversed easily and touched hands to show comfort with each other.

My social work training sensitized my interest over the years in news stories and movies about couples slipping apart. Friends knew of my listening intently to others whose marriages were crumbling, their eyes filled with tears, their hands limp. Details of hurts, wrong moves, bad decisions, and emotional wreckage were observable. Understanding others didn't remove blindness to changes in my own marriage. After twenty years of leaning inward, our bodies, our minds, touched less. We used fewer words at the dinner table, and after getting David off to college, Bob retreated further into himself, speaking and smiling less.

Years later, to others, "I didn't recognize our marriage's deterioration. Too busy at work." I had passed over small phrases in my conversations with Bob that invited a deeper discussion, left them ignored, until one day seven years after our La Ferme dinner, reality exploded in my face.

*

During the decade following our return from Togo, my mind focused on the Peace Corps: two-week-long travel schedules, half-day visits to remote Volunteer sites, new staff hires, reciting new Volunteer stories. Bob added long overseas assignments to his international development consulting portfolio: several months in Nepal, almost two years in Jamaica, a year in Sri Lanka. As teenagers, David and Kirsten watched us trade suitcases in the hallway. My brother Stephen willingly became a part-time substitute parent. During these years, friends asked, "How can you spend so much time apart? Don't you miss Bob?" My response: "Yes, I do. But we make it work."

In June 1984, just as I finished my Peace Corps regional directorship, the hot summer sun beat against the Peace Corps headquarters entrance as I stood in front facing Lafayette Park and the White House. Bill Hanson, my friend from Togo, was saying goodbye before returning to San Francisco. Like in Togo, Bill made me laugh with his raunchy and gossipy stories told with movements of a trained actor. He captivated me with his impolite words, stating truths I dared not say.

While walking away from the building, he tossed back the words, "Why don't you and Bob come and stay a few days on my farm?" He paused. "But don't come together." He disappeared behind the next building. Gone.

What did he mean? The phrase disappeared as work took over. Bill never said what he meant. In Togo, Bob gave Bill decoration advice for his house that hot Lomé afternoon. Their thinking, their actions meshed, a simple friendship.

*

A year later, Bob read *Goodbye, I Love You,* by Carol Lynn Pearson, a well-known and respected Church of Jesus Christ of Latter-day Saints author. He handed me the book and said, "I think you'll enjoy it."

Idly, I picked it up wondering why Bob suggested it. He didn't read many books for pleasure.

Pearson had written about her marriage, children, and husband, Gerald. She wrote about his coming out, their divorce, and her caring for him as he died of AIDS. They wrestled with the church as a gay man and his wife, trying to take part in the church's evergreen (gay-to-straight) program, his life as a gay man in San Francisco, and then contracting AIDS. How could he keep going to church, keep trying to be straight and stay married? How could Carol, after the divorce, take him back into her San Francisco home and nurse him lovingly until he died? What a caring person. Bob and I didn't talk about the book.

\*

We continued to manage work travel schedules, the kids, and the house, as our conversations lost the caring couples' need to hold together. We had fewer dinners with friends and with each other. Bob withdrew from events. His slow responses signaled depression. Rather than asking him what might be wrong, I remained silent. I didn't want to know.

My return to the Peace Corps as chief of staff forced me to focus more on work and travel and less on the home. Director Coverdell demanded full attention. His calm and even pace belied the actual speed of his movements. Luckily, both kids had left for college, David at the University of Michigan and Kirsten at BYU.

One September evening, a month before my first eastern European trip, I sat at the round white kitchen table, given to us as a wedding present twenty-five years earlier. This evening, Bob had come home early, leaving his slim black leather briefcase on the table. A plain brown paper bag with a paperback book inside poked out from the unzipped opening.

I held the phone receiver in my left hand, listening to my sister Christine. My right hand absently twirled the six-foot-long twisted white phone cord that stretched from the phone anchored on the wall across the room. Without thought, my hand dropped the chord and idly moved to the case and then to the paper bag.

"What did Lizzy say to you yesterday?" I had just asked my sister, focusing on the usual family stories. The bag and its contents lay inert on the table, oblivious to the conversation.

With my absent-minded touch, the book slipped out of the paper bag, the back cover visible: white, without graphics, and print too small to read. Still listening to Christine's story, I turned the book over and read the title, *Gay Husbands and Straight Wives.*

Christine's voice became faint, her words about Lizzy sticking together, crushing each other. My brain reached for conversation with Christine as it lurched back to the book's title. Say nothing. Sound normal. My voice squeaked, my body hot, then cold, then numb. Make the title go away.

The call ended quickly. "I have something on the stove," I said, lying, then gave the words "Talk soon." My fingers moved the book back to its brown wrapping and then into the open briefcase.

The thought "No one can know about this title" started screaming inside me, body motionless, limp. My hand, shaking, pushed the briefcase to the edge of the table. The book didn't exist, title didn't exist, problem didn't exist. "Make it go away," I screamed silently. Who is Bob, really?

After breathing deeply, eyes closed, my brain began rationalizing and planning. This emergency would disappear now. Denial. Think of work. Don't think of Bob.

The book sat in its paper bag, the bag sat in the case, the case sat on the table. No second glance at the front cover or pages inside. The chair grated along the floor as I stood. Moment over.

"Who is Bob?" still rattled in my head. "Just work harder," I told myself. "Don't let these questions interfere with being chief of staff: traveling, discovering, creating."

Rationalization is efficient until it crumbles with truth. Over the months, Bob's innuendos about outside meetings and nuances of conversations with other men forced back the vision of the book, forced back Bill's comment. More denial.

\*

Bob began attending a Friday evening male group counseling program. "I'll be at the St. Mary's Episcopal Church on Q Street." He declined further information but appeared relieved with the counseling. As Friday evenings passed, his stories returned, and his shoulders straightened. He walked taller.

"Ah ha," I thought, "the group counseling is working."

\*

Later that year, three friends from his counseling group joined Bob's fiftieth birthday celebration. In our living room, among the forty guests, these men did not mingle but stayed in their familiar group, animating points with sweeping gestures and laughter. Bob spent party time sitting with them, joking, the rest of the party largely forgotten.

\*

A month later, Andrew, one of the party trio, came to dinner asking to talk to me, his wife dying of cancer. He cried and grieved for the impending loss of someone he deeply loved.

Then Andrew went into the kitchen to help Bob prepare dinner. They nudged, smiled, and completed sentences as only those who are intimate do. My fear of knowing returned. Crush it.

That evening, we meticulously timed our household movement to avoid each other. I wanted what I feared to go away.

\*

Bob and I went to Madison, Wisconsin, in October 1991 to spend a weekend with David. He had graduated four months earlier with perfect grades from Michigan and now had a full scholarship for a computer science master's degree at the University of Wisconsin.

Paul had resigned the Peace Corps directorship the preceding Thursday to run for the U.S. Senate in Georgia, and the new Peace Corps director, Elaine Chao, wouldn't begin until the following week. I had a weekend with few work responsibilities.

Our planned Saturday schedule in Madison included a morning looking at the AIDS quilt exhibit filling Wisconsin's indoor football field, a walk to the state capitol a few blocks away, and theater attendance for the fall play *Kiss of the Spider Woman* by Manuel Puig.

On the thousands of colorful squares stitched together to create the AIDS quilt spread throughout the football field were stories of those who had died of AIDS. Families and friends had lovingly sewn into the one-yard squares illustrations of those lost. Photos, poems, songs, favorite foods, travels, and close companion stories brought to life those who had died and gave comfort to those preparing visual tributes. The vista of these squares, with their vibrant lines and shades of color filling the immense football space and of students slowly threading their way around the squares on the grass field, were both overwhelmingly sad and joyous—joy in celebrating the fullness of lives and sadness in lives shortened.

"Could my life, if twice as long, be half as full?" I asked David as we picked our path carefully, reading each square, learning of moments of lives lost to AIDS. We found the square for Carol Pearson's husband, Gerald. In one photo, he led the San Francisco Gay Men's Chorus, his face radiant.

The two of us absorbed the moments of each life, now gone: music, art, dance, travel, food, family. A collective image of the men represented in the squares took hold in my psyche. They might have been Bob.

From the field house, we walked toward the state capitol, the sidewalk lined with older men playing guitars, singing, and sporting long hair and dyed T-shirts. The 1960s had returned.

Unbeknown to us, this day and hour, gay rights advocates marched on the same street to the Capitol for speeches and slogans supporting gay-friendly state legislation. The three of us, with only the intention of admiring the Capitol's massive physical presence in a small college town, became part of a gay march of hundreds.

Bob stared at the marchers. He stayed close to David and me as we maneuvered to the side to make our way to the Capitol. As we crossed an intersection, Bob's body turned back toward the marchers, took a step, then turned to us.

We admired the Capitol's architectural features as we walked around the building, then back to the site of the gay rights gathering and its speaker, mic in hand, yelling into the crowd. Bob moved toward the speaker, leaning forward to hear.

"Let's head back," I said, not listening to the speaker. Near the campus, several pink triangles decorated the front window of a pastry shop.

"Do you know why they're pasted on the window?" I asked Bob and David.

Quickly, too quickly, Bob replied, "Hitler ordered gay Germans to wear the upside-down pink triangle, the marker identifying wearers as being deviant."

"Why are they on the windows now?" I asked, wondering how he knew.

"Gay people are embracing the symbol as one of pride," Bob replied.

*

The movie *Kiss of the Spider Woman* had tantalized me when it came out six years earlier. It earned its star, William Hurt, an Oscar. He played a homosexual (Molena) sharing a Latin American jail cell with a Marxist revolutionary (Valentin). In the cell, he told Valentin stories from movies he had seen using his body to create atmosphere for the stories. The beauty of Molena's body movements, stretching his arms and legs loosely intertwined with bright, billowy scarves, stayed imprinted on my brain. Bob had never seen the movie.

That evening in Madison, the university version of the play didn't have the same mesmerizing effect on me. But from our seats in the theater's front row, the power of the actor's sweaty body movements and tortured face showed the power of a gay man's fears. Bob remained fixated on Molena. Afterward, we told David goodnight without discussing the play.

\*

Bright sunlight through the high hotel windows gave a good beginning to the Sunday morning, our third day in Madison. I had exchanged the tiring day before with energy from a good night's sleep. We planned to meet David in an hour for breakfast before beginning our return to Washington.

Bob sat on a chair against the room's far window, looking at me as I awoke. When he saw me move, he rose, walked across the room, sat on the side of the bed, and said simply, "I'm gay."

There, he said the words. My memory of the moment is blocked. These two words still pull at my insides over thirty years later. Numb, hurt, rigid, silent. He sat still, no more words. I sat in the bed trying to make his words real.

"I wanted to tell you two years ago, but you were too busy being chief of staff. You didn't want to know." He was right. I was afraid to ask so buried myself further in work and in denial.

\*

Awareness is multilayered, and each layer has its own reaction. My awareness had grown over the years, unconsciously observing. But knowing without words differs from knowing with words. Words dashed denial, replaced by slow, controlled, unrecognized anger.

A false facade of normalcy covered my intensifying seething. What was to happen next? He's ruining my life. He had shared his secret, put me in the closet, and didn't talk further. Done. We would continue the lie of being a normal couple, my anger growing at his silent assumption that little should change.

We had breakfast with David, pretending to be happy. We visited a friend in the hospital later that day, smiled, chatted about the operation and our ordinary trip to Madison.

At work the next day, I pretended to be the same person who left the office the Friday before. Elaine Chao began as Peace Corps director and needed a chief of staff she could rely on, learn from, lean into. She had my faith in her, in the agency, and in my professionalism. No one would see weakness. No one would know about Bob.

Introverts process information internally, deliberately, organizing knowledge into actionable pieces before speaking. But introverts have emotions. Bob continued his routine, household conversations with me, preparation for a ten-month assignment in Sri Lanka, evenings celebrating with his other life, which he no longer needed to hide from me. David and Kirsten, both away, remained oblivious. When they returned for Christmas, Bob agreed to tell each personally. Until then, no words to anyone. We both hid in the family closet. My anger at him, the situation, and my being blind to knowing grew.

*

How did this happen? How could we be together for twenty-eight years, raise a family, oblivious to Bob's sexual identity? What was missed, denied?

During the fall, my mind tried to see the situation as a social science researcher might, as no action could be taken until the holidays. While waiting, I asked three gay colleagues to tell me their stories individually over dinner.

"Michael, I'll treat you to dinner. I'll tell you why over Legal Sea Foods' clam chowder."

"Their homemade rolls are even better. You're on."

As we sat at the restaurant table, napkins neatly in our laps and menus in front of us, I began, "Bob's gay. He told me three weeks ago."

"I know," Michael said. "I've known for at least a year." My stomach pitched.

I tried to hide my surprise. "You knew and said nothing. We work together. Why?" I took a breath and told myself to calm down.

"Sorry, Michael. Didn't mean to snap at you. I'm just surprised my friends knew before me. Am I the last to know?" I stopped, took a breath, looked at the menu without seeing the choices. "This makes me feel foolish," keeping my voice normal. Breathe. Breathe. "We don't see what we don't want to see," more to myself than to Michael.

He stopped, briefly squeezed my hand, and continued, "I couldn't tell you. You're my big boss." He smiled. "And it's Bob's responsibility. My telling you would have made it worse." He paused. "He's the one to say who he is. I can't." He spoke the truth.

Michael shared his story. "I knew I was different. No words. No one to reach out to. Went to the Peace Corps to get away. Found my feelings. Discovered. Lucky I figured it out before getting married."

Many of Bob's words about his own discovery mirrored Michael's but over more years. Bob's deep belief in the church and its expectations about marriage, children, the celestial kingdom in the hereafter, family, and community expectations all suppressed his admitting to himself his reality. Knowing this didn't help my new reality.

As we finished eating, Michael made an offer. "The Lambda Rising bookstore just off Dupont Circle has books by women about leaving gay husbands. I can get a couple for you."

"Can you?" I replied. "I'm afraid to go in the store, even though I walk by it regularly."

"That's why I offered. People look at who goes in and out and then make judgments. I'm keeping you safe."

A plain brown bag appeared on my desk the next day with two books. After reading a couple of chapters, I stopped. The women writing were not me. They talked about losing their purpose when their husbands came out, and then depression, heavy drinking, weight gain. They didn't know how to fight back, as it wasn't another woman but a man. Their husbands rejected their femininity, their identity. Unlike these women's experiences, my career had helped define me, not needing to lean on my husband for definition. I would face losing Bob still knowing who I was.

*

My two other dinners had similar themes of gay men's denial of self and final discovery. Tony confessed he had even taunted, ridiculed a gay Volunteer when he was Peace Corps country director. "My own religious beliefs made me hate him. I was older, had authority over him. I abused that authority to take out my self-hate on him, as I knew I wouldn't see him again." As he spoke, Tony wiped tears with the back of his hand, put his fork down, sat silent for a moment. He struggled to continue. "I knew what I was doing to that Volunteer." He picked up his fork, then put it down again.

"Five years later," he began again, slowly, still tearful. "I was at a gay bar here in DC, still not out to friends and colleagues but secretly testing who I was." He waited quietly another moment. "I saw on the stool at the far end of the bar the Volunteer I had taunted. Our eyes locked. He knew it was me." I watched Tony's face.

"I walked toward him, slowly, composing what I would say. Then quietly, I said, 'I'm sorry for what I did to you. I took myself out on you.'"

*

Each of my three dinner guests began their stories when they were teenagers. Each involved denial, self-misunderstanding, homophobia, trying to be "straight," and finally speaking truthfully, regardless of risk. These stories gave insight into Bob's self-journey. He knew he would risk everything, including his family, to come out, suppressing his inevitability for two decades.

In the fall, he told me, "If I didn't face the truth, I knew I would die." From these three friends who spoke so directly about their own experiences, I understood Bob's words.

In November, Bill Hanson came back to DC for a couple of days. He had dropped the first hint about Bob eight years earlier, in front of the Peace Corps office.

"The boy finally came out?" he said, sipping a glass of wine in the sunroom of my house, floor-to-ceiling windows. We sat across from each other, with a backdrop of lighted trees in the backyard reaching into the park. "I knew it before he did. Surprising, isn't it?" He continued, "We have radar. We know. We just wait for them to figure it out. I knew he would. I watched him sink into sadness, a year at a time."

My head dropped, shoulders crumbling. "I know it's not his fault, but I'm so mad at him. I'm mad at everyone who knew and didn't tell me."

"You didn't listen. You didn't want to know."

"I now have to do something about it, and Bob isn't helping. He wants us to go on as usual, hiding. Why doesn't he help?"

"He doesn't want to lose you."

"He already has."

*

I told three close friends.

"We knew," each said. Deedie added, "We asked each other, 'Should we tell her?' and decided not to. We couldn't understand why you didn't figure it out. But telling was not our right." That comment made me want to turn on my friends to hide my own rage.

Deedie said later, "When I walked into your living room for Bob's fiftieth birthday and saw the men sitting together with Bob, I knew Bob was gay. His body moved like that of my brother." She stopped for a minute, seeing how her words affected me. "Didn't you see it? So obvious." I was so smart and so, so, so stupid.

*

David and Kirsten came home for Christmas. Bob agreed to tell them individually after the Christmas Day celebrations. "I'm scared," he said.

"You have to. Not me," I said, getting angry. "You created this. I'm not gay; you are."

Bob told David, the person I thought would take it hard. Later that day, Bob said, "He shrugged and said, 'Okay.' I asked him if he still wanted to go to Sri Lanka with me in January. 'Sure, why not?' I'm so relieved," Bob concluded.

Bob couldn't tell Kirsten.

Each day, I asked, "Have you told her yet?"

"No."

"When will you?"

"Tomorrow."

Kirsten returned to BYU ten days later. She didn't know.

The next day, I said, "You have to call her today. Her best friend at BYU knows, David knows. You're cruel. You're her father." Standing in the kitchen, face tense, hands clenched, I said, "How could you not tell her?"

"I couldn't get the nerve," he said sullenly.

After the call later that day, Bob said to me, his face down, "Kirsten was upset. 'Why couldn't you tell me to my face? You told David. You hate me.' I had no answer to give her." He left the room.

"I'm so mad at him. He didn't have the nerve to tell me. He couldn't even trust me. I'm not upset that he is gay, but I'm furious he didn't have the guts to tell me," she said to me in a subsequent phone call.

She hurt bad. I hurt bad. We didn't know how to hurt bad together, two thousand miles apart.

Bob and David went to Sri Lanka in January, David for a month, Bob for almost a year. Decisions about our marriage went on hold. Fear of ending the marriage immobilized me. The Peace Corps consumed me.

That summer, Kirsten called. "I started going to PFLAG [Parents, Families and Friends of Lesbians and Gays] so I can hear what families are going through. Greg Louganis was our keynote speaker last night."

"The two-time Olympic gold medalist in diving?" I asked. "I remember when he won. He's gay?"

"Yep. And speaking out. I liked his words. The small group meeting afterward blew me away."

"Go on."

"A guy in our group said he had dinner with his parents every Sunday night. He wanted to tell his parents he was gay, practicing the words carefully in the car ride over. He came home having said nothing. 'Okay, next Sunday night.' That Sunday came and went. 'I'm sure I can do it this Sunday night.' Nope, he couldn't. He did this every week for a year without courage to tell them." Kirsten softened her voice. "Finally, he wrote a letter and mailed it to them. He said, 'I couldn't do it face-to-face. I chickened out.'"

She breathed softly into the phone. "I now understand why Daddy couldn't tell me at Christmastime. I'm still angry, but I understand. The speaker had said, 'You don't know if your family will end, your life will end when you tell someone you love that you're gay.' I'm his daughter. He knew telling me would hurt me, and it did."

Kirsten's healing came slowly.

With dread and fear, I opened the door as Bob returned home from Sri Lanka after several months. I had practiced painful words that finally had to be said. He smiled and reached out for a hug, but I didn't respond.

"Take the bags to the basement bedroom. You will begin sleeping there." The words hung in the space, finally spoken. "Staying together won't work. We have to separate." I spoke before my carefully rehearsed resolve crumbled. In the hallway, he stared at me, as if made of stone, shocked. His two lives, a normal-looking family life hiding a roaming gay nightlife, ended. He couldn't accept who he had become. Thus, he denied me mine.

To friends and work colleagues, I looked calm but lost my humor and usual quick step.

"I'm managing fine. We'll get through the separation," I said to Deedie. She knew I lied. But I couldn't break my facade of self-control. My life depended on it.

When angry, I get sullen and quiet. My voice gets tight and offers little zingers. For me, angry is being out of control, not allowed.

"This is terrible. Are you angry?" a friend asked.

"No, I'm not angry" was my common response. No one believed my answer except me. Months later, after Bob had moved out and met Bruce and the two had moved to Baltimore, I drove Kirsten to the airport. Bob was to meet us to say goodbye before Kirsten returned to college.

As I drove, she looked at me and said firmly, "Mother. You. Are. Angry. Very. Angry."

"No, I'm not," I replied. "I feel fine."

"You're not listening. You're angry."

"Nope."

"Believe me."

"I'm fine."

When we arrived, Bob saw us through the crowd and walked up to the ticket counter where we stood. "I've been here for about ten minutes."

I interrupted harshly, "That's your problem. We're on…"

Words stopped midsentence. A wave of heat and tightness in my stomach took over, moving up my chest, through my neck, and into my face. My voice rose. The noise of hundreds of voices in ticket lines disappeared.

My fisted hands, my feet heavy on the expansive tile floor, and my dry mouth that had just spat out words all said, "Anger." Is this what anger feels like? Am I furious? Should I scream, run, hide, retch? Unnoticed in the crowd, I stood still, not listening, not looking, taking forced, slow breaths, feeling my fingers, feeling my face, feeling my stomach. Months of rage rushed through me. Stand, feel inside, let it come, let it go. Bob and Kirsten continued to chat, no notice of me.

Calm came slowly, very slowly, fingers loosened, feet moved, body heat diminished, crowd noises returned. Minutes, more minutes. Cautiously, slowly, I stepped forward and entered the conversation, any conversation they were having, just plain, regular, untangled spoken words.

But my unknown anger had been so strong that even seeing Bob striding toward us twisted my face, balled my fists, raised my voice. Kirsten had told me this was anger. Now I knew this feeling. That moment of feeling rage, surging in my body, began my healing. Talking, being, sharing could begin.

*

Over subsequent months, when conversations became more relaxed, Bob added details about his growing up, ones he had hidden, even from himself. We had separated our lives as a family and replaced them as friends.

One evening, as Bob came over and we sat in the sunroom, Bob added details about his confusion while growing up. He said, "I liked the book *Kon-Tiki: Across the Pacific in a Raft*, by Thor Heyerdahl. It sat on my living room bookshelf, loved by Mormons, as it's the true story about building a primitive raft made of forty-foot balsa logs and sailing across the Pacific."

This well-known book added truth to the ancient story in the Book of Mormon and was cited in our church services.

Bob continued, "I didn't read the book. Instead, I looked at the photos of the six sailors over and over. These sailors, hot and sweaty day after day on the boat, were almost naked. The photos made me feel good."

Devout Mormons in Provo, Utah, in the 1950s did not seek self-discovery that countered church beliefs about marriage, children, and eternal families in the hereafter.

"When I grew up, I had no words for my feelings; no vocabulary existed. Without words, I didn't feel." He talked of trying to express the emptiness. "I knew I needed to meet my family and Mormon expectations. They loved me. Loving meant college, mission, marriage, a new family. I wouldn't disappoint."

His early feelings followed him into adulthood but still without meaning. Then he had a career, a wife, two children, and to everyone else, happiness.

"When we returned from Togo, something happened. My strange feelings grew, and I didn't know what to do with them." I pieced together my own memories of this time.

"You watched me withdraw, you saw me go into gloomy silence. I know you did, but you carried on. We both carried on." He knew this hurt me to hear.

He continued, "I walked into the bookstore Lambda Rising and felt comfortable with myself for the first time I could remember. I looked at the customers, books, discussion boards and wanted to stay and stay. I couldn't drag myself away." He stood up for a moment, adding energy to his voice. "Something on the bulletin board caught my eye. It read, 'Group weekly sessions are being offered for gay married men. Friday nights. P and Twenty-Second Street.' I knew I had to go, went every week for a year, finally said to the group, 'I'm gay,' the first time I said it, even to myself. I felt free."

*

The lawyer, me, Bob, and one witness assembled in the divorce courtroom in Rockville, Maryland, on a bleak April morning, 1994. I had pushed for the earliest divorce date possible.

"I want to be your friend, Bob, but only after severing all financial ties—no legal requirements to each other."

My lawyer didn't want him to come to the divorce hearing. "Talk him out of it."

Bob said, hurt, "After thirty years of marriage, I want the mark of closure. I'm a partner, even in divorce." He came. My lawyer didn't understand our kind of divorce or why he agreed to whatever she and I decided.

"I talk everything over with Bob, and we agree before I come to your office,"

"You're going to check with Bob to see if he's okay with our decisions before you sign?" she asked, puzzled. "Don't you want to get as much as you can? You were wronged."

"We have two adult children and years ahead to celebrate parenthood together. No more being wronged. I'm tired of being angry," I replied truthfully.

Before the judge could drop the gavel, completing the divorce hearing, he called me to the witness box to confirm we had been physically separated for twelve months, a Maryland law. In my nervousness, I gave the wrong date, only nine months of separation.

The judge looked startled, called my lawyer to the bench, and then announced loudly to anyone in the chambers, "The Olsens haven't met the separation agreement. I can't approve of this divorce." The lawyer walked quickly to the bench while Bob, the witness, and I went to the courthouse cafeteria for juice and sticky buns.

"How could I plan so carefully for this day and then screw it up?" I said, taking my last bite of the sticky bun.

"These things happen. It's okay," Bob said. He always supported me.

"You can all come back in," the lawyer called to us forty-five minutes later. "Bob, you need to sign papers confirming a one-year separate date. Jody, you need to sign the same papers." She added, "If Bob hadn't come, you would have had to stay married for three more months." She finally smiled.

The gavel fell, the judge said to the chamber, his voice echoing into the void, "You are now divorced."

Bob turned to me, gave me a smile, and then asked, "When should I pick you up for the Chromys' dinner tonight?" The lawyer rolled her eyes as she walked out.

*

Since that cold spring day, our family, including Bob's husband, Bruce, have taken vacations, celebrated both David and Kirsten's weddings, watched grandchildren being born, run marathons (I cheer, the others run), shared meals and guest bedrooms, and talked weekly. Bob lived through my anger. He kept the family as one—certainly different, but together.

We are lucky. Many ask, "How do you stay friends?"

"We care about each other, about David, Kirsten, and the families they have created. We overlook our imperfections to hold the lives we live and celebrate together." I knew, even during the worst times, we wouldn't lose each other.

*

The divorce also ended my active church membership. My theological devotion to church teachings began waning as a Volunteer and continued even with decades of regular attendance. My own belief didn't understand how a "one and only true church" with a significantly less than 1 percent global reach and a distinctive American-centric history could offer the only assurance of a strong afterlife. But the congregation friendships, support for family, and religious training for David and Kirsten kept me attending Sunday school and giving weekly religious lessons to women attendees. I encouraged the women in the congregation to talk about their struggles and joys of raising children and maintaining spiritual household harmony and opened lively discussions, not necessarily in tune with the church leaders' admonitions. The congregation knew me to be a renegade, demonstrated by my working full time and earning advanced degrees. As always, I remained silent about my doubts as to the church's one and only religious truthfulness. These doubts complicated life, but they wouldn't go away. My questions were my own. I never challenged others.

My parents were part of the same congregation, devotedly so. We sat together as a family each week, same bench, same spot, for twelve years following our return from Togo. My father taught religious classes, performed holy church functions, and served as the Washington Temple president for three years. As my theology slipped away, family pressure continued my attendance, but each year with less fulfillment.

My spiritual hypocrisy ended when Bob came out. The church had condemned the practice of alternative lifestyle behaviors and officially ended membership for those who did (including for Bob). He and I had been a loving family for thirty years, and once we recovered enough from the divorce's grief and anger, we would continue family support. Our children, adults beginning separate lives, wanted and needed parents who cared for each other.

I no longer wanted to be part of a congregation that condemned the father of my children for being gay. My newly revised family was my priority. I stopped attending church and have rarely returned, with only a few regrets. I am at peace with the decision.

# PART SIX

# *Peace Corps Presidential Appointments*

# 13

# It's Dark in the Desert at Night

2002–9

Leading the Fulbright Senior Scholar Program for five years after I left the Peace Corps chief of staff position offered me experiences with hundreds of faculty from countries throughout the world. In conferences and presentations, I nudged scholars to approach their experience by listening, observing, and celebrating differences, regardless of academic discipline.

My subsequent five years as senior vice president at the Academy for Educational Development (AED) brought me little joy. Responsibilities focused on business development, proposal writing, fundraising, and budget negotiations. I pretended to smile, gave encouraging words, but felt approaching darkness, sadness, and a need for antidepression pills. My recent divorce, redefined family, and loneliness contributed to the malaise.

George W. Bush's presidential victory offered me hope for a way out of AED proposal negotiations and back to the Peace Corps, a place to renew my global engagement spirit. Maybe as an associate director or... didn't matter. I missed its mission and energy.

\*

Two White House Presidential Personnel Office (PPO) staff on the Eisenhower Executive Office Building's (EEOB) second floor offered me a government-issued armless chair. The chair defied the image of a building completed in 1888 to house State, War, and Navy Departments, with massive skylights above grand circular stairwells, individually crafted doorknobs, and carved marble fireplaces. Presidential staff crowded together in its grandeur while occasionally moving back and forth through the underground tunnel to the White House West Wing.

In this crowded corner of the ornate white room, I nervously introduced myself, fearful of not sounding Republican enough. Then, midway through expressing my love for the Peace Corps, one interviewer interrupted me midsentence.

"Yes, yes, we know your history with the Peace Corps. No need to say more." Then she paused, moved her desk chair closer, and looked directly at me. "We asked you here because President Bush would like to nominate you for Peace Corps deputy director. Are you interested?"

Shocked, silent, taking short breaths, then with a forced serene face, I replied, "I would be honored to accept the nomination. And if confirmed, I would be proud to serve President Bush's administration." This was said as if responding to a question about the weather. My body wanted to stand and dance with joy, but proper protocol kept me still.

I began thinking about papers, clearances, a White House announcement, meetings with senators, a confirmation hearing. The interviewer continued, her words passing by me. My mind had already moved into the Peace Corps office, ready to begin.

No words about the offer for two months, even to David and Kirsten.

*

A month later, on September 12, 2001, Gaddi Vasquez, the Peace Corps director nominee, and I met for the first time at a coffee shop a block from the Peace Corps office's newest location at Twentieth and L Streets.

We sat at a small, low, round table, our backs to a modest gas fireplace, its flames appearing frail. Even full sunlight streaming through the west-facing windows could not shake the terror of the attack on New York City and in Washington the day before.

"I was in the Executive Office Building yesterday afternoon, just hours after the attack," Gaddi said. He and I had shaken hands, ordered tea, moved our stuffed chairs closer. Gaddi continued, "As we talked briefly, my PPO officer's voice shook, became less focused." Gaddi paused, thoughtful. "Our conversation, after the attack, seemed irrelevant." He stopped and lowered his head. "I'm scared. I don't understand what's happening."

"So am I." We looked at each other, fearful. "I'm afraid for our country and for us." The enormity to the nation and the world of what had just happened wasn't yet understood but would be soon.

The morning before, September 11, I had been sitting in the dental chair at Eighteenth and Eye Streets, only three blocks from the White House, when the planes hit the Twin Towers. The dentist laid aside the drill as we both listened to the shaky announcer's voice describing the details of the moment-by-moment horror.

An hour later, walking the twenty minutes back to the AED office, I passed workers crowded on the sidewalk looking at live TV screens in store windows now facing outward. The Pentagon had been hit moments before, and a fourth plane was still unaccounted for.

"It's aimed for the White House," one person shouted, "just two blocks away." But we stayed frozen, staring at the TV screen.

Later that morning and into the afternoon, alone on the tenth floor of the AED executive office space staring out over the city and Northern Virginia suburbs, I watched first flames from the Pentagon, then heavy black billows of smoke covering a fourth of the sky. Hour by hour, it burned as radio reporters described the three crash sites. I watched the smoke, not moving, not eating, not calling David and Kirsten, frozen in space.

Gaddi and I shared that moment of fear we each experienced the day before and what it meant for tomorrow and the next month. We didn't know details, only the sights of towers falling and the Pentagon burning. The Peace Corps seemed inconsequential. We had been strangers meeting for the first time, but that hour gave us a common drive to protect the Peace Corps's global presence. Together, over the next few years, we worked to keep that promise.

*

The 9/11 tragedy changed the Peace Corps. Recognition seeped in slowly over the year following as fear of more attacks on Americans became direct challenges to Volunteers being safe anywhere in the world.

Immediately following the attack, Volunteers reported host families and colleagues protecting them. They and their communities mourned the loss of life together.

One health care counterpart told a Volunteer, "An attack on America is an attack on the world, an attack on us." The country or region of the world made no difference in the outpouring of love and support for the Volunteers.

A Senegal Peace Corps Volunteer said, "The information came to us on shortwave radios. It was delivered by men riding horses, holding transistors to their ears. It was passed along by word of mouth in Wolof and Mandinka and Pulaar and Seereer, and we thought surely it was the vocabulary we didn't understand. But the words were very simple. 'America has been attacked.'"

Slowly, fear replaced horror, anger replaced grief. To some families in the United States, their Volunteer sons and daughters appeared isolated, alone, targets for attack. They expressed their fears to members of Congress who repeated them to Gaddi and me in hearings.

"Joanna is alone in a savanna village in Niger," one congressman stated firmly, looking Gaddi in the eye. "She isn't safe. I know it," he continued firmly. "What are you going to do about it?"

Gaddi stayed calm. "Joanna is with six hundred people who love and care for her. She has a host family reporting her safety." He continued, "No Volunteer is alone anywhere. They are not with other Americans but are with families and communities who watch out for them day and night." The congressman saw isolation, the image of a white, young American female alone among dark-skinned natives. Gaddi saw love, respect, family bonds between Joanna and her community. This congressional exchange began the Peace Corps's deliberate shift toward reinforcing the why of a Volunteer integrating into the community and being part of a system to sustain it. Gaddi asked me to lead this global Peace Corps effort to strengthen the Volunteer's integration and show the safety and security model it brought. This idea remained foreign to many in the United States, who visualized Americans living together behind walls.

Volunteers living in a community, often the only American, working side by side with those being served, sharing cultures and traditions, drove how the agency approached safety and security. The Peace Corps's core values could have been at risk if we followed other agencies' responses of constructing barriers: building walls, bringing in more guards, discouraging embassy staff and officials from leaving the compound, and closing streets around embassies. Americans also talked of war against Afghanistan, Iraq: deterrence. The nation needed to exact revenge and get even. The 9/11 attack and national and global responses added pressure on us to show aggressive action to keep Volunteers safe. Gaddi's police background gave credibility to actions we could take, making congressional and anxious parent responses easier.

*

July 2002, sunshine came in through the broad west-facing windows, brightening the director's office. Gaddi sat behind his large mahogany desk, smiling, impeccably dressed, as I sat across, facing him, to begin the discussion that would affect the Peace Corps's approach to safety and security to this day, more than twenty years later.

"You asked me to shape the agency's new formal safety and security strategy, but to do so, I need your guidance and thinking," I began. Gaddi, as a former police officer, had seen rough Los Angeles neighborhoods and knew what bad guys did. As a social worker, I learned how to heal minds, save marriages, not construct safety programs. Our two minds with divergent backgrounds had to merge.

"News stories suggest Americans now fear the countries and communities in which our Volunteers serve," I began. "Before 9/11, living with those who talk, look, eat, and live differently had an allure, an appeal." Gaddi reached for a pen and paper, jotted ideas. I continued, "Now we see state and other agencies building more barriers, creating more distance between American staff and others in-country. These barriers place Americans in a cocoon and tell foreign leaders we are afraid to be in their countries, that harm awaits in these countries." I talked faster. "The heart and soul of the Peace Corps and its three goals is the Volunteer's community living experience," I said, pushing forward and not waiting for a response. "Building walls and huddling together inside won't work. Congress is clamoring for more protection for Volunteers, but doing so risks that very security and the program's future."

He looked up, smiled, and said, "You're talking too fast." He sat back in his chair, looked out at workers carrying buckets on the roof of the building across the street, and then said, "Police work requires the community to trust you. You learn the neighborhood. How did I do my job?" His voice rose slightly, his face firm. He continued to speak with pride about his own police work, his school assembly presentations, his lectures to teenagers being drawn into gangs. Bilingual, Gaddi understood the kids, used their own words in both languages to guide them. He showed his trust in them. He already knew what the Peace Corps needed to do to keep Volunteers safe. I learned from him.

For thirty minutes, we suggested themes for staying safe while living in communities, themes that framed the agency's culture. We had been alert to issues of safety and security for years. Now we had to promote the concept as integral to Peace Corps's mission and describe it in our promotional materials. Community integration hadn't been seen as a safety tool before, only a phrase describing Volunteers in communities. Now it was core to the Peace Corps's survival.

*

Michael, a Peace Corps mental health clinician and expert on staying safe in dangerous situations, became my safety and security mentor. He had been a Volunteer and later a hostage in Sierra Leone and knew how to build trust, even in hostile situations.

As he sat across the desk from me, I asked, "Paint me a picture of what the phrase safety and security looks like. How does it fit Peace Corps's mission?"

Michael grabbed a pen and paper. "Here goes," he said. "You asked for a picture." He then drew a triangle and labeled each point. The words *Barriers* and *Deterrence* anchored the bottom corners, the words *Community Integration*, *Trust*, and *Respect* described the top. "There you have it," he exclaimed as he handed me his diagram. "Walls are an example of barriers, guns are an example of deterrence, Volunteers in a community are an example of integration. Each is a tested safety and security method." I sat back, framing the concepts.

He continued, "We can take this to Congress if we have to. It works. We already do it."

"Okay, now we figure out how to convince others it works. The idea is counterintuitive to the country's mood right now."

The next week, Michael had borrowed staff from other offices to be a makeshift safety and security team of ten and brought them to my office. Early morning, coffee and muffins, the latter cut in half to be more tempting.

I asked the group, "How do Volunteers stay safe now?" The agency's medical health experts and desk officers held cups of coffee and talked.

"The host families care for Volunteers as their own."

"The Volunteers know everyone, speak their language."

"Trust each other, protect each other, as they do their own families."

Examples continued, stories added. The families, communities, schools, health clinics acted as protective barriers, invisible shields over each Volunteer. A memory rekindled from thirty-five years earlier, my own Tunisian experience: the Zinelabedines, the stall keepers near my front door, the clinic health care workers had been my informal protective barriers. They had watched out for me.

Michael added, "We need some barriers—not just walls but accessible phones and emergency evacuation procedures developed by Peace Corps staff. Also, let's add a new staff member at each post to stay in touch with Volunteers, local police, and security officials." More questions, more ideas. More muffins eaten. We had begun.

We built our program around integrating into the community to change lives and keep Volunteers safe.

But we needed to show others this worked. Rumors of war with Afghanistan and Iraq increased and, with it, public fear. Editorials and op-ed pieces reflected the public wanting to pull back, disengage.

In a later meeting, we mulled choices. "Let's use both data and stories. Congress asks for data, particularly when they don't believe our stories."

After reviewing Volunteer survey data, our statistician, Jamie, announced proudly to the group, "Volunteer satisfaction is positively proportional to their communities' distance from the capital and other large cities. They like being the only American in their towns and living away from large gathering places." She smiled, pulled up another table. "Look here, Jody. Congress will like this part. Volunteers report their safety, measured by the absence of incidents of burglaries or physical attacks, increases proportionate to their distance from big cities." She then added, "And Michael's triangle image is right. Community integration works. As a Volunteer, my coworkers in Jamaica took great care of me. I felt totally safe."

We created testimony for a doubtful Congress, had conversations with inquiring parents, and added safety and security to our recruiting materials for potential Volunteers.

But we needed a stronger backup evacuation plan for natural disasters or other emergencies, the barrier point of the triangle. We had to show the doubters we could move Volunteers out immediately if a province, a country, or a region was threatened. We had moved Volunteers quickly before, including evacuating six countries ahead of the Gulf War in 1990 and as Hurricane Mitch approached Central America in 1998. These methods had worked well enough, but 9/11's global impact required us to codify emergency procedures, test them quarterly, train Volunteers and staff on the procedures, and add trained staff.

The core to its ultimate success was in every Volunteer's hand, the newly available cell phone. We could add emergency procedures to each Volunteer's phone.

*

"What, Volunteers have cell phones?" I had asked Amanda, the West African support desk officer, a few months earlier when I became deputy director. I had been gone from the agency for nine years. Much had changed. With the invention of cell phones, communication changed.

"How will they become part of the community, learn the language, if they are on the phone to their parents every day?" I asked. "They can't have my kind of Volunteer experience."

"Cell phones are what's happening," Amanda answered, rolling her eyes at me as she sat in her Ghanaian fabric–decorated cubicle. "Host families have them. Some coworkers have them. Why not Volunteers?" She asked me to sit. "You've been gone a long time."

"I know, but change is difficult."

"We can't go back."

I reached for a homemade cookie on the coffee table.

"They'll get phones no matter what we say. Cell phones are just a few dollars. The inexpensive Nokias have the global market covered." She pulled out the Nokia she brought back from Ghana. "And the flashlight on the end makes nighttime latrine trips safer."

"And electricity?"

"Amazing what car batteries and tiny solar panels can do. Volunteers are creative. They even hook up computers for their students."

The cell phone became the centerpiece of our new safety and security program. These thousands of cheap phones in the hands, pockets, and backpacks of Volunteers were core to regular community-based emergency drills. Before cell phones, emergency messages to Volunteers might have gone by bush taxi, donkey, motorcycle, or foot, sometimes a two-day journey. As we codified our new system, contact times dropped to a few hours, then minutes. Both families and Congress slept easier. So did I.

\*

Fifteen years later, as Peace Corps director, I attended the Peace Corps's biannual global safety and security conference in Houston, Texas. Two host-country safety and security officers from each country, regional U.S. safety officers, and headquarters safety staff filled the Hyatt grand ballroom. Flip charts with arrows, circles, and scratchy writing hung on walls and on the edge of the stage. The safety and security officers from the Pacific island nations shared a round table with me at the conference. The Vanuatu officer who sat next to me talked of how local police on the islands would call in.

"Damien's fine. Just saw him playing soccer with the school kids." Then he added, "Seems we missed the hurricane's edge. Lucky again." This table had representatives from three of the most storm-turbulent countries of the world: Vanuatu, Fiji, and Tonga.

As we continued sharing island safety stories, I asked those near me, "How long have you worked for the Peace Corps?"

"Fifteen years," said one.

"Twelve years," said another.

"Ever since the safety and security program began," said a third.

I grinned, leaned forward, looked at the faces around the table. "You and I began this journey together." They looked puzzled. "When you get back home, look at your position descriptions. I wrote the position descriptions in 2003. The program's beginning... after 9/11."

Now they laughed. "You!"

"We figured it out together, all of us here," I replied. They picked up this theme and talked over each other with stories of the 2004 Boxing Day tsunami, the 2007 Peru earthquake, the Philippines earthquake, and the 2000 Solomon Islands government coup. They talked of saving Volunteers, being able to bring programs back, keeping the Peace Corps's presence as countries rebuilt.

"You've helped keep Peace Corps stable, country by country, over these years as risks have grown. I respect you all for your work."

\*

Each country team found its safety rhythms through seas, mountains, drought, and tribal conflicts within its own national borders. We prepared the plan's outline in Washington. Posts filled in the specifics. Country staff communicated ideas across the world drawn from generations of history on Pacific islands, South American mountains, or West African deserts. No two safety and security plans were the same, as were no two Volunteer experiences.

*

How did the cell phones' presence change the Volunteers' experience overseas? Did it affect their child nutrition demonstrations with new mothers? Their shared cooking time with host moms? Should a Volunteer take a call from his brother in Atlanta while his host dad talks of garden fences? Can Volunteers live two lives at once?

My Tunisia experience was without phones, even the black rotary kind. I walked to houses or cafés for conversations, looking people in the eye when I talked. I listened and watched their faces. My stories included smells of cumin and sounds of teacups as we talked, phrases connected to places we shared. I hoped Volunteers, even after 9/11, would have similar experiences burrowing into a village and finding its soul. Would the cell phone end that experience?

These choices affect our memory of the experiences years later. A phone call is as different from a letter as an electronic chat is from an intimate group eating from a common bowl. Cell phones change the experience and how it lives on. They don't make the stories better or worse, just different.

Will these Volunteers have the same rich experience I had in Tunisia? My stories have influenced me to this day. Will theirs do the same? I was about to find out.

*

In 2007, as deputy director, I crossed Mauritania in a two-SUV caravan. The sand begins at the Atlantic Ocean; stretches through Nouakchott, its capital; and continues a thousand miles across the Sahara Desert to the Mali border and beyond. Hot sand moves with the winds, its dunes reforming across villages, roads, and isolated herder tents. Sahara sands cover everything in its way. The government had ten snowplows, imported from the United States, to defend the highways. The sand usually won.

The country's reputation for "hot" is well earned, as temperatures reach 120 degrees by day. However, the dry air doesn't hold the sun's heat, and the nights drop to a cool 70 degrees. If they get three storms during the "rainy season," it is considered a lucky year. For ten months, green is only an abstract idea.

Amid the barren rocks extending from distant treeless mountains, nomadic Mauritanians herd animals: camels, cows, donkeys, and goats. They live in eight-foot-high tents close to palms marking watering holes. The heavy gray flaps are tied up during the day to let in breezes and down at night to hold warmth and protect against sand storms. Children carry water in earthen jugs from nearby oases. Families cook, eat, and wash clothes by sun or lantern. Except when under a full moon, herders go to bed early. Lanterns tire the eyes, and fuel is expensive.

Our two Peace Corps SUVs drove through the desert, stopping at weathered tents to meet Volunteers and their host families. We shared plastic bottles of water, peanuts, and oranges.

After my youth in Utah and two years in Tunisia, the desert's dryness smelled familiar, comforting. The wind's sounds through twisted bushes, the only break in the stillness, were common in climbing Wasatch Mountain slopes. In Mauritania, the stillness, the loneliness, extended thousands of kilometers. This desert was endless.

Mauritanian tents were colorful, intimate. My shoes stayed outside the entrance as my bare feet felt the hooked rug entering my first tent.

"Aslemma," my host said, offering me hot Turkish tea in a tiny clear glass. "Welcome to the desert. I know America is far away. You honor us here." Preston, the Volunteer, beamed from behind the host.

"Alikoom salem" ("And welcome to you"), I replied, eager to move further inside, away from sand and wind. "What colors, what designs, what vibrancy," I stammered after my eyes adjusted from the bright sun, stunned by the vivid color. Elaborately designed woven carpets of red, orange, and yellow covered the desert floor. My host, Mr. Ben Ali, pointed to the rugs. His full-length embroidered djibbah rustled as I remembered from Tunisia. "My grandmother and mother made these carpets. They're our tradition, our connection to the past."

Preston pulled me aside and whispered, "Look up at the ceiling. See how the fabric's lines and colors match the carpets? They are also handcrafted." He said this proudly, as if he owned the tent and crafted the fabrics. "I love coming into the tent after working in the desert. The smells, the colors, the intimacy of this tiny space—it is home. The family embraces me."

\*

The next evening, Preston and I attended a dinner for our traveling Peace Corps staff caravan and thirty-five Volunteers living in the region. Adrian, a newly married second-year Volunteer, and her Mauritanian husband's family graciously hosted our staff and Volunteer group.

We arrived at the family compound in total darkness, not even a moon. "Can you find your mat?" Preston called out. Then touching my arm, "Let me put your hand on the straw mat. It's right here." He added, as would a guide, "I'm used to the darkness. I'll keep guiding you."

Our mats covered a space used during the day for washing clothes, cutting wood, sharpening field machetes, and raising chickens. A couple hours before our arrival, this space had been cleared and mats laid out for the hungry Americans. A few weak Nokia phone flashlights appeared as fireflies, revealing the small pillows for groups of six surrounding nine-inch-high wooden tables.

"I feel helpless," I commented to Preston. "As if blind."

On the edge of the compound, beyond profiles of Volunteers, hung two lanterns. Below them, swaying bodies stood at a table cutting meat, stirring pans, stoking charcoal fires. Dinner, sometime. We waited.

In the darkness, words by my immediate companions broke into the low hum of indistinguishable voices. An occasional laugh encouraged louder noises, then back to the low hum. For two hours we shared words, floating without faces or bodies. With no other cues, I listened for accents, phrases, tones to understand who spoke.

"My mother wishes I would come home," the Volunteer next to Preston said to me. "She calls and tells me this every week." Parents always worry about their children in a strange country. "I need help to tell her I want to stay. Jody, could you call her when you get back?"

About the time dinner had become just a dream, a figure rustled near us, placing a large bowl on our table.

"I'm sure it's mutton and couscous," the Volunteer whose mother wanted her to go home said. "In this valley, it's always mutton and couscous." I scooted my pillow closer to the bowl and listened as others did the same. We felt each other's hands go in and out of the bowl, grabbing a handful of what we could feel: mutton, bone, grain, onion, and Sahara sand.

"Jody, do you know what to do?" Preston asked, laughing.

"Sure do. I have Tunisia and Togo to thank. Feels like home." Experience guided hands to take turns, eat slowly, but our hunger bent the unspoken rules of only one hand in the bowl at a time. Another full bowl replaced our empty one. We kept reaching.

"Jody, do you want to see what you're eating?" Preston asked as the second bowl arrived. He laughed. "It might surprise you. Be ready." A movement, a slight click, and then the small flashlight revealed a piece of stomach among meat chunks. Another mysterious shape lay half buried in the couscous. "Don't ask," I thought. "I'm happy not seeing what I eat," I said. "No need for light."

As we continued, the nearby Volunteer reached her hand to me. "I apologize, but in five minutes, you'll hear my cell phone ring."

"That's fine," I replied, trying to get my mind off of sheep stomachs and other body parts.

"My parents call each week at this time. They're in Denver, an eight-hour time difference." She said this to me as if cell phone calls from Denver under the Sahara Desert stars and with no electricity were normal. They were. Five minutes later, I heard Bach's Fugue in G Minor, and then "Hello?" Then another ring, another, and another. Each was a parent, a brother, or a good friend in the States calling on Sunday evening as we ate couscous with Sahara sand in the darkness without moonlight. In this desert, eight thousand miles from home, Volunteers stayed connected to family recipes, shopping trips, and moments of joy and sadness.

"I told Volunteers their families could check in once a week," Obie, the country director, said. "Train your families not to call more often." He chuckled. "Sounds like these guys have trained their families well. I'm proud of 'em." He continued, "We couldn't be here without the phones. We need emergency contact. And Volunteers get how to use them carefully."

Two years later, even with phones, the Peace Corps had to leave Mauritania for Volunteers' safety and security. But phones bought us a few extra years in the country, time for Volunteers to eat couscous, mutton, and sand (it was gritty) from common bowls with host families and colleagues.

Three years later, in Salt Lake City, I listened to Preston and his bride, who had been a fellow Volunteer, share these stories. Following the wedding ceremony, the twenty-eight other Volunteers from their Mauritania group hugged and laughed with the newlyweds as their words stumbled over each other. "Do you remember?" "No, this is even better." "I still call my host family, and I can speak to them in Arabic." I listened and laughed. Peace Corps would continue to thrive with cell phones.

*

After the dinner in the dark, Obie and I walked to the Peace Corps SUV. He asked me, "Do you mind having a courtesy call with the minister of health this evening?"

"Delighted," I responded. "But it's almost ten."

"It's just a courtesy call. He is in the village visiting family and staying at the hotel nearby. The visit would be important to the Peace Corps program." And he added, "He knows this is after normal courtesy visiting hours, but he wanted to say hello. Five minutes max. He will be in casual clothes, maybe even in his pajamas."

"Sure." Travel duties came first.

Thirty minutes later, Amir, the Mauritanian program staff director, and I drove the gravel path to the dimly lit, one-story hotel. "I don't think they see many guests here," I mentioned to Amir as we opened the car doors.

He laughed. "The minister and you will probably be the two fanciest people the hotel has ever seen. Travelers rarely pass through this rugged part of the desert."

As I slipped out of the car, I asked, "Amir, should I wear a scarf for this brief visit? What's the protocol?"

"No need tonight. He knows this is after hours and you are coming from a casual Volunteer event. And he'll be casual."

Walking to the hotel door, I stopped, turned to Amir. "I'm thinking I might wear the scarf after all. Let me run back and get it."

"But I don't think it's necessary."

With the scarf loosely over my head, we entered the hotel sitting room. The minister sat comfortably on the couch, reading. As he stood, the elaborately carved wood armrests caught my eye.

"Aslemma, my friend," the minister said as he walked to us, giving Amir a bear hug while kissing both cheeks. Amir still wore his white djibbah from dinner, but the minister now had on a Western casual cotton shirt and jeans. This friendship between Amir and the minister kept Peace Corps programming engines running strong.

Amir introduced me to the minister as we moved to the chairs facing the couch. "You enjoying it here? Are we treating you well?" the minister asked eagerly in Arabic and French. I groped for my forty-year-old Arabic words of greeting and then drug up rusty French.

"Everyone is gracious, generous. And I feel almost at home." He looked at me, surprised. "Oh, I was a Volunteer in Tunisia for two years. Fell in love with the country. Mauritania reminds me of that happy time."

We compared food, dress, and Arabic greetings, laughing as I described the red hot peppers in Tunisian couscous and the milder form in Mauritania. "I had tears down my cheeks from the peppered couscous in Tunisia. I had to take tiny bites. Here I can scoop up spoonfuls. I love it."

We continued back and forth, stories. Finally, Amir suggested the hour was late, and we said our farewells. Neither had mentioned the Peace Corps, but we each showed our mutual support in the visit itself.

The next day, Amir pulled me aside. "Did you hear what the minister whispered to me as we left last night?"

"No." I smiled. "I wouldn't have understood it. I fake my language knowledge."

Amir smiled. "You did something very respectful. The minister noticed and was pleased."

"I can't think of anything unusual I did. I try to be natural."

"You wore a headscarf." Amir paused and added, "You showed respect for his beliefs. He knew it was your choice. You didn't need to wear it."

After that experience, I thought about the visit, the headscarf, each time meeting with country officials. My visits represented a program, a mission, bigger than myself. The visits weren't about me, an American woman and leader, but about the Peace Corps in a country with its own culture and traditions. How do I make the other person feel comfortable, respected, trusted? Volunteers learn to do it every day. Top Peace Corps officials should do the same.

\*

On a Saturday in March 2008, the country director in Kazakhstan received notice he had twenty-four hours to leave the country. The rarity of such an event suggested major maleficence, but the reason for removal stayed quiet. The following Monday morning, Director Tschetter walked into my office. Ron Tschetter had followed Gaddi Vasquez as agency director after Gaddi became ambassador to the World Food Program in Rome. I missed

Gaddi, but Ron's Volunteer experience in India parallels mine in Tunisia. We also worked well together.

"Jody," he began in seriousness, not sitting down, "yesterday, we let go the Kazakhstan country director." Ron carried a medium frame with the casualness of manner and sparsity of words known as part of the culture of the northern Midwest, his home.

"I woke up at three this morning with a great idea." He paused, his hands holding the edge of the desk. He took a long breath. "Would you like to be country director in Kazakhstan for a few weeks?" Talking faster, "You have been a country director. This could be an adventure and good for the agency…"

I mentally created a travel checklist all in a split second before asking, "When do you want me?"

"This week."

More questions filled my head, such as why the post was suddenly open and why a current staff member was not taking over, but why ask? The details would not change my answer, which needed no thought. "Delighted," I said. Another unexpected adventure to an unknown part of the world.

That evening, over a dinner I had cooked for my parents, they asked, "What, where, how long?" And most fearfully, "How will we get along without your help?" They had moved to a nearby condo as my father, at ninety, had failing health, and Mother struggled with his care. My thrice-weekly visits and food shopping created stability in the small apartment and kept me connected to parents I could soon lose.

"Christopher and Stephen will be here for you," I said, crossing my fingers behind my back about their availability. "They come regularly anyway."

I organized tasks to be done, asked others to take my place at meetings, and for my parents, checked food, medicines, emergency numbers, and Stephen's and Christopher's availability. All worked. Six weeks later, back home again, when my parents and I had dinner together around the small dining table, they hadn't even remembered that I had gone.

*

Four days later, the plane landed at 11:00 p.m. at the Almaty International Airport, located in the southeast edge of a country half the size of the

United States, with eighteen million people. The dry semidesert Kazakh Steppe across the country defined the country's vastness with nomads, horses, cattle, and yurts. Volunteers lived in the visual richness of the loneliness of open fields and mountain peaks without end.

The Kazakhstani staff gave me a Nokia flip phone as my feet touched the tarmac.

"This is your most important tool while here," Alana, the safety and security officer, said, assuming I knew how to use it. I didn't. The staff's late evening introductions came after the ceremonial gift of the flip phone. They knew Peace Corps priorities.

"On this phone, you have names and phone numbers of all staff, Volunteers, embassy officials, and key people to call in an emergency," Alana continued. The first flip phone lesson began under the airport's bright night-lights.

*

Thirty-eight Kazakhstani staff smiled hesitantly as I walked into the conference room the next morning. The mammoth wood-carved conference table revealed the opulence of the former occupants. Two three-story, fully carpeted, side-by-side houses told the demise of a former wealthy family with a falling out. Peace Corps was the lucky recipient of their misfortune.

After introductions, one staff member asked, "Are you here to punish us?"

Startled, "I don't understand. Why would I?" wondering at such a strange question.

"The country director suddenly left last Saturday. We didn't hear a word about why. And Peace Corps sent you, the deputy director, the big Washington boss. What did we do wrong?"

"Absolutely nothing. I'm the lucky one to be here with you."

Hands relaxed on the table, backs leaned back into chairs. They looked at each other, relief on their faces, then cathartic shouts and laughter as their fear dissipated.

The staff gave me their stories during subsequent staff meetings: parents forced to move from Moldova, Ukraine, Georgia, to Kazakhstan under the pre-1992 USSR. Some were Kazakhstani because they had happened to be here when the Soviet Union fell; others had generations of proud Kazak heritage. The Russian language and view of the Tian Shan mountain range outside our window united the group.

The staff turned to me at our second meeting. "And what is your story?" Our mutual trust was developing quickly. It had to, as I only had six weeks to rebuild a team to support this strong fifteen-year-old Peace Corps country program. I smiled, reaching into my bag for eight-by-ten family photos carefully assembled before leaving DC. Family stories united the most disparate backgrounds.

"Here is my family reunion at the beach last year," pointing out children, grandchildren, and Bob and Bruce. The photos lay along the middle of the table and were then picked up and looked at by staff members. "Bob and I stay close, even as he is with someone else." I told the story, not knowing if it would offend Kazakhstani cultures, beliefs, or laws. Follow-up questions were as normal as those asked of any other family.

"What does your daughter do?" or "Where do Bob and Bruce live?" I had made myself vulnerable, asking for their trust to share my secrets. Six weeks later, they were my new family saying goodbye.

\*

I became close to Victor, the Peace Corps medical doctor. Of average build, he moved with his former USSR military officer precision and smiled only reluctantly. Volunteers listened to his medical orders, fearful of consequences but knowing how much he cared.

"Take these pills daily at 8:00 a.m. sharp, and text me in a week to verify," he said to a Volunteer, his face stern.

"Yes. Oh yes, I will," the Volunteer replied, quickly turning away.

"Don't let me down," Victor called out as the Volunteer left.

"He has a scary look," the Volunteer told me later. "I would never disobey Victor."

Victor laughed when I told him about the Volunteer's comments over tea that afternoon in his medical office.

"They stay healthy. That's my purpose." He continued, "They know I love them all, but some need a hint of my military face to comply."

Over dinners and at concerts with him and his wife, Sophia, I learned their history, not unlike those of other Kazakhstani staff. Almost two decades earlier, as chief of staff, I had seen, from an American perspective, the immediate change from Communist dictatorship to early democracy in central and eastern Europe. Victor described the side I hadn't seen. His earlier professional career had been as a doctor in the Soviet Army.

From Victor's letter to me following my return to the States:

> My mother had been sent to Moldova by the Soviets at the end of World War II to teach.... There she met my father, ethnic Bulgarian, and they married.... Technically, that makes me Moldovan.
>
> The USSR collapse was confusing to me. I had served in the army for a long time, being sent from location to location. Kuibyshev, Kaliningrad, Angola (three years in southern Africa), Leningrad, Chernobyl, Bishkek, Riga, Moscow, Kyiv.
>
> I considered myself a citizen of the Soviet Union, a country that would never collapse. That country was my motherland. Suddenly, it was gone. I woke up one morning without having something big behind me, something I had worked and served for all those years. I had no country.

Before meeting Victor, I had never thought of losing my country. What if the United States ceased to exist? What if, as Victor described, I woke up one morning to no America, just states fighting with each other? What if I became a citizen by default of the state I happened to be in that day? That could never happen.

Victor described his next steps following the USSR's collapse. "I went from Moscow back to Moldova and lived next to my mother on the land on which I was born. However, Moldova had changed: war in Transnistria, ethnic clashes, slogans like 'Russian pigs, go home to Russia' [addressed to anyone not Moldovan], and the introduction of a new state language, Romanian. My family had to adjust, stay calm, learn a new language, and hear bad words from local nationalists."

What if the state I happened to be in when America fell apart didn't want me, tried to return me to somewhere else? This is fantasy, but Victor's words, "I woke up one morning without having something big behind myself," have continued with me, hauntingly calling. A decade later, as the Peace Corps director under the Trump administration, I knew what could happen. Victor's story reminded me of how the loss of a nation might feel.

Victor joined the Moldavian army and came to Texas on a military exchange.

He said to me, "I witnessed every morning the U.S. soldiers raising the U.S. flag at the Lackland Air Force Base. My mind told me these people must be proud of their country and proud that they have this country."

Every day when I read the news, Victor's words return. Does it take an outsider to remind us of the worthiness of our nation?

Victor ultimately becomes the Peace Corps medical director in Moldova, Kazakhstan, then Morocco, where he continues Peace Corps medical leadership. He remains a mentor.

*

The novel *Snow*, by Nobel laureate Orhan Pamuk, describes physical and emotional entrapment, blinding whiteness, and cold. The book could have been describing Kazakhstan's winter. Volunteers told me that reading *Snow* had been a prophetic preparation for their two years on the Kazakh Steppe, with up to a hundred days of annual snowfall. Childhood memories of Utah's Wasatch Mountains' snow did not prepare me for my Volunteer visits to northern Kazakhstan.

In one small northern town, snow had taken over and added chilly winds to slow people's walks, their faces bundled behind thick scarves. Mike, a second-year Volunteer, had invited me to see his tiny nongovernmental organization (NGO), which arranged activities for those with disabilities. The plane from Almaty to this northern region skidded on landing in the snowstorm. The taxi driver in the tin-can-looking Russian Lada came within a couple of inches of a roadside ditch... more than once. Snow kept falling.

After the harrowing drive, Mike greeted me at the office's entrance, a small three-room wood building at the top of a hill overlooking a road to the park several blocks away. His slight frame got lost in his too-large white hand-knit sweater, staying warm a top priority. He offered me a comfortable stuffed chair near the warmth of the colorfully painted traditional Russian stove in the room's center.

The center's director, Lyazzat Kenes, sat facing Mike and me, adjusting her prosthetic left leg for greater comfort.

"Thanks for coming," she began. "I know it's a long trip in the deep snow." She reached for a cup of tea from Mike with her right hand. Then

I noticed. She had no left hand. The sleeve of her cabled sweater hung limply at her side.

She noticed my eyes looking at her sleeve. "I almost lost my life in a car accident. I'm lucky to be sitting here today." She said it with a normal voice, smiled, and then continued, "We are lucky to have Mike with us. He speaks Russian well, listens, and…" She paused. Tears appeared, a catch in her voice. She leaned forward, took a sip of tea, and continued, "Mike cares about me, about all of us who work here. Few people do."

"We're a family here. You're like my mom."

The director became quiet.

She cleared her throat, sat forward, looking at me. "I want to say more about Mike while you are here. Mike, you haven't heard this before, but don't be embarrassed.

"In this neighborhood, Saturday mornings at nine o'clock, I watch Mike go to a half dozen cottage doors, one by one, asking parents to share their sons or daughters with him to go to the park. I watch the little group grow as each new child emerges, one limping, one without sight, one with limited hearing, one slow to move." She looked at Mike, smiled, and continued. "They weave through the streets to the park for two hours of play side by side with other children. Then they return by the same route, and one by one dissolve back into their family homes."

"You see me do this?" Mike asked. "It's nothing special. I enjoy being with the kids."

"It is special. Mike, you don't know how unusual it is," she continued. "This isn't normal here in Kazakhstan." Mike rose and fetched cups of tea. He looked uncomfortable with this attention.

Lyazzat continued, "Most children with disabilities are hidden in shame in the backs of cottages. Families lose face and hide what they cannot acknowledge to others." She took the tea and sipped as she continued. "We with disabilities are not to be seen. And yet Mike, with his blue parka, tasseled wool hat, and mountain boots, laughs, skips, and holds hands with his charges as they jump snowdrifts the distance to the park. For these children, this could be their first time being outside playing with others."

"I'm embarrassed," Mike said, his face getting red.

Lyazzat did not stop: "The neighbors see these children with some-one, an American, who shows his respect and joy for each child." The director's eyes glistened. "I watch Mike from this office porch." She turned to Mike. "Did you know I watch you carefully?"

"I didn't think anyone watched. It's just the kids and me."

She continued, her voice now strong. "His courage has become my courage, his walks have become my walks, his caring for the kids has become my caring for all with disabilities. My voice is stronger and more outspoken. I reach farther across the country." She turned to Mike.

Mike whispered, "Thank you. I now know why I had come to this small, cold, white town."

Two weeks later, Mike sat in my office in Almaty with his laptop open. "This is a recording my friend made of our ball last Saturday for those with disabilities... broadcast on national television." I looked for Lyazzat on the broadcast. She stood in a blue floor-length gown, ready to speak... speak to the country about rights for those with disabilities. I didn't understand her words, but I heard her power.

"Now watch this next scene, Jody," Mike spoke up excitedly. "Aset and I created a floor show dance for the hundreds of attendees. We had to practice hard. I'm not a good dancer." In the video, I watched Mike and Aset enter onto the dance floor.

"Look, my tuxedo's bright-red cumber bun and bow tie are the same fabric as Aset's gown. To match." As the music began, Aset's arms reached up to Mike. Their heads and upper bodies moved in perfect rhythm, her smile magnetic. I stopped seeing her wheelchair, just saw two people as one to the music, an image all Kazakhstan could see.

*

The three-day in-service training for community development Volunteers brought Mike and twenty-five first-year Volunteers to Almaty. These Volunteers had finished their three months of preservice training in November and traveled by air, train, and bus to sites scattered throughout the largest landlocked country in the world. Now the first week of April, they were seeing each other for the first time in five months, many having just lived through a northern Kazakhstan dark Siberian winter. What held them in isolated communities during twenty hours of night at twenty degrees below zero, one of the most challenging Peace Corps assignments anywhere?

Volunteers got out of taxis and paid their drivers as I watched from the steps.

"Tom, wow, it's great to see you," said Grant, running up the steps toward Tom.

He turned. "Grant, you've lost weight but look great." They hugged and continued into the building with arms around each other… words, phrases, parts of sentences.

"How's your sister? Didn't she…?"

"And your cold? It sounded awful."

"That text asking how I was brought me out of my funk. How did you know?"

"Glad you could use the lesson plan I texted. Did the kids like it?"

The snippets of conversation gave one answer to why the Volunteers stayed through the winter: flip phones. They texted each other across miles of the blistery steppe, blinding whiteness, long nights, to encourage each other, share brief stories, take others out of funks. The texts helped them connect to a few words from another American living the same experience when they weren't sure how they could survive until spring.

On the last training day, Alana said proudly, "I'm in awe of everyone's Russian and Kazakh language ability. I had doubted their skill."

"How could that have happened so fast?" I asked, surprised at Volunteer skill.

Alana smiled. "Think of those long days and nights near the center stoves sitting next to families, staying warm and telling stories. You can't be in a room alone in the winter. You freeze."

Any doubt about Volunteers using phones ended in Kazakhstan.

*

Seven weeks earlier, Director Tschetter had walked into my office to offer me Kazakhstan. I said yes without pause. Maybe out of curiosity, maybe because of the adventure, or maybe because Kazakhstan was there. A sense of wonder had shaped many life decisions. Once made, there was no looking back. Kazakhstan gave me a stark perspective on freedom, democracy, and a country that "was something big behind me." It gave focus to my experiences two decades earlier in central and eastern Europe. My future leadership depended on those insights.

*

Nine months after I returned from Kazakhstan, Barack Obama became the forty-fourth president, and the White House approved me as acting

Peace Corps director to serve eight months until Obama's chosen director, Aaron Williams, was sworn in. Unknown at the time, this was a practice run for eight years later when I would become director.

As acting director, swearing in new staff, leading meetings, giving speeches, and getting good budget news from Congress and the administration filled most days. It's the other days that tested leadership.

The Honduran president was unceremoniously ousted in a coup on June 28, 2009, an action roundly condemned by the secretary of state and the Organization of American States. Two days later, we had a group of forty new Volunteers sitting in Miami, ready to board their flight to Tegucigalpa. That morning, Secretary of State Clinton's office sent word they were not to board the flight.

"Do you have a safety and security concern for the Volunteers?" I asked the official on the phone.

"No, but we don't approve of the new government," the official replied. "Arriving Volunteers two days after the coup suggest the United States condones the action."

"But we have been invited by the government, an invitation still in place. And forty Americans have just volunteered two years of their lives to work side by side with Hondurans." I continued, a hint of anger in my words, "Volunteers are not political pawns. Using them as such risks a negative message to Peace Corps countries throughout the world and a risk to Peace Corps itself."

"Do not let them board the plane tonight," he said, finishing the conversation and hanging up.

The State Department didn't have authority over the Peace Corps, but we were dependent on embassies, ambassadors, and regional bureaus for our own work. And as is true with all official Americans working in a country, our three American staff were under the ambassador's mission authority while in-country.

"What should we do?" I asked Kathy, my chief of staff. "This is precedent setting and ugly. But we risk a rupture with the State Department if we go ahead."

Staff talked back and forth with officers at the State Department and the ambassador to Honduras, himself less certain Volunteers should be held back. No solution emerged, and we had only a few hours left.

That evening, the Shakespeare Theatre Company presented the most powerful and disturbing play I had seen, *King Lear*. Leaving the theater, my mood matched that of the play.

My phone rang as I left: "This is Kathy. Shall I tell State the Peace Corps director authorizes the Volunteers to fly? We worked out for Volunteers to arrive at the airport without announcement and quietly go to the training site. They will not pass through Tegucigalpa. No chance for press, photos, stories that give legitimacy to the new government." She hesitated and then added, "State still says don't go."

My *King Lear* mood seeped into my response. "Okay, Kathy. Tell the team in Miami that the Peace Corps director gives permission for them to board the plane." I let out my breath and then added, "My being fired by the White House is the worst that can happen. I only have two more months on the job anyway."

Kathy laughed and added, "Right call. We'll get through it."

The Volunteers arrived with no public mention, completed training, and went to villages as usual. The ambassador quietly continued his in-country support for the Peace Corps program. And we never heard another word from the State Department.

*

While acting director, my personal time attended to my ninety-one-year-old father's mental and physical deterioration as he slipped from the vibrant religious and political leader that defined his identity to being unaware of his surroundings and needing full-time care. My drive to their condo took ten minutes, done almost daily the last few months, exchanging in that time thoughts of international negotiations, Congress, and Volunteer crises to thoughts of helping my caregiver mother and supporting a dying father. He had offered me courage as a teenager to speak out and then continued unconditional support and guidance as I took tenuous steps toward leadership. His having me at his side in the 1950s defied conservative Mormon tradition and his own beliefs but showed me examples of what was possible, regardless of gender. Now we had changed places. I could give the love back by stroking his hands, helping him eat, sitting at his side, letting go of all else. At the right time, he quietly slipped away with Mother and me at his side.

*

At 6:00 one morning in March, having just showered and dressed for work, I received a call from my chief of staff.

"We have a Volunteer death in Benin. It looks like murder."

I sat down on the kitchen stool, held my breath, body tense. My worst nightmare. And murder? "What do we know?" I asked.

"She was found at her house... with her throat cut."

"Oh my God."

"Come in quickly. We are waiting for you to make the call to the parents."

Thirty minutes later, I walked into the office, knowing what had to happen. This would be my eighth call to parents about a son or daughter's death. Rather than easier, each call brought me closer to my trauma from my brother David's death. Each time, as I punched the numbers on the black desk console phone and waited for the "Hello," I knew my news would change the life forever of the voice at the other end of the phone. The space in the family that had been a vibrant young person with a future would now be a deep hole that never heals. These families would have the same wrenching feeling I had forty years earlier. This breath-stopping pain came back each time. For me, it could never go away.

How do I share initial sketchy details about a murder? The murder of a talented, well-respected, and loved Volunteer? One whose photo Peace Corps had been using for recruitment? One who led her fellow Volunteers and guided her mother through her village a few months earlier? I didn't know who would answer the phone. Father? Mother? Where would they be? At home? In the car? At a party?

I punched in the phone numbers at 7:00 a.m., reaching the father, who was in the hospital with a chronic illness. By the tone of my voice, he knew it was bad. But I had to say the words. He screamed. I cried.

At the funeral, I spent a day with the family. We looked at photos of a Volunteer laughing with her students, hugging her host parents, smiling to show her joy at being a Volunteer. The family told stories of her generosity. Monumentally unfair.

The murder details came in slowly, each one worse. The State Department and FBI took over the investigation; newly discovered details were required to be held back from the grieving family, the fear of possible press stories and public attention. This tragic story and its Peace Corps fallout outlasted my time as acting director. It greeted me again eight years later when I prepared for my hearings as the nominee for Peace Corps director.

*

My responsibilities quietly ended in August 2009, leaving by a side hallway from the director's office. One assistant joined me. The conference room had been taken over with preparations for Aaron Williams's swearing in later that day. I had said goodbyes the day before. My time with the Peace Corps had ended. Retirement. I thought.

# 14

# Run Silent, Run Deep
## 2018–21

The watch vibrated on my wrist: call coming. My phone showed "Blocked Call." "Should I take it?" I thought. At that moment, our University of Maryland Center for Global Engagement team stood together in the university's student lobby talking through our next event, not a time for a scam call. But Elaine Chao had submitted my name to the White House for Peace Corps director two months earlier. Could this be...

*

Days after leaving the Peace Corps in August 2010, the University of Maryland School of Social Work's dean offered me a visiting professorship. "Join us this year, teach a course, mentor faculty and students interested in international opportunities." Retirement slipped off the table, exchanged for eight years of teaching, mentoring, and building the structure for a new campus-wide global engagement center. A reverse commute resumed, Silver Spring to Baltimore. Midway through the decade, my daughter and son-in-law moved from Los Angeles into my home's terrace apartment. Two Hungarian pointer dogs came with them. I tried hard to like these fifty-pound dogs.

Colon and breast cancers, fifteen months apart, interrupted my teaching. These challenges bonded our family, understanding that life is lived in moments: use every day well and show appreciation.

As we drove to the hospital at 4:30 a.m. for the colon cancer surgery, Kirsten said, "Now I know why I moved back. I'm needed." She became my anchor for all that followed.

Now in the fall of 2017, as I stood in the student lobby looking at the blocked call, my cancers were almost history, one remaining drug and a fading limp. Third ring. I swiped the accept button.

"Hi, Jody. This is Kajka. You won't believe I left retirement, and I am back in White House personnel." I remembered Kajka, with a deep voice and slight accent, last seen at my father's funeral ten years earlier. As a neighbor to my parents, Kajka gave support and friendship during his last year of life.

"Good to hear your voice, Kajka. It's been a long time. Congratulations."

We caught up on families, my recent eight years at the university, her retirement and then unretirement.

"I have your résumé for Peace Corps director in front of me." My heart sped, needing to be alone. I turned my back to my colleagues, trying to disappear.

Kajka continued, sounding casual, "Are you interested?" After a pause: "What luck. I am here at PPO. Yesterday, they gave me the Peace Corps account, and here is your name. Come in. We can talk." The call ended. I looked back at my colleagues, pretending nothing had happened, and picked up their conversation midsentence.

With that call, my life changed again: three years of exhilaration, political and pandemic trauma, and a thousand Zoom meetings. I would make it to the Peace Corps director finish line at noon, January 20, 2021, emotionally exhausted and eminently proud to have led the Peace Corps under a tumultuous administration. No one knew as the presidency began that this nation's global leadership risked being diminished by a president who, among other international outrages, called many of Peace Corps's countries of service "shithole countries."

My three previous political appointments, under Reagan, H. W. Bush and W. Bush, did not foretell this turmoil. I had not campaigned, having been living an academic life out of politics. My Republican registration since 1981 had not changed. Maybe I unconsciously watched for this opportunity. Kajka knew none of my recent cancer history. Nothing said. Unfortunately, during the nomination process, opposition research uncovered the health scare and spread detailed information on social media. I then owned my cancers and celebrated the medical profession for my full recoveries.

\*

From the PPO call to swearing in took less than five months, a miracle by today's Senate's broken confirmation standards. Donald J. Trump had been president for thirteen months.

My appointment process focused on preparing for the Senate Foreign Relations hearing, the time senators ask whatever they want of nominees. As nominees, we prepare, practice answers, and hope. On the day of the hearing, I sat in the Senate hearing greenroom waiting, repeating two thoughts: "Don't limp when you walk into the hearing room with two hundred people watching, and keep smiling at the C-SPAN camera," the latter more challenging as the camera is hidden without an on light. No matter the questions to me or to the Department of State nominee beside me, I sat tall, hands clasped on the table, unmoving, constant smile.

The most common comment from friends watching on C-SPAN was "You looked great and always smiled." No memory of what I said, by me or anyone else. Unknown then, that was the easiest part of the Peace Corps director path.

A few weeks later, Elaine Chao swore me in at Peace Corps's headquarters. She shared her own experiences as Peace Corps director, my role as her chief of staff, and our friendship. Twenty-five years later, the relationship continues.

\*

The continued investigation of the circumstances and fallout from the Benin Volunteer's murder nine years earlier, when I was acting director, had profoundly impacted Peace Corps. New legislation instructed the director to create a whole-of-agency sexual assault/harassment support system. But the news stories about the murder lived on as headlines made tantalizing reading.

At my hearing, the senators knew I had made the family call. In anticipation of questions about the circumstances, my opening remarks included the reference. It worked. Rather than questioning, senators added support for the importance of women's safety. However, as I had prepared my remarks, trauma and grieving returned, as if it had happened the day before. I choked up reading the words about the tragic event to the senators.

That moment in the hearing brought back the eight times I had called families with life-shattering news. Directors made the calls, a tradition since 1961.

From my first day as director, normally a period of new leadership celebration, I drove into work each morning wondering, "Will a Volunteer die today? Will I have to make a call?" The fear grew, taking the joy out of happiness to be back in the Peace Corps. Trauma from years past grew.

Two weeks after the swearing in, at my one-on-one with Carl, a senior advisor, I asked for help. We had worked closely years earlier. He would sit in my office as I made the tragic calls to families as deputy director, coaching me with whispers and gestures.

"Stay calm. It's okay to show your emotions" or "They will remember the sound of your voice more than words." We had a bond.

Now sitting across from Carl, I began, "I'm struggling." There, confession. "I grow cold when a duty officer walks in with a serious face. I worry—a death? I'm afraid to be here." He paused, never having heard that phrase from me before. He waited, silent.

Finally, he said, looking at his phone on the table as if thinking about the past, "I saw its impact when you were here before, a stronger impact than for other Peace Corps directors." He added, "You're sensitive. That's good. But it hurts you inside."

I waited a moment, then said, "I need to make the calls. Everyone expects me to. But I'm afraid to do it. Nutty. With the director's title comes hard work. But it's eating me up inside."

With his hands against the table, Carl pushed his chair back, sat quietly, thinking. He looked straight at me. "I'll make the calls."

More silence as we both realized what this meant.

"Will you?" I whispered, sensing myself relaxing.

"Of course." He reached out, briefly took my hand, quickly squeezed, and let go. "I see it rips you apart. You care so much. I care but can put it aside once done. You're different. You can't. It's what makes you you."

"Thank you, thank you." I stood up, breathed more slowly, then as we walked to the door. "Will staff think I'm weak, not up to the hard stuff?"

Carl stopped, smiled, and then almost laughed, his bald head wrinkling above his eyebrows. "Your reputation precedes you. Don't worry. You're fine."

*

One more person needed to know, the director of special and mental health services. Jill led the office that provided logistics and support for families and staff once a death happened. Her work began once the Peace Corps director made the call to the family.

"Jill, I've decided that Carl will call families instead of me," I began after settling across from her desk in the cramped office two floors below and after chatting about our families.

She leaned back, looked at me, and then asked, "Why?"

The words came out without thought, all I had kept inside for years, not knowing how deep the wound was. "My brother died suddenly in a car accident, and the short sentence with the news, carefully said by my husband, stays in my mind. The bolt of pain sears." I stopped, put my face in my hands. Jill stayed silent.

I raised my head, grabbed a tissue from her desk, wiped my face, and then said haltingly, "Every time I tell a family, the pain returns. I'm striking them with the same bolt I felt over fifty years ago, destroying who they have been up to the moment their phone rings. And I know they will never be the same. I know. I'm not the same, no matter how long I live." This was the first time I used these words. Fifty years earlier had become yesterday again.

"Jody, you're still in trauma. No wonder you can't do this. You shouldn't do this."

"But the agency, I'm letting down the agency."

"Let me tell you something," Jill said. "I wondered why the Peace Corps has this tradition. These families are in shock. They don't remember who is telling them. Seared in them are the voice, the tone, and some words. You don't need to be that person."

"I'm still in trauma?" I asked, repeating her words, not wanting to believe it.

"Yes, and that's okay." Jill continued, "You don't need to keep bringing the trauma back. Reach out to the families the next day when they need the special comfort only you can give. You are a caring person and the Peace Corps director."

That became our system. Driving into work each day, joy replaced fear.

*

My assumptions about how to serve a president drew from earlier affirming experiences under previous administrations. Peace Corps remained independent and nonpolitical, a standard renewed by each White House. The differences the Trump presidency brought to national leadership came in drips, first slowly, then quickly, like a leaky faucet. Procedures and discussions thought normal by other administrations were challenged or abandoned.

As the summer of 2018 turned to fall, Trump's demands of Congress for over five billion dollars for a border wall grew louder and angrier, an entire federal budget caught in the crosshairs.

"No wall, no federal budget," he said to crowds across the country. Congress had until September 30 to give Trump what he wanted without shutting down the government, no money to operate. Americans watched this game of chicken between the wall and federal funding, not believing government programs could be sacrificed for a wall. They were.

The showdown came December 22, three days before Christmas, forcing eight hundred thousand federal workers to go home without a paycheck, as if fired from their jobs. On the eve of the holiday, federally funded programs across the country, from food stamps to drug approvals to education programs, halted, closed. This had happened before. Under Reagan, three days; Bush, five days. Then employees returned, shutdown forgotten.

Not this time. Trump dug in deep, and so had Congress, the federal government, with its four-trillion-dollar budget, caught between them, including the Peace Corps.

To staff questions, as late December approached, I responded with answers such as "Yes, you have to go home," "No, you will not be paid," and "When home, you cannot access your Peace Corps computers, you cannot do Peace Corps work. Pretend you don't work for the agency."

"But it's the holiday season."

"I wish I could magically fix this, but the White House won't take my call." I feared a national train wreck with the Peace Corps as one car.

Ninety percent of Peace Corps headquarters staff, eight hundred workers, went home, locked out of work, no pay. Ten percent came in, "essential" by government definition, to manage emergency tasks without pay.

I sent gentle preparatory emails to all staff as December 22 arrived, hopeful the shutdown could be averted. "I know this is tough. But we will make it work." To the sixty-one host-country staff, I said, "You can go to work. You directly support Volunteers. We will pay your salary from the last of last year's budget, but not American staff. The law doesn't allow it." Keep Volunteers and host-country staff calm, despite social media's constant pounding about American Armageddon, read on smartphones in Bangkok, Pretoria, or Kyiv.

Parents texted Volunteers directly: "Coming home?" "No money?" "Are you safe?"

My emails to in-country staff: "We're using the rest of last year's budget to support you and the Volunteers. We have no 'this year's money' until either Congress or the White House folds. We have resources to support you for twenty-five days, if careful." I said to the CFO, "Twenty-five days is forever. This will be over before then." Wrong.

Day five, I wrote the field, "You're not hearing much because 90 percent of us can't legally work: furloughed." I gave examples: "We have one desk officer and no assistants for all of Africa, down from ten. Be patient. We have no recruiters or placement officers, so postpone questions about your incoming Volunteer classes. No answers to give and no one to give them." Safety and security fell under the definition of "essential." I assured the field, "We can ship medicines, support medical evacuations, and manage the duty officer system. But no training and new programming." I felt like the Grinch at Christmastime.

The field understood and raised questions, solved problems directly across central Asia to South America and West Africa. "How are you holding up?" a country director asked me. "I worry about you all in Washington. We're pitching in here in the field. We'll make it."

Like eight hundred thousand other federal workers, the furloughed Washington-based Peace Corps staff could have no contact with the agency, furloughed on Christmas Eve, with a stern warning to "make no contact with the Peace Corps."

We wouldn't let them lose faith, find other jobs: keep them updated on Volunteer activities; give advice on unemployment insurance, food banks, diaper and formula supplies; and assure them their plants were being watered, desks being watched over. We wanted them back. How without legally contacting them? Federal law had banned them from official contact. Day by day, Congress and the president dug deeper verbal trenches.

The Peace Corps is creative. RPCVs had to survive and thrive in villages. Washington? Sure. The Information Technology Office had installed a Peace Corps communication app connected to personal staff phones a couple of months earlier, not sure about its use.

Five days into the government shutdown, the border-wall tantrum drove Congress and the White House further apart. Congress didn't have agencies to run; the White House didn't care. Only a massive constituent uprising would move anyone to action, and heated rhetoric had kept that at bay for now. We needed to keep seven thousand Volunteers safe in sixty-one countries without most staff.

"What can I do tomorrow? The next day? And the next? How do I stay calm, steady? How do I keep Volunteers safe?" I asked myself every morning as I stayed in touch, borderline illegally, with those temporarily forced out of the agency. A Volunteer death, a country coup, a major earthquake would put Volunteers at added risk without the backup staff in Washington. We held our breaths.

Those disconnected and sitting without paychecks at home wanted to come back, wanted to be missed. We had an answer: messages from the director to their personal phones via the recently installed app.

Our one-person communication team and I wrote thrice-weekly news and supportive brief personal messages to the private phones of furloughed staff with copies to overseas posts. No work discussed: that would be illegal. We didn't know what other agencies did, but communication, cell phone by cell phone, could hold us together until a budget passed Congress and staff could return, as long as the prior year's rapidly dwindling budget resources held.

Our few staff members with family members working in other agencies mentioned to me they were hearing nothing from their own agency leaders.

"My wife feels adrift from her position in the Department of Commerce," Theodore, the staff trainer, said as we waited for the toaster in the eighth-floor empty kitchen. "She waits for our messages, reassuring us the government's still there. 'Doesn't my agency care?' she asked me yesterday."

We prepared the next staff note. "Keep thinking of our younger staff, those with children, with no savings," Mark said as his hands reached for the keyboard. "Yeah, and that's a third of the staff," Patrick said with a wan smile.

We scoured websites, message boards for offers of reduced and free groceries and household items to add to staff messages. Companies gave away paper goods, Chef José Andrés opened a meal kitchen near Thirteenth and Pennsylvania Avenue for furloughed workers, and federal credit unions offered loans without interest. Mid-January, Christina, my assistant, brought a message from the USAID director to his agency staff, those whom he could reach.

"This just came to me from a friend at USAID. Haven't read it yet, but I bet we can borrow quotes from it for our message tomorrow." She stood by my desk as I read it.

I smiled, then laughed. "It's our message from Monday with their logo." Giving it back to her: "We'll keep leading, and the big agencies can follow."

The Department of Commerce secretary thought differently about supporting staff. On January 24, Secretary Wilbur Ross said he was puzzled by reports of federal workers turning to food banks and other forms of relief, suggesting they should get bridge loans to tide them over.

"True, people might have to pay a little bit of interest, but that it's paycheck or zero is not a valid idea." Secretary Ross continued, "While I feel sorry for the individuals that have hardship cases, eight hundred thousand workers... if they never get their pay, you're talking about a third of a percent on our GDP, so it's not like it's a gigantic number overall" (*Washington Post*, January 24, 2019). Trump supported Secretary Ross. Ross, secretary of commerce and a billionaire, didn't seem to understand or care about workers. Nor did the president.

Christina checked the going interest rate at the Commerce Department credit union. "It's 9 percent," she said. "No reduction offers." The secretary's words, widely read in the *Washington Post*, stung.

My dismay with the president stayed unspoken. Words travel, and an agency director's words travel to the White House. Paranoid? Maybe. Cautious? Yes. Watching appointees from other agencies fired for words of truth justified paranoia. I would not leave. I would protect the agency to which my soul belonged. Stay politically silent, every moment, hour, day. Keep the rage inside. Look calm even when walking in the silent halls. No one can know, except my daughter, Kirsten, to whom I let words, anger, hurt come out each evening.

\*

My walks through the building each day to cheer on the 10 percent of the crew, essential workers, brought me energy. Their faces showed long days and fears of Volunteer system failures. Guy, the only IT field support specialist allowed to work, had brought a cot that sat next to his desk.

"I'm on call. Host-country IT staff represent all time zones as they hold their countries' computer systems together. Communication is literally life and death for Volunteers in the field." He laughed as he looked at his cot with a small pillow, light blanket. "I need to do this," he said. "I would feel personally responsible if even one post went down for a few hours."

By January 18, the twenty-eighth day, angry voices against Congress and the president rose as federally funded services ceased. The remains of last year's Peace Corps budget necessary to support Volunteers during this national farce reached a dangerously low level. We had postponed leases and large purchases to stretch out the rapidly dwindling last year's monies, but Volunteers had to keep receiving monthly living allowances to survive. Our budget team wrote scenarios for bringing home Volunteers and drafted and filed emergency messages to Congress. "We can squeeze by until day forty," my CFO said. "Coffers will be empty by day forty-five."

White House/Congress negotiations became an obsession with the news, coffee chats, social media posts. No one blinked.

"This false drama will end the moment millions of people feel it personally," I said to Mark. "We're hurting inside. Systems are grinding down, but those in the political bubble are not personally affected yet." The political bubble finally burst. Day thirty-four, airlines announced significant to total shutdowns because the Transportation Security Administration (TSA) and airport control tower staff wouldn't continue working. They had not been paid since Christmas. The president signed the bill funding the government, no money for the wall, nothing. The Congressional Budget Office estimated the shutdown, the longest in history, cost taxpayers eleven billion dollars... and for nothing.

Peace Corps senior staff greeted returning staff with balloons, welcome signs, and sweets the first morning back. After buying food from the closest COSTCO, I hosted a lunch next day in Shriver Hall, thanking everyone, one by one, for their endurance. Office plants alive, babies born, furloughed staff's short-term Uber responsibilities discontinued—we were whole again. A few days later, opening a Shriver Hall all-staff meeting, I said, "Working without everyone in place and without the building humming with activity, I have gained an even greater appreciation for the importance and value each of you give the Peace Corps's mission, the Volunteers, and the agency."

The emotional damage from the government shutdown lasted, dismay with the White House grew, and the Peace Corps kept its head low.

\*

After the shutdown, Ivanka Trump created the Women's Global Development and Prosperity Initiative (WGDP). To celebrate it, she announced a White House presidential signing in the Oval Office. Peace Corps was part of the initiative and invited to have a recipient join in the celebration and signing.

"Ella, founder and leader for ten years of the Budala Women's Group, Malawi, will be our representative," I announced at the all-staff meeting. "She and her recent Volunteer counterpart, Anna, will join me to honor Peace Corps's role toward women's economic empowerment."

Ella, a grandmother from rural Malawi, had never left her village home, had no passport, and had never been on a plane. She had limited English. However, her energy, resolve, and gift for encouraging hundreds of women to build an economically viable food co-op made her famous across southern Malawi. Her force of will awed Peace Corps Volunteers.

On February 8, she; Deena, the Peace Corps Malawian staff member and informal interpreter; Anna; and I climbed into the Peace Corps director's black Chevrolet for the five-block ride from our office to the White House.

"You look beautiful, Ella," I said. She turned to Deena to be sure she understood. Her colorful *chitenje* two-by-three-meter cotton cloth wrapped around her as a floor-length skirt, matching the handmade blouse of identical fabric, a traditional dress. She had wrapped her head in the same chitenje cloth, adding a half foot of height to her diminutive five-foot-one frame. Cut glass stones encased in imitation gold around her neck gave additional elegance as she carefully slid into the front seat. She seemed practiced at this ritual.

Thirty minutes for White House clearance, a long walk around the back of the Eisenhower Office Building with a view of the Mall and the Washington Monument, and then under the blue awning and directly through the doors into the White House West Wing.

A few minutes later, about four dozen individuals packed the cabinet room, awaiting permission to enter the Oval Office two doors away—cabinet secretaries, White House aides, agency heads from programs being featured, and women representing women's empowerment globally, each of these women in national dress. Two presidential aides described the event's Oval Office standing chart to the anxious participants, arranged for a presidential photo op when the president sat at the Oval Office resolute desk. They assigned Ella to stand directly behind the president, center back in the photos to be taken that day.

With instructions, we took our places in the Oval Office and waited for the president to arrive. Small agency heads, staffers circled the wall to the president's left, cabinet secretaries and more important dignitaries to his right. Ella, directly behind the president's desk, only needed to stand and smile. I stood on the far left, next to the National Security Council director, Ambassador John Bolton. In person, Ambassador Bolton matched his photo with his larger-than-life bulky white mustache tightly clipped at the edge of an unsmiling mouth. His bushy white eyebrows communicated a sternness not to be interrupted.

"Ambassador Bolton," I said, then introduced myself. "I met you once before as undersecretary of state."

He smiled. "And you are the Peace Corps director. Great organization."

We both looked around, assessing the level of national political leadership attending Ivanka Trump's signature event in the most powerful room in the world.

Ambassador Bolton continued, "Years ago, I designed the USAID/Peace Corps's small project assistance program for Administrator Peter McPherson."

"I remember well, Mr. Ambassador. I did the same for the Peace Corps's side of the agreement. We must have attended the signing ceremony together thirty-five years ago." I sighed with relief that we found a common topic. "Our two agencies just celebrated their anniversaries," I continued. "The USAID representative told us it was and continued to be their most successful project."

Ambassador Bolton smiled, then joked. "I sometimes think it was the only really significant thing I've done."

At that moment, a voice announced the president's arrival. He walked in, suit fitting loosely, pants legs a hint too long, smiled at Ivanka and the cabinet secretaries he passed as he moved to the desk and sat, continuing a quiet conversation with Ivanka, standing at his right.

As the event began, dozens in the press corps hovered on the outside portico, awaiting the glass doors to the Oval Office to open, giving them direct access to the president. Photographers, cameras, phones, fuzzy microphones on poles, elevated lights streamed into the room; cameramen set up equipment, sat, stood, flashed camera lights, recorded a few words from the president, and then left through the same door. Only C-SPAN and White House photographers stayed.

The president, his script written on a single sheet of paper centered on the desk, began his remarks, continuing a smile toward Ivanka. He spoke, then called others to speak: cabinet officials, a grant recipient from Armenia, a congressman. The moment for his signing of the Women Empowerment Initiative had come, the highlight of the event. His stack of black Sharpies, his signature imprinted on each one, sat in a wood file outbox on the desk's left corner.

He reached for a Sharpie, beamed, and said, "We are ready." He picked up the black Sharpie, then added, "Does anyone else have anything to say?" Protocol suggested silence, his question only a formality, then the president's signature. Ella didn't know Oval Office protocol.

She took a step forward, stood between the president and Ivanka, and said quietly, "I have something to say." I thought to myself, "This is an Oval Office disaster in the making," looking at the door to the portico, the press corps outside. Could I walk out? Hide behind the blue curtains? But I stood still, afraid.

She began, "I'm Ella Zanda. I'm honored to…" The president, looking surprised, turned to her. This wasn't in the script. Ivanka smiled, not knowing what to do, but then watched Ella speak. I stopped breathing. She continued: "Be here and represent…" I listened to her clear, quiet, accented voice as she described her project, the Peace Corps Volunteer, the significant impact it had on women in Malawi. She spoke clearly for one minute, then said, "Thank you, Mr. President," and stepped back. I began breathing again.

The president said, "Thank you," picked up the Sharpie, and signed the initiative. He held up the Sharpie, turned slightly, and said, "I know who should get this pen," looking toward Ivanka.

Ella put out her hand, took the pen, and said, "Thank you, Mr. President."

The president looked surprised but smiled, turned, and rose. As he did: "Ella, would you also like my speech?" He handed her the script. "Thank you again, Mr. President." Ella, a Malawi village woman, a force for local women's business, had just given a speech to the most powerful person in the world. Unprompted.

Unknown to me, Peace Corps staff had prepared the speech for Ella, hoping she could recite it earlier in the day. When that didn't happen, Ella gave the speech, unasked, in the Oval Office to the president. She shone.

Later, as we left the White House, Ella, Deela, Anna, and I walked the pathway from the West Wing back to Seventeenth Street. Ella clutched the pen and the speech, walking tall.

I asked Anna, "How do you feel being here? Did you think as a Volunteer you could have this impact?"

Anna, still walking, thought a moment and said, "When you volunteer with the Peace Corps, you accept you will never see the outcome of the work you do in your community. Today, I count myself among those lucky enough to reconnect with their counterparts. I am merely a single representative of the thousands of Volunteers who impact the lives of their host-country neighbors every day."

I have quoted Anna often, knowing that quietly, we make an impact with someone, somewhere, even if we never see it. And Ella impacted me that afternoon and, hopefully, the president.

The next morning, we said goodbye, rewatched C-SPAN with Ella and Deela to affirm it had happened, and called Ivanka's office to thank her. Three days later, Carol Spahn, the Malawi country director, told me how excited Ella felt about her experience in Washington, DC.

"She loved the electric stairs, trains that ran underground, and elevators. Couldn't believe such things existed." Carol continued, "That's all she talks about."

\*

A few months after the president used the term "shithole countries" for most of Africa, I led a six-person White House delegation to Sierra Leone for the inauguration of President Julius Maada.

"What do I say to President Maada, as he knows I'm representing the president?" I whispered to another delegate, a former ambassador and fellow RPCV, as we sat in the transit lounge at CDG, France. "Might he refuse to see me?"

"Diplomacy gets us through these situations," my colleague said gently. "Trust your gut."

Our plane landed at the Lungi International Airport at 9:00 p.m., then one twenty-minute, diesel-powered, open-top boat ride across the Sierra Leone River to the capital, Freetown, then a fifteen-minute car ride to the national preinaugural ball being given by the new president. Our delegation, still in rumpled travel clothes with reminders of diesel fuel from the boat, was to meet President Maada in a side room off the dance floor while celebratory music overpowered most party guest communication. Last-minute plans.

At 11:30 p.m., the new president walked into the side room, flushed with inaugural excitement and wearing a long traditional white robe. He sat, looked at my wind-blown hair and walking shoes, and put out his hand.

After formal introductions by the American ambassador, I began a stilted but practiced speech: "I represent President Trump here to…"

"I know," President Maada said, cutting me off. "I know who you represent. I know what you're supposed to say. But aren't you also the Peace Corps director?"

"Yes, I am," I said. "And…"

"Well, that's what I want to talk about. Let me tell you about my own Volunteer experience." He continued talking without stopping for ten minutes, stories and words of gratitude tumbling out faster as minutes passed. Finally, he said, "We need you now. Can you double the number of Volunteers here this coming year? Tell me yes."

"I'll try to make it happen."

"Thank you, and a pleasure to meet you."

He rose and was off again into the dancing crowd.

He trusted Peace Corps. Sierra Leone had trusted Peace Corps for sixty years. U.S. presidents come and go.

*

Both of my mothers passed away while I was director, both having lived into their nineties. They saw families flourish: fifteen grandchildren and twenty-four great-grandchildren. Francine and Mother met only once, at the arrival gate at the Salt Lake City airport a couple of years before Mother's death. Francine leaned over to Mother, sitting in her wheelchair, and said, "Thank you for raising Jody and David." They both smiled, reached out their hands, then parted. During the years before, they had each asked me of the other, curious mostly but with growing tenderness.

For several years, my sister Cindy worked at the same small Salt Lake City company as my brother Matt, which brought the two sides of the family together. They remain good friends. No more secrets, hiding.

I was in Europe when, in Provo, Utah, Mother passed away. Over the years, family dinners and gatherings gave the two of us time together and, with that, understanding and deep love. A delayed funeral offered time to share my goodbye, gratitude... and peace.

Francine passed away a year later in Salt Lake City. I was in Paraguay. She had left Paris after forty-five years to live her last decade and a half near Cindy. Francine created a new home with colorful fabrics, paintings, and furniture that brought joy similar to that of her Paris apartment but without the Eiffel Tower. My frequent Salt Lake visits, more stories, laughter, and trips to funky used clothing stores made us as one, more than mother and daughter. My strength as director came in part from her love, strengthened because of a twenty-year loss of each to the other and then a decade to build, step by step, trust to become as one.

*

In 2003, a request came to the Peace Corps for a program in Vietnam, thirty years after a war that divided the nation. Even though surprised by the possibility, we excitedly began negotiations, taking small trust-testing steps. In 2010, as my acting director position ended, these same steps kept repeating with little forward movement. Nine years later, as my directorship began, bigger steps taken, now fifteen years. Some said, "It won't happen. Trust is too tenuous. War has a long memory."

With continued negotiations, our two nations agreed enough for me to visit the country for an "almost" signing ceremony and, unknown at the time, for my penultimate trip before the COVID-19 pandemic. Even as leaders continued negotiating legal fine print interpreted through nuances of two languages with generations of cultural interpretation, I traveled to the countryside to live a few moments of future Volunteer experiences. As I watched in a high school English-language classroom, the teacher incorporated the basics of grammar and vocabulary using Facebook texts. Facebook had become the communication vehicle, and its English, the entry to a global community.

Standing in the high school courtyard after class, the headmaster expressed his enthusiasm for having Peace Corps Volunteers: "And we want to give them our best hospitality. We have a few well-furnished dorms here on campus."

I interrupted gently, "Volunteers traditionally live with host families, share in community experiences, and speak in the language of students and colleagues. We respect your offer, but…"

As I spoke, three English teachers behind me immediately raised their hands. "Me, me, I will be a host mom."

"So can I."

"I have kids who I know want them in the family."

I saw in these exchanges people wanting to share, bringing strangers in, being part of each other's lives and teaching experiences. Most were too young to remember the war. If only I could have bottled their excitement to take back to Hanoi.

We did not sign an agreement on that visit; more negotiations were needed. Seven months later, in a Department of State conference room, twenty people sat each six feet apart, each fully masked, with the country agreement printed in both languages, ready to be signed by myself and the Vietnamese ambassador: seventeen years to completion. Now two years following COVID-19, Volunteers are beginning service in the Peace Corps's newest country.

*

The unknown virus originating in Wuhan, China, appeared in Chengdu Province, our headquarters for Peace Corps China. Several days earlier, headlines from Wuhan with hints of the virus's discovery, fatal outcomes, caught our medical office's attention. We watched carefully but were not alarmed by this not-yet-named local virus. But now, in late January, our 146 Volunteers teaching English in technical schools in Chengdu and the surrounding provinces were at risk. The Chinese New Year added health risks to Volunteers traveling throughout the country on vacation. Three days later, on January 29, we ordered a full, immediate Volunteer evacuation to Bangkok.

"Tell the Volunteers to pack for two weeks," I said to the China country director by phone. "I'm sure it'll be settled by then, and Volunteers can return to their teaching. No need for goodbyes to students." Hopeful, I didn't see what lay ahead; I focused just on the next day.

\*

The China Volunteers arrived at the Bangkok airport on a chartered flight, met by Thai Peace Corps staff who said later that day, "We saw fear in the eyes of arriving Volunteers as they read headlines about the virus for the first time. They had no information in China."

"I'm scared. Am I getting sick?" They asked the Thai staff, but no one had answers.

\*

A week later, at 8:00 p.m. DC time, I walked nervously into the Peace Corps conference room, sat, and looked directly at the computer screen and into the faces of the evacuated China Volunteers. They sat in rows in the Bangkok hotel conference room at 8:00 a.m.

I took a breath, straightened my back, and began the painful words: "We don't know when you can go back to China as lockdowns there are continuing indefinitely. Thus, we are planning your return to the United States." Volunteers' faces sagged, voices groaned, hands reached to each other for support. With that sentence, their lives changed. My eyes closed sadly. It was unknown at the time, but this moment did not end emergency evacuations; it began them.

Earlier in January, we had restricted Volunteer travel to emerging hot-spot countries amid Volunteer grumbling. A new agency-wide task force tracked the virus. They recommended posts receive medical, security, and logistical emergency procedures, just in case.

"Isn't this overkill?" I asked the medical director, reading sketchy virus medical details in the email she was about to send. We stood in the medical unit's dark corridor late at night. "This will scare people. Do they need it? Tonight?"

"Yes," came the firm answer. "We have lives at risk."

Country staff gave headquarters a daily virus count report for all Peace Corps countries. I tracked the counts, watching numbers increase. January 30, the day after the China evacuation, the World Health

Organization (WHO) declared the virus a public health emergency. We prepared for evacuations in two other Asian countries. We suspended all nonemergency international Volunteer travel. The virus threat grew.

*

In early February, posts in Asia reported additional constricted movements within and between countries. Our Peace Corps COVID-19 task force prepared daily guidance; talking points for Volunteers, their families in the United States, and Congress; global updates; and updated medical, travel, and self-protection procedures. The virus consumed us, but the determination to keep programs as normal as possible stayed strong.

Even without active COVID-19 cases, by late February, the Mongolian government closed schools and imposed confining local and international travel restrictions. The country didn't want COVID-19 inside its borders. On February 28, we brought Volunteers in Mongolia back to the U.S. I updated my China evacuation points and used them for Peace Corps Mongolia Volunteers, but the conversation did not get easier.

The Peace Corps country director in Mongolia wrote, "The clincher was when flights from Seoul were canceled. I told the embassy, 'If people need to be medically evacuated, we're not going to be able to get them out.' The farthest part of the country is normally a forty-hour bus ride. It took five days, with help from embassy cars, to caravan all Volunteers back in. And, of course, there was a blizzard.... My communities said as Volunteers left, 'We want the Volunteers back as soon as possible.'"

In the first days of March, news of national borders being closed and flights canceled began as ripples, then waves, and finally, a tsunami as countries prepared to close transportation options, borders, and internal movement. Countries announced decisions with only a day's or even a few hours' notice.

Asian and European countries began restricting international flights, limiting in-country travel, requiring travelers to quarantine, and closing schools and other centers. Volunteers could no longer work.

As the second week in March began, we organized departures for other countries in Asia, then eastern Europe. By now, I had sadly memorized the China talking points, giving them to a growing number of fearful Volunteers. I believed we could still stay in most countries and sent daily messages to the field affirming this belief. Emergency plans were in place, practiced, and not needed.

The country director in Ukraine wrote, "Friday the 13 of March, and only three cases confirmed in Ukraine. The Ukrainian government acts quickly and is banning foreigners from entering, effective in 48 hours; 170 border checkpoints closed. We go to alert stage. Overnight, a nationwide lockdown is imposed. Saturday morning, airports close. I tell Washington, time to evacuate. We have 274 Volunteers serving."

This same week, U.S. newspapers headlined the growing COVID-19 cases. From the *Washington Post*, March 14, 2020, "A surge in coronavirus patients is threatening to swamp U.S. hospitals, as Oregon, Virginia, Louisiana, and New York all reported their first coronavirus-related deaths on Saturday."

While the agency focused on the safety and security of Volunteers and staff globally, the U.S. pandemic situation deteriorated. We had no federal government precaution guidelines. The Peace Corps was on its own. I had a responsibility for seven thousand Volunteer lives around the world, almost a thousand staff in Washington, and double that many host-country staff globally.

The task force outlined a new emergency COVID-19 plan with the hopeful name, Peace Corps Everlasting, to guide actions for staff at headquarters and all posts. Up to this point, we had focused on the Volunteers. Now as the pandemic spread in the United States, focus increased to include the safety of our Washington staff as well.

On March 11, I ordered the 950 Washington staff members home, each with an encrypted laptop and phone. IT had worked the previous forty-eight hours nonstop to make working remotely possible.

"How do we work?" a concerned desk officer asked that afternoon, running into my office. "I have Volunteers in transit. The field staff needs guidance. I can't abandon them." Then "Can you really do this to us?"

"Yes, the only responsible action given the rising COVID-19 numbers in DC. We'll figure it out as we're in this together. We will manage, somehow, remotely," I said without knowing what I meant.

That afternoon, my assistant, Izi, handed me a preprogrammed Peace Corps phone. "Here is everything you need to get in touch with us, conference call-in numbers, post emergency numbers..."

"Thanks. But I don't need it. My phone works fine."

"Yes. You. Need. It. This is serious." My assistant had never spoken to me that way.

"But we'll be back together in a couple of weeks. I know it."

Izi just rolled her eyes. She knew. And she was right—when I walked out that afternoon, I would not step foot in any office in the building for the duration of my tenure, eleven months. Agency staff in the United States and from sixty-one countries saw me from my upstairs home study, forty masks from my travels on the wall behind me; owls, cardinals, and black squirrels in the trees outside; and my face on Zoom all day, looking professional with a scarf, makeup, and dangling earrings. March 12, 9:30 a.m., I opened the computer, brought up the system, found Skype, opened the virtual senior staff meeting, and greeted thirty-five staff members. If I could do it, so could others, no excuses made. This group, three days a week, same time, one hour, became the agency lifeline for the thousands of decisions made over the following weeks and months that brought home seven thousand Volunteers in nine dates from sixty-one countries and supported their unanticipated COVID-19 U.S. reentry.

March 12–15, the global public health collapse grew.

Friday, Saturday, and Sunday morning, the emails became more frequent and alarming. March 15, 2:00 p.m., Sunday, Patrick, the associate director for international operations, called me. He sounded hesitant, nervous, knowing what he had to say to the director. He didn't want to say it.

"More countries are closing borders, canceling international flights, and restricting internal movement." He paused. I could hear his measured breath. "I have just talked to the three regional directors who have talked with their country directors. We agree we should put out the order to evacuate all seven thousand Volunteers."

His words from the speakerphone reached through my sunroom, behind plants, next to paintings, under chairs. The words couldn't be stuffed back into the phone. They couldn't be swept into a dustbin. They now filled the space. I sat still in my leather chair, holding the phone in front of me, thinking. My mind did what it does in emergencies: make quick checklists. Making lists postponed emotion.

"Patrick, who have you talked to?" Before he could answer, I continued, "When did you talk to them? Do they all feel the same?" I knew the answers, needed more time to think, to absorb. Now, no more stalling.

I said, slowly, deliberately, clearly, "I will order all Volunteers to evacuate tonight. Have the team prepare the Peace Corps global email message for me to review by 10:00 p.m. to be sent by midnight. Monday will have already begun in most countries."

"Do we need to ask permission or even tell anyone outside the agency first?" Patrick asked.

"No," I said firmly. "No one else needs to know before we send out the notice. No one needs to approve, not the White House, not Congress, not the Department of State. Once the worldwide announcement is sent, it'll be too late to be challenged. We know what we're doing. I won't be second-guessed."

"Thanks," Patrick said. "No one wanted this to happen." His voice stopped. Then "But now it's here."

I said, "We have to move fast, fast. No sleep for anyone during the next two weeks." After more instructions, I added, "Thank you again, Patrick. I know how hard this call was for you to make." We hung up, neither being able to predict the implications of a full worldwide evacuation.

I stood, walked to the window, stared at the trees with their first hint of green. It will be a beautiful spring. I sat again. Tears began, came faster. I sobbed, having made the most difficult decision of my life. This decision closed down part of my soul. We began what had never happened in sixty years of Peace Corps, a complete worldwide evacuation. Peace Corps had been my touchstone for fifty-four years, since being a Volunteer in Tunisia. The agency had the reputation as a national and global treasure, protected and honored. As its twentieth director, I respected those who preceded me and hoped to give an even stronger Peace Corps to whoever followed. Instead, on this Sunday afternoon, I ended all Volunteer service, leaving only an empty shell of global service for the future.

*

That afternoon, I created my mental checklist, small next-day decisions, then the following day's decisions. The long-term impact emerged slowly in my head, its implications difficult to visualize. Better not to know.

Emergency actions begin now. Focus on now. Now. Tonight. Show calm. Be present. By midnight, seven thousand Volunteers and thirty-five hundred staff in the United States and in sixty-one countries would begin emergency evacuations. The White House, Congress, and Volunteer families would be told moments and hours later. Too late for them to intervene. That was my plan.

No one, not Congress, not the White House, not families, gave us pushback. Instead, support.

A State Department official called me four days later asking about our emergency charter planes for Volunteers. "How did you know the decision had to be made Sunday?" he asked. "Here at State, we're already too late. International flights canceled, charters full." I smiled to myself, saying nothing. We knew. Local government officials looked out for us. Months later, word circulated that Fulbright faculty and students had to quarantine in the country for up to four months before finding flights home.

*

The next nine days, through March 25, we evacuated 6,892 Volunteers and Trainees to the United States. We had little time as international travel choices closed hourly. If no scheduled flights, Peace Corps in-country staff chartered planes. Forty percent of the Volunteers returned to the United States on charter flights.

We drew on ambassadors, embassy staff, taxis, local banks, guest-houses, hotels, restaurants, host-country counterparts and families, and local and national host-country officials. Their gracious help affirmed their support for the Peace Corps and Volunteers.

Peace Corps staff in-country worked continuously to make sure Volunteers could leave posts safely, quickly, and with the dignity of service the Volunteers had given.

The country director in Ukraine wrote:

I was in Kryvyi Rih at a training with Volunteers and Ukrainian partners, took a seven-hour train back to Kyiv Saturday morning. Peace Corps in DC finds a charter plane from Jordan, to arrive Monday. PC Ukraine had 274 Volunteers serving. We tell all Volunteers to get to Kyiv by Sunday night; they do. We get them to the airport—which is closed, skeleton staff. We wait. Flight delayed several times, then, about midnight, canceled. Hotels were closing. We found rooms; staff brought PCVs [Peace Corps Volunteers] water and food, since restaurants were closing.

Tuesday's charter: delayed, then canceled. Wednesday: flight delayed several times, then canceled last minute. The government of Jordan wouldn't let the plane leave because of new COVID-19 restrictions.

Thursday, nineteen cases. We're getting inquiries from congressional offices about concerned Volunteers' parents: What's going on? Thursday: delays, cancelation. Peace Corps HQ locates a different charter company from Spain. Thursday night, 10:30 p.m., wheels up, Madrid. We move PCVs in six different buses, with police and Regional Security Officer escort, since it is now illegal to gather more than ten people. At Kyiv airport, they can't issue or print boarding passes, systems down. So airport staff write them out by hand. Check-in took ten hours. Friday morning, 6:20 a.m., plane departs. Kyiv to Madrid to Dulles to homes of record.

Some Volunteers left their country of service within a few hours. Others remained for several days. Some completed formal close-of-service activities and/or physical exams; others did not. We provided ceremonies of closure, such as ringing the Peace Corps Volunteer end-of-service ceremonial bell, if even on the tarmac. We wanted to honor each Volunteer's and trainee's time in-country.

*

Peace Corps Washington staff, working from home, became one family of action. As core evacuation staff worked without stopping, other offices tasked staff to help them. Volunteer recruitment staff supported duty officers, who themselves came from other offices to take up responsibilities. Management staff supported travel; regional staff supported country staff. I virtually attended emergency team meetings; encouraged finding planes, charters, emergency supplies; then jumped to the next team meeting and helped make decisions about messaging Congress, getting legal authority for our actions, hour after hour, day after day as Kirsten brought stories to help me stay calm. "The baby owls out back have just been born. They know how to screech! Ugh."

"We can't fail," I said to myself with each meeting, each decision. I feared an accident, a lost plane, an airport disaster. We counted each Volunteer as they arrived safely on U.S. soil, each a success of individual staff and Volunteer tenacity, grit, and luck. These Volunteers all recounted their experiences:

Lucy Baker, a Volunteer in Mongolia: "Wednesday, February 26, walking home from visiting a friend, my site mate called me in tears. 'Lucy, we're being evacuated,' she said. Then I received the email. I had about thirty-six hours to pack up everything and say goodbye. Teachers came over at midnight to say farewell. That was hard. All that could be said was, 'I'll be back.'"

Diane Glover, Volunteer in the Philippines: "Then came the email. Peace Corps staff flew from Manila to Cebu City to ensure that Volunteers consolidating there got home safely. They just wanted to support their Volunteers till the very end. The evacuation has given us a snap of realization: your relationship is your success—the relationship that you create in your community. And suddenly, that was gone."

Rok Locksley, Volunteer in the Philippines: "I firmly believe that one-to-one relationships built at a grassroots level between people who are fundamentally different is the best pathway to world peace. But I forgot how much it hurts to leave your friends."

Volunteers and trainees showed honor, dignity, selflessness, and courage. This evacuation was a disruption to them of a two-year life-changing commitment to service.

*

Everyone returned safely to the United States. Thousands self-quarantined for fourteen days.

Once back in the United States, many Volunteers were angry, sad, confused, and fearful. Many had no plans. They expressed justifiable anger and confusion on social media, in emails, on calls, posts too painful for me to read. All were natural grieving processes. We were all hurting... badly.

I knew anger, grieving, confusion. I knew their feelings, wished I could make the evacuation go away, could send Volunteers back and kill the virus. I could do none of this, only absorb their anger.

A letter to the agency from the mother of a returning Volunteer brought me perspective. At that moment, I loved parents:

> Thank you for your kindness and heroic efforts. I just picked up my daughter from the airport. As the events of the past few days have evolved, I, like many mothers around the world, have been worried about our children. You all have mothers... you may even be mothers yourselves... so you know what I am saying here. I cannot thank you enough for helping my child get home.

[Her time in the Peace Corps] was nothing short of transformative. Right now, with the jet lag and emotional adjustment, her soul has yet to catch up to her body. When her soul has time to catch up and her quarantine here is over, you will certainly be on our minds. And the story of your efforts will be told over and over.

\*

Our legislative mandate, our legal structure, and our internal policies had no protocols or decision tools for evacuating all Volunteers at the same time. We creatively interpreted rules for this emergency. Our teams had to find airlines to get wheels up, manage airport arrivals, give onward tickets, provide access to U.S. cell usage and immediate cash, and share onward quarantine locations without breaking quarantine rules.

Everyone continued to account for each returning Volunteer as needs shifted from getting home to accessing U.S. medical doctors and clinics, medicines, evacuation allowance ($10,000), and trauma-related emotional support. Volunteers arrived having been out of the United States for up to two years and without U.S. dollars, U.S.-activated phones, or appropriate clothes for March weather. An unprecedented American health crisis confronted them. Their families had not expected them, and the Volunteers did not plan to be home.

A senior Department of Transportation official, whose department was helping other agencies get two hundred thousand Americans back to the United States, told me later, "If you had pulled the Volunteers back any later, it would have been mass pandemonium. You made the right decision at precisely the right time." Host-country officials had watched out for the Peace Corps, gave us a warning, and then stayed with us until everyone was safely home.

I didn't know the implications of the March 15 decision—good, bad, safe, deadly, overly cautious. Decisions are part experience, part gut—they are made with available information at the moment. No one knew COVID-19's future, only as of that day.

Decision results included hard work, leadership, and luck. We worked hard to influence the luck.

Supporting evacuated Returned Peace Corps Volunteers (eRPCVs) remained my priority, our staff's priority. To support their reintegration home and help find necessary services, we reinterpreted the rules. When necessary, we went to Congress and Office of Management and Budget (OMB), armed with stories of returning Volunteers without resources. A few days earlier, they had been Volunteers. They had been evacuated early; some, after being in country only a few weeks, had not been allowed to complete their two years of service. Thus, they were not legally eligible for support. I made personal calls. Agencies came through, tweaking rules, getting congressional legislative action supporting these Volunteers. The March 2020 Coronavirus Aid, Relief, and Economic Security (CARES) Act gave them access to state unemployment benefits. The Office of Personnel Management helped negotiate access for all returning Volunteers to non-competitive eligibility for federal service for one year. The OMB supported our adding two more months of health insurance and evacuation allowances.

Thousands of families and friends across the United States offered informal support to the eRPCVs. Many who gave support had been Volunteers themselves or family, colleagues, and friends of Volunteers.

We maintained full staff in the United States and in each overseas post. This ensured that every one of our Volunteers returned as soon as possible. Congress approved our budget to support host-country staff and the return of Volunteers. We continued to work on laptops, phones, kitchen tables, and porches throughout the world. Despite our hopes, returning Volunteers to countries of service was not to be before I left my position eleven months later, a month before the FDA approved the first COVID-19 vaccine, and thirteen months after the pandemic began. We had set dates, canceled dates, set new dates, and gave up setting dates. Without a vaccine, COVID-19 could be fatal. The world closed down. No one moved.

*

The murder of George Floyd on Memorial Day 2020 brought a nationwide and then worldwide tide of anger, fear, and Black Lives Matter (BLM) marches. I watched the marches on my screens, large and small, from my home study. Seven thousand Volunteers had been home less than three months, angry, frustrated, and waiting for jobs or graduate school. Their responses to the murder poured into social media accounts, and the frequency and intensity grew daily. Their support for BLM and disdain for institutions not supporting the movement focused on the Peace Corps, an institution they had joined and that now let them down: bringing them home and not supporting the protests.

Anger turned toward me, the director and a Trump appointee, unwilling to speak out forcefully for the movement.

The communications office shared summaries of the evacuated RPCV posts but said, "Don't look at them. You'll get depressed. We know how personal this is to you… and you can't respond directly to them."

"You know me too well. Thank you," I replied.

President Trump had said, "Black Lives Matter is a symbol of hate," further infuriating the eRPCVs toward me. I remained silent. Personally, I supported the broad message of BLM, but as an appointee, I could say nothing.

As businesses and nonprofits posted their support for BLM and racial equality in the weeks after Floyd's death, communications tracked federal agency sites for similar statements. Nothing. Pressure mounted from RPCVs and staff for a Peace Corps website statement: "Where is it?" "Why don't you make a bold statement?" "You speak of equality, and you say nothing." "You're weak." And worse.

On day nine, I approved a website post highlighting our commitment to diversity, equity, and inclusion without mentioning BLM. My general counsel said the agency legally couldn't use the term. Before posting the message, three of my political appointees reviewed the post to see if it would upset the White House.

"Good luck. This should pass," one remarked. "Our Peace Corps constituency is crying out for it… and more." We posted it, probably the only agency in the federal government to do so.

From the Twitter feed: "This is weak." "Your statement is timid." "Don't you believe in your own institution?" "Where is support for BLM?" "We don't trust Peace Corps to do the right thing by our mission." "Shame." And so on.

From the White House two days later: "We don't support your posting the message. Don't do or say any more." They guaranteed my silence.

In the thrice-weekly senior staff meetings, I opened with a clear statement: "We are here as senior staff, as an agency, for the long haul… returning Volunteers to the field." I paused at this moment, looked to ensure their faces were attentive. I then slowed my words, raising my voice. "Until we do, we are vulnerable to those in Congress, only a few—but a powerful few—who could hold, cut, or eliminate our budget and our agency. A handful in the White House National Security Council would support this congressional wrecking crew." I paused again. "Congress and the NSC could now do grave damage to us. In business terms, without Volunteers, we don't have a product to protect, and our agency is funded with taxpayer money."

Responses came: "But our staff want our statements. They're hurting inside. Many of our staff were Volunteers. Silence from you and from us challenges values they are here to uphold." And "They don't understand. Our agency is nonpolitical. We should have space to speak out."

More spoke. I listened for the depth of agency-wide rage. I expressed understanding of their feelings but could not express my own. Speaking up would end my leadership.

I then added, "Think for a minute. Staff can discuss among themselves, within their Zoom spaces, quietly, the anger, hate, and sadness. You can support their doing so. But remember, if we lose our agency, we have nothing. We are in this for next year, years afterward. We must focus first on our staff overseas and returning our Volunteers. We cannot make public statements, nor can I, personally."

I had no place to be me, Jody, no private personhood; I can only be the Peace Corps director, a public leader. Leadership is lonely.

*

The summer of 2020 remained tortious throughout the United States: marches, fights, vicious headlines.

I acted strongly on what I could control: internal changes. These changes said what couldn't be said in words: I believed. We could be better ourselves. Our staff, at headquarters and in the field, focused on internal changes toward equity and greater diversity. Our new sixteen-person task force interviewed individuals, conducted surveys, reviewed results, and prepared recommendations. These recommendations included diversity training for staff, outreach to minority employment organizations for Peace Corps job announcements, higher reimbursements for preservice medical exams, and strengthening minority recruitment staff at colleges and universities.

Staff engaged, shared ideas, saw decisions, some of which had languished. The new diversity training contractor began work sessions, and field staff joined meetings and nudged conversations toward other countries' viewpoints and reactions to the videos of street demonstrations headlined globally. Peace Corps host-country staff saw the nine-minute video of George Floyd's death. They asked questions: "How could that happen in the United States?" "We believed in your country. Can we now?" "What do we say to host families here in Thailand, Rwanda, Kosovo?"

We tried to better understand what we thought we knew about each other, but this understanding was difficult. We couldn't properly see how the world saw us, how they interpreted this country after watching George Floyd's slow death. Painful. I became lonelier, no place to speak my feelings, except to my daughter, Kirsten.

*

Friday, September 4, 2020, 6:00 p.m., three months following George Floyd's death, the OMB sent a directive to all federal agency heads:

> It has come to the president's attention that executive branch agencies have spent millions of taxpayers' dollars on "training" government workers to believe divisive, anti-American propaganda.... Employees have been required to attend trainings where they are told that "virtually all white people" contribute to racism or required to say they benefit from racism.... The president has directed me to ensure that federal agencies cease and desist from using taxpayers' dollars to fund these divisive, un-American propaganda training sessions....
>
> All agencies are directed to identify all contracts or other agency spending related to any training on "critical race theory," "white privilege," or other training or propaganda effort that teaches or suggests either (1) that the United States is an inherently racist or evil country or (2) that any race or ethnic is inherently racist or evil... to cancel any such contracts or divert federal dollars away from these un-American propaganda training sessions.

These words stung. Who uses these phrases? Could this administration call our work at the Peace Corps un-American propaganda? Or share these vile words with the entire federal workforce, workers who care about this country and represent its rich ethnic and racial diversity?

Yes, they could, and they did—and at a time only cowards send edicts: 6:00 p.m. Friday evening, the time least likely for news headlines. Our three months of rebuilding a fractured workforce, day by painful day, torn apart by George Floyd's murder and the racial discrimination it exposed, were called out as "un-American propaganda." All I believed, had been taught, and experienced were wrenched away with those words.

Saturday morning, I ordered Peace Corps management to cancel the diversity training contract. Monday morning, an email went to all department heads, putting our task force and its work on pause. It quoted the OMB directive. The agency should know this decision belonged directly to the Trump administration. The hammer on top of our work dropped. The door slammed shut. We put the task force on hold.

The reaction was minimal. Over the almost four years of the Trump administration, our overseas staff had gotten used to news about the administration's disdain for darker skin hues, other languages, different cultures. This announcement confirmed the disdain. Why react?

The in-country staff had shared their attitudes in conversations with the headquarters desk officers. They looked for help in understanding.

"How do I respond?" one officer asked me during an Africa region virtual desk officer meeting I attended a few months earlier. Another officer added, "The words uttered by the president three years ago, 'shithole countries,' have seeped into host-country attitudes toward this powerful man." She added, "He's now seen as little, petty."

The poll numbers favoring candidate Joe Biden winning the presidency in November contributed to the staff's mild reaction to my email.

My assistant said, "Countdown, two more months." I didn't react, couldn't react. I said nothing.

The word "pause" in my email to department heads deliberately suggested, without words, that I, too, believed a new president would occupy the White House in four months, and the task force could spring back to life. If so, I could not be there to lead its renewal. Agency leaders leave when their presidents leave office on January 20 every four or eight years. I would leave on that date.

*

Even knowing my job would end if Trump lost the election, all in me prayed for Biden to be successful. I had seen the innards of the government crumbling during the last several months before Trump left office, firing people who cared about the government, exchanging them for his supplicants who supported his arbitrary decisions. Even with only a month left, the administration could bring government operations to a halt.

After the election, the agency and I watched the news carefully, the daily movement of elector certification as it moved from the communities to state houses and then to the Capitol on January 6 for final certification, for some a civics lesson not learned in high school. If we got through that date, we could make it, even though Trump had two more weeks in office to create havoc.

On that day, we worked from home as we had for over ten months, Zoom meetings filling each day. During my lunch break, I saw the headlines about the event on the Mall, heard words of Trump encouraging the audience, but being optimistic, I assumed the final certification would go smoothly.

At 3:15 p.m., my associate director, also a political appointee, Skyped me, saying he needed to talk as soon as possible.

I slipped out of my Zoom staff meeting and Skyped him, who then said, "Do you know what is happening at the Capitol? It looks like a coup." His voice sounded tense, frightened. "I fear for our country," he continued, then paused, his voice cracking. "I didn't sign up to be part of the Trump administration for this." He stopped again, his voice becoming quiet. "I want to submit my letter of resignation now, this afternoon. I can no longer affiliate with this president."

His words were direct, fearful. What's happening to us? He doesn't exaggerate. My heart rate rose with his news, and my panic about Biden not being certified and Trump not leaving on January 20 rushed forward.

"Please don't resign," I said with the most even tone I could muster. "We need you. Now. We have to make it through to the inauguration."

The associate director continued to describe what he saw on TV.

"I cannot support this assault on the Capitol. I can't," he said, describing the events.

"We are here for the Peace Corps, not the administration. We must ensure the Peace Corps survives. You are part of our survival. Stay," I said too loudly.

"I'm so angry. They can't do this. But…" He trailed off. The TV voices in the background covered our silence. "I will stay." He paused again, then "I believe in us, in our mission."

"Thank you. You're needed. We all have each other."

After the call, I brought up coverage and listened silently, feeling more anger at what such a mob could do to a nation. Because of COVID-19, I had been confined to my upstairs home study for the past ten months. The park outside, with the owls, squirrels, deer, and mammoth trees losing and then renewing their green canopy, had substituted for direct human contact. Now listening to this impending capital building chaos brought me a sense of helplessness as I sat in a chair eight miles north of the Capitol. My life championed democracy with its trust in humans respecting each other. Could this end today?

The Peace Corps building guards had reported to the security team their early morning January 6 observations of men shouting and swearing to each other as they walked through the parking garage to the exit. The number of flags, signs, sticks they carried had alarmed the guards, three of whom had seen similar potential violent anger in men in their home African countries.

"It's okay. This neighborhood is well policed. And the nearby Capitol is fully protected," Shawn had told the guards that morning. When he talked with me at 5:00 p.m., he said, "I didn't know these were the men on their way to the Capitol." His voice cracked. "This is hell. What's really happening?" He began speaking more to himself than to me, his voice breaking. He paused, then asked, "Should I have reported these men to the police this morning? But I had nothing to report." As we talked by phone, Shawn second-guessed his earlier decisions.

"It's okay, Shawn. We respond based on what we know. None of us could have guessed the atrocities we're seeing. I'm sickened as I listen." Shawn then agreed to bike to the Peace Corps building to ensure its safety as the angry, rowdy men seen in the morning returned to the garage.

As the afternoon chaos unfolded, staff sent me emails describing fear for themselves and that the election results would be overturned. My two staff assistants watched events directly from their apartment windows, two blocks north of the Capitol.

"What country are we in?" one texted. "I'm watching the anger, the fighting near my front doorstep. I'm scared."

Some Peace Corps staff had seen coups and violent national leadership uprisings during their years overseas as Volunteers. They talked about these experiences in our work conversations, assuming these stories wouldn't be repeated in our own democratic system. As director, I assured the staff of this belief. I knew little and believed much. Did I trust too much?

*

As with others, I listened intently hour after hour through the evening and into the night, fearful of when Congress could reconvene and certify the election. By midnight, most of us watching understood the awful reality that the mob wanted to shut down Congress to violently prevent the certification. Like almost all other Americans, I stayed close to news accounts of mob rule in the Capitol and the slow return to order, all culminating in Vice President Mike Pence's certification of the Electoral College vote at 3:40 a.m. January 7.

Calmness didn't come, couldn't come as words of denial continued out of the White House through the night and on through the next fourteen days to January 20, Inauguration Day. The president determinedly created government havoc with last-minute agency leadership changes and denial of access to agencies by the presidential transition team.

The morning of January 7, only hours after Vice President Pence had certified the election, Secretary of Transportation Elaine Chao resigned in protest to the president's actions. The administration had been creating governmental fear and distrust since the election, most notably firing senior officials in the Department of Defense, including the secretary of defense. With Chao's resignation, several emails arrived in my inbox. "Will you resign? Will you make a statement?" Staff knew of my relationship with Secretary Chao and asked about a resignation "in principle" against the president, as did the secretary.

Despite deep anger at what happened since the election and fear for the future of the electoral process, I did not, would not resign. Even in the two weeks before the inauguration, a new person, a Trump person, replacing me could end the Peace Corps. I had met a couple in the administration who would do it without guilt. With no in-country serving Volunteers, outcries of the demise could be muffled until too late.

A fifty-eight-year national treasure had been given to me when sworn in, and I would proudly pass that treasure, even though temporarily shy of full sparkle, to the next director.

\*

Despite the Presidential Transition Acts of 1963 and 2015, the Trump administration had not let the Biden transition team begin serious work within the agencies. Even the day after Vice President Pence certified the final election count, we at the Peace Corps, like other federal agencies, were required to continue acting as if no election had occurred. We could not prepare for our successors.

Kirsten listened to my growing anxiety and fear about the administration's election results denial: "I have to be calm with my staff, but I'm afraid they can read my face. On Zoom, it's right in front of them. I know how alarmed they are."

"Let me do a countdown for you. Give you a morning smile and calm you." I heard her clinical social work voice. A yellow Post-It note appeared on the top of my coffeepot on November 18 with the number "63." The yellow sticky "60" appeared on the hallway mirror, and "59" on the front door window, November 21. These early numbers seemed so forbidding, a long way from the inauguration with growing news headlines of denial.

"Two more months of this president's election denial," I said to her as the "59" came into view. "I'm not sure I can stand the tension... but I have to," I kept repeating to Kirsten.

Sticky "56" adorned Baby Yoda's midsection as he sat next to the milk in the refrigerator. Sticky "55" had a place of honor with the turkey at the Thanksgiving table, and "52" adorned Buddha's forehead under the second-floor stairs.

The Christmas holidays brought added fear of the president not leaving office. The Electoral College met on December 14 to formally elect the new president, but with that legal milestone, no White House admissions of defeat, and no permission to begin agency transition.

With the holidays, the election denials grew louder. My birthday, December 16, was celebrated with "35" on Kozy Shack pudding in the refrigerator and a "Happy Birthday" balloon, but no proper celebration until after January 20. A carefully wrapped priority mail shoebox had only "26" inside, my Christmas present.

Getting close, only the vice president's Electoral College certification remained. This was the day it was to happen, the final certification. Sticky "14," January 6, sat in the middle of a partially finished puzzle on the dining room table. It had a picture of a flower garden with white, red, and yellow butterflies in the completed top third, their colorful wings belying what would happen only hours later. On it, Kirsten had written, "Congrats, GA Democrats," the state that made Biden's victory assured. This morning brought a smile, then terror hours later. Even the puzzle's butterflies stopped flying.

January 7, the Buddha wore a mask hiding the nose and mouth. "Speak no evil," whispered behind sticky "13" under the bust.

Each workday, our Peace Corps meetings continued on Zoom, my forced tranquil face hiding anxiety, even paranoia, of democracy's demise. Host-country staff asked questions reflecting their bafflement and concern about the president's behavior and the labyrinth-like constitutional routine to certify and swear in a new president. "Why?" they asked often enough for the Americans on the calls to wonder themselves. We were drained of rational responses to questions, even our own questions. The twenty of us who were political appointees still could say nothing about our leaving the agency on January 20. We could make no agency transition plans, only a couple of weeks away.

"Will you be here after next week? Will President Trump be here after next week?" an international staff member asked on January 8.

"I follow the president's term of office, whatever that means" was all I could say. My insides begged for the president to be gone. I had seen broken political, democratic systems in other countries and trusted ours to stay strong. Having seen the alternatives and their stultification of citizen freedoms, the potential of our own president not leaving office terrorized me for what my country could become.

I kept looking for the stickies from my daughter. Their shrinking numbers gave me hope.

Sticky "7" adorned my Peace Corps mug in the cupboard, sticky "6" covered three brownies with the hopeful words "Less than one week left."

The last week became almost normal again. The Biden transition team had finally been given permission by the Trump administration to talk to the staff, two months after the election and two months after the law said they could do so. The entire federal government had less than ten days to transfer leadership among dozens of agencies with a multitrillion-dollar national budget. The president's denial of transfer encouraged more chaos. We prepared sign-offs and had a virtual farewell party with the political appointees, all of whom would leave on January 20.

A few days earlier, I gave an agency-wide Zoom farewell speech, seen by staff on home computers in sixty-one Peace Corps countries as well as in the United States. COVID-19 continued to keep in-country offices and Peace Corps headquarters empty.

I come to this moment humbled and honored to have served as Peace Corps director. I am proud of what we have accomplished in the last three years and a little sad to say goodbye to an agency I have cared about for fifty-four years, close friends with whom I work, and our teams here now as we return to our global mission of Volunteer service. You all know how much I care for each of you.

This trust and these relationships, shown in strength this last year during COVID-19, have flourished because we have committed over sixty years to our core values, mission, and goals. People have joined the Peace Corps for more than five decades because they trust and believe in the organization's mission and three goals and know that staff will always work hard to provide them a safe, healthy, and productive service.

Nations and communities trust the Peace Corps to provide qualified and committed Volunteers to work alongside their professionals at local and regional levels to improve the quality of life of all. We have done so for so many years, and they know we will continue to do so. Agencies, companies, NGOs, and educational institutions want to engage in relationships and partnerships because they believe we can be a transparent, trustworthy, humble, and powerful partner.

Trust and respect are not easy to establish and perhaps even more difficult to maintain over decades.... The Peace Corps has done that, we have done that because we honor our mission and our respect for everyone with whom we live and work.

Last Wednesday, we all witnessed a horrific event at the U.S. Capitol. We know that there is a lack of trust, with cynicism and deep divisions existing across the country. However, as I said last Friday, democracy was shown to be strong Wednesday night and in these subsequent days. We know the Peace Corps and, in particular, RPCVs have a role, obligation, to contribute to the repairing of our country's colorful and vibrant fabric using all the skills, sensitivities, and experiences gained through our service and work with the Peace Corps. We must continue to challenge each other to do so.

*

Inauguration Day met all but one tradition established over generations of the U.S. democratic transfer of leadership. The president had dishonored the outgoing presidential tradition, left from Andrews Air Force Base at 8:00 in the morning to ride in Air Force One for one last time and to not have to meet or shake hands with his successor, President Biden.

My "o" sticky reminded me of normal and a new beginning for me without the Peace Corps. It was stuck to a yogurt jar in the refrigerator with only the words "Inauguration Day." The next morning, January 21, I slept in, peacefully, for the first time in three years.

# Epilogue

January 20, 2021. By midmorning, I had removed my personal effects from my office in Peace Corps headquarters. The last to be packed was a batik painting from Tunisia and a framed photo of my children. I reflected on my decision on March 15, 2020, to recall all Volunteers to the United States as the COVID-19 pandemic raged. I recalled my fear they might not return, that the Peace Corps could disappear, would be sacrificed by an administration with little interest in the countries where our Volunteers serve.

By noon on that day, I knew the Peace Corps would survive. The incoming administration would honor JFK's commitment, made in an executive order on March 1, 1961, sixty years earlier. It would return Volunteers to the field as soon as the pandemic eased.

I look back with pride and forward with hope—and remain active in support of the Peace Corps and its mission. I am the copresident of Women of Peace Corps Legacy, an NGO I helped establish before I became Peace Corps director. Its members have joined to honor Volunteer and staff service and promote its values to newer Volunteers and to women and girls around the world.

The Institute of Politics at Harvard gave me the opportunity to spend twelve weeks on campus as a fellow in a venue engaging with young scholars interested in international service. Their excitement about a strong global future that they will shape ensured my belief in the next generation of leaders and in America's robust international engagement. My continued student mentoring on both the University of Maryland and the University of Utah campuses reinforces that belief.

In the three years since I left the Peace Corps, I continue to reflect on the difference we Volunteers and staff have made. What have we done? There are hundreds of thousands of stories to be told multiple times by those in communities, homes, and schools where Volunteers have served. Each is framed through the lens of teaching and learning in diverse cultures and traditions and bringing home that experience to shape our nation.

Today, over three thousand Volunteers are serving in fifty-eight countries, and numbers continue to grow by the month. Current countries have welcomed Volunteers back, and new countries have asked for the program. Eagerness for these family and community relationships is told with each Volunteer serving and each counterpart in schools, clinics, and centers.

Has my experience changed me? By reading this book, you know the answer. Have I changed the world as JFK intended? Surely a little here and there. Now multiply that by the experiences of another quarter million Volunteers—and know that we have collectively made a difference.

# Index

# About the Author

Josephine (Jody) Olsen, served as the twentieth director of the Peace Corps between March 2018 and January 2021. With the beginning of the global COVID-19 pandemic, she made the decision to evacuate all seven thousand Peace Corps Volunteers from sixty-one countries safely back to the United States.

Jody began her career as a Peace Corps Volunteer, Tunisia, from 1966 to 1968. She has also served the agency in five other senior-level positions, including deputy director.

Prior to returning to the Peace Corps in 2018 as Peace Corps director, she was a visiting professor at the University of Maryland, Baltimore, School of Social Work and director of the University's Center for Global Education. In the 1990s, she was director of the Council for the International Exchange of Scholars (CIES), the organization that manages the Fulbright Senior Scholar Program.

Jody received a BS from the University of Utah, a master's in social work from the University of Maryland, Baltimore, and a PhD in human development from the University of Maryland, College Park.

Among her many awards, she has received the University of Maryland President's Award, the University of Utah's Alumni of the Year Award, and two honorary doctorates. She spent a semester as a resident fellow at the Institute of Politics (IOP) at the Harvard Kennedy School in Spring 2022.

She currently lives in Silver Spring, Maryland, with her daughter, Kirsten, and son-in-law, Nels Andersen. Her son, David, and daughter-in-law, JaneAnne Peterson, live in Portland, Oregon. Jody has three grandchildren, Anders, Leif, and Berit.